HON. LEWIS CASS.

Second Governor of Michigan

THE

# EARLY HISTORY

OF

# MICHIGAN,

## FROM THE FIRST SETTLEMENT TO 1815.

BY E. M. SHELDON.

NEW YORK:
A. S. BARNES & COMPANY, 51 & 53 JOHN-ST.
DETROIT:—KERR, MORLEY & CO.
1856.

RICHARD C. VALENTINE,
STEREOTYPER AND ELECTROTYPIST,
17 Dutch-street, corner of Fulton,
NEW YORK.

GEORGE W. WOOD, Printer,
No. 2 Dutch-street.

TO

HON. LEWIS CASS,

SECOND GOVERNOR OF MICHIGAN,

WHOSE JUDICIOUS MANAGEMENT OF THE

NUMEROUS INDIAN TRIBES OF THE NORTHWEST

SECURED TO THE

PENINSULAR STATE

ITS PEACEFUL SETTLEMENT AND CONTINUED PROSPERITY,

This Volume

IS RESPECTFULLY DEDICATED.

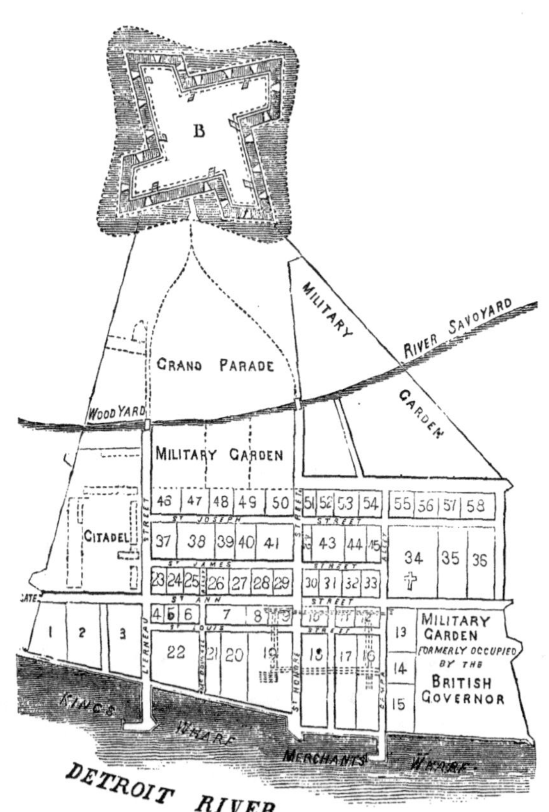


DETROIT IN 1796.

# PREFACE.

---

THREE years since, while editing a literary periodical in Detroit, I commenced the publication of such facts as I could obtain concerning the early history of Michigan. Hon. Lewis Cass becoming interested in them, generously presented me with a large collection of manuscripts, containing official and narrative letters relating to the early French settlement, which he procured from the Colonial Archives at Paris, during his residence there as Minister Plenipotentiary. On examination of these papers, I found them interesting and valuable, furnishing many links in the broken chain of the early history of the Northwest.

Encouraged by the commendation and proffered assistance of Rev. H. D. Kitchel, Capt. E. B. Ward, Rev. O. C. Thompson, and Messrs. U. Tracy Howe, George F. Porter, Henry Hurlbut, and Robert E. Roberts, of Detroit, I undertook the task of translating and compiling the manuscripts, hoping thereby to be of some service to the American reader, and especially to the inhabitants of Michigan and other portions of the great Northwest.

In this translation I was assisted by a native Parisian, and by an accomplished French scholar from Boston, Mass. The translation was made with the greatest possible care, every sentence being revised and compared with the original. Whatever the work may lack in beauty of diction, and gracefulness of expression, unwearied pains have been taken to make it historically correct.

I have chosen to embody in the work the manuscripts themselves, rather than to give the facts in a more modern style, partly because the unique mode of expression often used has attractions to my own mind, and partly because most historical readers love that which has the savor of antiquity, and prefer the original of an old book to the most polished modern version. The names of all persons and places, and of some few words having a local signification, have been spelled as in the original manuscripts, except Michilimackinac, which in some instances was spelled *Missilimakina;* but, this being an Indian word, I have preferred Schoolcraft's orthography.

Though a large portion of this volume is composed of the manuscripts, much research has been necessary to obtain corroborating testimony and connecting facts. The principal authorities which have been consulted for that purpose, are "Hennepin's Travels," Wynne's "History of the British Empire," Parkman's "Conspiracy of Pontiac," Schoolcraft's "Thirty Years with the Indian Tribes," Lanman's "History of Michigan," Ingersoll's "Second War," and Bancroft's "History of the United States."

The facts concerning Detroit, after its occupation by the Americans, were obtained from Hon. S. Conant, Major Joshua Howard, Major Abraham Edwards, and Hon. B. F. H. Witherell; and from Mrs. M. McCarty, and Mrs. Robert Abbott, daughters of Peter Audrain, first Secretary of the Territory, all of whom were then residents of Detroit. By the politeness of Mr. Amos T.

Hall, Register of the city of Detroit, I have also had access to the old records, and have brought thence a bundle of gleanings.

I am under many obligations to the "Mechanics' Library Association" of Detroit, and to the "New York Historical Library," "Mercantile Library Association," and "Astor Library" of the city of New York, for the use of books contained in their several valuable collections. Mr. Joseph G. Cogswell, librarian of the Astor Library, has also kindly rendered essential service, by a patient examination of many of the manuscripts, and by reliable advice concerning the plan of the work.

And by no means of the least account in the sum of obligation, is the gratitude due to Rev. Joseph P. Thompson for an introduction to my publishers; to whom I am indebted for the handsome appearance of this volume, and by whose liberality the public are presented with the life-like portraits of some of those distinguished men, whose names are well known in connection with the early American history of Michigan.

Hon. Lewis Cass, second Governor of Michigan—whose portrait, engraved from a daguerreotype taken during the present session of Congress, will be immediately recognized,—retained his office as governor, from the time of his appointment in 1813 till he was appointed Secretary of War in 1831. In 1836 he was appointed Minister to France, and returned in 1842. In January, 1845, he was first elected to the United States Senate.

Hon. James Witherell, one of the "Board of Governor and Judges," was a native of Massachusetts, and was appointed a Judge of the Territory of Michigan, April 23d, 1808. His term of office expired July 1st, 1824, after which he was reappointed for four years. On the 1st of February, 1828, he was appointed Secretary of the Territory. He died January 9th, 1838.

Hon. James May was appointed Chief Justice of the Court of Common Pleas, about the year 1800. He held that office for seven years; and his name often appears in the subsequent public records of the Territory. He died in January, 1829.

Rev. Gabriel Richard, Vicar-general, Sulpitian, was born at Saintes, in France, October 15th, 1764. He was educated at Issy, near Paris, and became a priest of the Society of St. Sulpitius in 1791. With a number of priests of the same order, he arrived at Baltimore, in the United States, June 24th, 1792. After laboring some time as missionary among the Catholic missions of Illinois, he came to Detroit in June, 1798. He closed a long and laborious life at Detroit, on the 13th of September, 1832.

All efforts to obtain a portrait of Hon. Augustus B. Woodward, one of the first judges, and author of the "Woodward Code of Laws," have been unsuccessful, and it is believed that none exists. He was a native of Virginia, and was appointed a Judge of the Territory of Michigan in 1805. His term of office expired in 1824, and he was soon after appointed one of the Judges of the Territory of Florida, and died there three years later.

Far from considering this volume above criticism, yet believing that it contains historical facts which will be appreciated by the reading public, and especially by the inhabitants of the great Northwest, this portion of the Early History of Michigan is respectfully submitted.

NEW YORK, March, 1856.

# CONTENTS.

## CHAPTER I.



## CHAPTER II.



## CHAPTER III.

## CHAPTER IV.



## CHAPTER V.



## CHAPTER VI.

## CHAPTER VII.



## CHAPTER VIII.



## CHAPTER IX.

## CHAPTER X.



## CHAPTER XI.



## CHAPTER XII.

## CHAPTER XIII.



## CHAPTER XIV.



## CHAPTER XV.

## CHAPTER XVI.



## CHAPTER XVII.



## CHAPTER XVIII.

## CHAPTER XIX.



## CHAPTER XX.



## CHAPTER XXI.

## CHAPTER XXII.

# EARLY

# HISTORY OF MICHIGAN.

---

## CHAPTER I.

Francis I. grants a commission to Jacques Cartier—Voyage of discovery—Second voyage—Ceremony of embarkation—Tempestuous voyage—Discovery and naming of the river St. Lawrence—Island of Hochelaga—Indian account of the Far West—Cartier names New France—Charter granted to Roberval—He proceeds to America—Erects a fort on the coast—Colonization Company formed in 1603—Expedition under the command of Champlain—Emigration of the Franciscans—Jesuits—Champlain appointed governor—Missionaries visit Saut Ste. Marie—Death of Raymbault at Montreal—Jogues attempts to return to his missionary work—Taken prisoner by hostile savages—Ransomed by the Dutch—Réné Mesnard visits Lake Superior—Mysterious disappearance—Establishment of a mission at Saut Ste. Marie by Allouez and Marquette—Speech of Allouez—Death of Marquette.

THE enthusiasm awakened in Spain and England, at the beginning of the sixteenth century, by the discoveries of Christopher Columbus and Sebastian Cabot, was soon communicated to impulsive France, and Francis I. granted a commission to Jacques Cartier, of St. Malo, to prosecute discoveries in the unknown regions of the New World.

Cartier's outfit for this expedition consisted of two ships, of sixty tons burden each, and a crew of sixty-one efficient men. He set sail from St. Malo on the 20th of April, 1534.

The Spaniards already occupied Florida; the English had taken possession of the middle portion of the continent; the more northern regions, therefore, alone remained for the French, and thither the adventurous commander directed his course. His first voyage was merely a survey of the northern coast of Newfoundland, which was prosperously accomplished; but fearing the disastrous effects of the autumnal storms upon his ships, he turned prow homeward, and arrived safely at St. Malo on the 15th of September, 1534. The favorable account which he gave of the voyage was well received at court, and preparations were immediately commenced for a second expedition.

During the winter of 1534–5, three vessels were fitted out, which were to constitute the squadron of M. Cartier. They were the Great Hermina, of about one hundred and twenty tons, which was the flag-ship; the Little Hermina, of sixty tons; and the Hermirillon, of forty tons.

The day of embarkation, May 15th, 1535, at length arrived—a most important day at St. Malo. The adventurers, who were about to embark for the just-discovered, yet almost unknown world, were objects of general and enthusiastic interest; and in this hour of separation from kindred and country, the priests of their religion had prepared a gorgeous pageant for their future support and consolation. The officers and crew of the whole squadron, having confessed and received the sacrament, presented themselves before the altar in the spacious cathedral of St. Malo, where the bishop, arrayed in sacerdotal robes of the most costly magnificence, bestowed on them his benediction.

The voyage was very tempestuous. When the fleet arrived within sight of Newfoundland, they still continued to sail to the westward, and entered a broad gulf on St. Lawrence day, in commemoration of which event they gave the name of St. Lawrence to the gulf, and to the river that flows into it.

Crossing the gulf, Cartier ascended the river to the island of Orleans, where he arrived in September. Here the natives made him bountiful presents of corn and fish, but strongly opposed his farther progress. Disregarding their opposition, he continued his course until he reached the island of Hochelaga. He found this beautiful island in the possession of a band of Wyandot Indians. Their principal village was circular in form, and contained about fifty houses, built of wood, and thatched with strips of bark ingeniously joined together. This village was at the base of a hill which commanded a magnificent prospect, to which Cartier gave the name of Mont-royal—the site of the present city of Montreal.

Cartier was told by the natives that "there was, far away to the westward, a country called Saquenay (Saginaw ?), where were great stores of gold and copper; and that there were three great lakes, and a sea of fresh water so large that no man had ever found the end."

Before leaving the island of Hochelaga, Cartier erected a cross, and a shield emblazoned with the *Fleur-de-lis*, emblems of Church and State, and named the region of his discoveries New France.

He departed on the 5th of October, wintered on the St. Croix river, and the following summer returned to France. On his arrival he reported that the country he had explored was destitute of gold and silver, and that its coast was bleak and stormy.

The representations of Cartier, whose candor was known to be equal to his judgment and energy, so far checked the progress of French enterprise, that not until four years after his return was another expedition attempted.

Early in the year 1540, Francis I. granted to François de la Roque, Seigneur de Roberval, a charter covering all the region north of the British occupancy, and investing him with supreme power within its bounds.

During the summer of the same year, a squadron, consisting of five vessels, under the command of Admiral Cartier, and furnished with all the necessary men and provisions for founding a colony, bore Roberval to his new possessions. The voyage was prosperous. On their arrival, a fort was erected—the location of which is now unknown—and Cartier was appointed commandant.

Roberval immediately returned to France, and the same year brought thence a reinforcement of men, and a large supply of stores and arms, for the relief and protection of the fort. Nothing farther is known of this colony: indeed the history of New France, from that period to the founding of Quebec, is almost entirely lost.

In 1603, a number of merchants of the city of Rouen, in France, formed a Colonization Company, designing to realize large profits from the fur-trade. A charter was obtained granting them the same privileges which, sixty years previously, had been bestowed upon M. de la Roque.

The first expedition of this company was made the same year that the charter was granted, under the command of Samuel Champlain, a member of the company, a bold, energetic man, and one well fitted for the arduous duties with which he was intrusted.

In 1608, Champlain founded the city of Quebec. His

time seems to have been employed during a few of the succeeding years in strengthening and improving the colony, and in making farther explorations. In 1611, he discovered the beautiful lake which still bears his name.

Champlain made a voyage to France in 1612, and on his return brought with him four Franciscans, or Recollets, for the conversion of the savages in the vicinity of Quebec. Five years later he brought over his family, and entered with renewed vigor upon all the enterprises connected with colonial life. The colonists were greatly encouraged to find their governor willing thus to unite all his interests with theirs, and pursued the arduous labors, and endured the privations of their lot, with an energy and fortitude hitherto unknown.

The adventure-loving and persevering Jesuits had formed a part of each emigrating band, and, in 1611, had established a mission among the savages. During many subsequent years, despite the efforts of Champlain and others who favored the Franciscans, the Jesuits exerted a controlling influence throughout New France; though Hennepin asserts that "from the arrival of the Reverend Father Martin de Valence, one of the first of the Franciscan priests, to the year 1621, there had been five hundred converts of the Recollets established in the New World."

In 1622, the Duke de Ventadour, who had taken orders for the avowed purpose of aiding in converting the savages, sent over to Canada a large number of the Jesuits; and in 1635 a college of the order was founded at Quebec, under the direction of the Marquis de Gamache.

Samuel Champlain, first governor of New France, died in 1635. Under his administration the colony had been uniformly prosperous, and his loss was justly considered a great calamity. Lanman, in his History of Michigan, pays the following tribute to his memory:

"With a mind warmed into enthusiasm by the vast domain of wilderness which was stretched around him, and the glorious visions of future grandeur which its resources opened, a man of extraordinary hardihood and the clearest judgment, a brave officer and a scientific seaman, his keen forecast discerned, in the magnificent prospect of the country which he occupied, the elements of a mighty empire, of which he had hoped to be the founder. With a stout heart, and ardent zeal, he had entered upon the project of civilization; he had disseminated valuable knowledge of its resources by his explorations, and had cut the way through hordes of savages for the subsequent successful progress of the French toward the lakes."

M. de Montmagny succeeded Champlain as governor.

The fur-trade was the principal object of his attention, and to prosecute this most effectually, the wilderness in the region of the St. Lawrence was explored; and rude forts were erected as a means of defense to the trading-houses. Not far remote—a never-failing auxiliary—was the chapel of the Jesuit, surmounted by a cross.

Gradually these explorations were extended westward until, in 1632, Father Sagard, a Jesuit missionary, ascended the "great river of the Ottawas," and after enduring many hardships, reached the shores of Lake Huron.

In September, 1641, Charles Raymbault and Isaac Jogues, two other Jesuit missionaries, who had previously established a mission at the head of Pentanguishine Bay—at that time the western terminus of the traveled route between Montreal and Lake Huron, by the way of the Ottawa river and Lake Simoe—embarked in a frail birch canoe, and pursued their course northwest, through the Georgian Bay and among the countless islands of the St. Marie's river. After a voyage of seventeen days, amid scenery of unequaled beauty, the crowning glory of all, Saut Ste. Marie, burst upon their enraptured vision. Here, where the evergreen of the unbroken forest was contrasted with the matchless beauty of the foam-crested waters, and the handiwork of Deity was everywhere strikingly manifest, the weary voyageurs found a settlement of two thousand of nature's own children, the hospitable Chippewas. The chiefs of the tribe gave the travel-worn missionaries a cordial reception. "We welcome you as brothers, and will profit by your words," was their assurance, when the object of the long, wearisome journey had been explained.

A few days' observation convinced the missionaries that the peculiar facility afforded by the rapids for catching the white-fish that abounded in those waters, more than any other advantage of the location, was the great attraction which made the Saut de Ste. Marie the abiding-place of so large a number of the roving Aborigines.

The Chippewas informed their guests that, beyond the foaming rapids and the clear, placid Ste. Marie's river above, was a lake, called by them *Gitchi Gomee* (Great Water), larger than either Lake Huron or Lake Michigan, which was then called by the French *Lac des Illinois*. Beyond the western limits of *Gitchi Gomee*, the country was said to be destitute of trees, while countless herds of deer and buffalo roamed over the vast prairies. But that favored portion of the earth was inhabited by the Sioux, a warlike band, between whom and the Chippewas had long existed a deadly hatred. Thus were those choice hunting-grounds, to the Chippewas, like paradise to our first parents, protected from intrusion by the weapons of destruction.

Very late in the autumn of the same year, 1641, the two missionaries returned to Pentanguishine, intending to revisit the Saut early the following spring. But the devoted Raymbault was already the victim of that insidious disease, consumption, induced, no doubt, by the exposures and privations he had suffered; and the following year Father Jogues accompanied him to Quebec, where he died, in October, 1642.

After the death of Raymbault, Father Jogues attempted to return to Saut Ste. Marie, but while ascending the St. Lawrence he was captured by a marauding band of Mohawk Indians. A small number of Huron Indians, who were with him, were also captured, and were burned at the stake. The missionary himself was subjected to the most ignominious treatment, but was finally ransomed by the Dutch in the vicinity of Albany. He returned to France, and subsequently revisited the scene of his labors in the New World.

On the 28th of August, 1660, René Mesnard, another Jesuit missionary, left Quebec, resolved, if possible, to make greater progress than his predecessors in the exploration of the Northwest. He took with him only a scanty supply of the necessaries of life; "for," said he, "I trust in that Providence which feeds the little birds of the air, and clothes the wild-flowers of the desert."

Soon after his arrival at Saut Ste. Marie, he ascended the river in a birch canoe, and coasted along the southern shore of *Gitchi Gomee.* On the 15th of October he reached the head of Keweenaw Bay, to which he gave the name of St. Theresa—the day of his arrival being the anniversary of that patron saint.

Here in the wilderness, far removed from the comforts of civilization, did the old man (for he was past the meridian of life) spend the long dreary winter, with no other companions than the untutored red men.

In the spring, accompanied only by a single Indian, he started for Chaquamegon Bay, near the head of the lake. They took the route through Portage Lake; and while the Indian was engaged in carrying the canoe across the portage to Lake Superior, Father Mesnard wandered into the woods, and was never again heard of. The presentiment that he should never return to Quebec, which he had often expressed in letters to his friends, was thus verified, August 20th, 1661.

Undaunted by the melancholy fate of his predecessors, resolved to gratify his own love of adventure, and at the same time benefit his fellow-men, Claude Allouez embarked at Three Rivers, August 8th, 1666, in company with about four hundred Indians, who had been to

Quebec for the purposes of trade, and were now returning home. Allouez was devotedly attached to the Order of Jesuits, and unwilling that any of their plans should fail to fully accomplish the desired object. No doubt his enthusiastic mind, in its solitary day-dreams, pictured hordes of savages converted from heathenism by his instrumentality.

The missionary and his savage companions arrived safely at Saut Ste. Marie early in September. From thence Father Allouez proceeded immediately to Lake Superior. "This lake," said he, "shall henceforth bear the name of M. de Tracy, in token of the obligations the people of this region owe to him." Accordingly, the first map of Lake Superior, drawn in 1668, and published in 1672, supposed to be the work of Allouez and Marquette, bears the name of *Lac Tracy ou Supérieur*.

Of this map, Dablon says: "It was got up by two Fathers, very intelligent and observing, who did not wish to incorporate any thing except what they had seen with their own eyes. That is the reason why they have only inserted the upper parts of Lakes Huron and Illinois, although they had coasted much on both."

In "Foster and Whitney's Report of the Lake Superior Region," are the following observations: "When it is considered that these men were not engineers, and that to note the geographical features of the country formed no part of their requirements, this map may, for that age, be regarded as a remarkable production; although, occasionally, points are laid down half a degree from their true position. The whole coast, sixteen hundred miles in extent, as well as the islands, were explored. Even Caribou, a low island in the midst of the lake, and not visible except within a few leagues, did not escape their observation."

"The savages," remarks Allouez, "respect this lake as a divinity, and offer sacrifices to it because of its size, for it is two hundred leagues long, and eighty broad; and also in consequence of its furnishing them with fish, upon which all the natives live, when hunting is scarce in these quarters."

That the discovery of copper in those regions is not a recent event, is evident from the following description of Allouez. He says: "It frequently happens that pieces of copper are found, weighing from ten to twenty pounds. I have seen several such pieces in the hands of the savages; and, since they are very superstitious, they regard them as divinities, or as presents given to them to promote their happiness, by the gods who dwell beneath the water. For this reason, they preserve these pieces of copper, wrapped up with their most precious articles. In some families they have been kept for more than fifty years; in others, they have descended from time out of mind, being cherished as domestic gods.

"For some time there was seen near the shore a large rock of copper, with its top rising above the water, which gave opportunities to those passing by to cut pieces from it; but when I passed that vicinity, it had disappeared. I believe that the gales, which are frequent, like those of the sea, had covered it with sand. One savage tried to persuade me that it was a divinity, who had disappeared, but for what cause he was unwilling to tell."

At the bay called by Father Mesnard Ste. Theresa, Father Allouez found "two Christian women, witnesses of Mesnard's labors, who had preserved their faith, and sparkled like two stars in the midst of the darkness of infidelity. Having refreshed their memories with our mysteries, we proceeded on. After having traveled one hundred and eighty leagues along the border of the lake, on the southern side, where the Lord often tried our patience by means of gales, famine, and fatigue, both day and night, we landed, on the first day of October, at Chaquamagon, a beautiful bay, on whose margin dwelt numerous savages. Their warriors amounted to eight hundred men."

Chaquamagon is the old La Pointe of the voyageurs. There this self-denying missionary lived two years. He built a chapel, and zealously prosecuted the work of winning converts to his own faith. When he first arrived, he learned that the Chippewas were about making a warlike expedition against the Sioux; but being permitted to advise, he had the satisfaction of diverting them from their bloody enterprise.

The fame of Allouez extended to all the surrounding tribes, who gathered around the mission-house to gratify that curiosity which is an inherent quality in every human breast, mingled, no doubt, with an indefinable desire to be benefited by his instructions.

Some time during the two years of his sojourn, he visited *Fond du Lac*, where he met a number of the Sioux, who informed him that there was a vast country still farther west, spread out in beautiful prairies, over which roamed immense herds of buffalo. They also told him of a great river called *Messepi* (Mississippi), along whose banks dwelt the beaver.

Allouez also extended his labors to the Nipissisiniens, on the north shore of the lake. Becoming more and more deeply interested in the spiritual necessities of the Indians, he returned to Quebec in the fall of 1667, to obtain aid in establishing missions in different parts of the Northwest. So successful were his appeals, that only two days after his arrival, having accomplished his object, he again set out on his return to the wilderness.

The following year, 1668, Claude Dablon and James Marquette proceeded to Saut Ste. Marie, and established a permanent mission. From this period, therefore, Saut Ste. Marie dates its actual settlement, being, according to Bancroft, the oldest in the State of Michigan.

In 1669, Marquette succeeded Allouez at Chaquamagon, or La Pointe, and the latter established himself at Green Bay.

"In May, 1671," says Foster and Whitney's Report, "a grand council assembled at Saut Ste. Marie. The chiefs from fourteen of the tribes of the Northwest and the soldiers of France sat in council together. M. Fallon, then governor-general of New France, had sent there M. de Lusson, to take possession, in the name of His Majesty, of all the lands lying between the east and west, and from Montreal to the south, as far as it could be done. When the tribes were assembled, the ambassador selected a hill above the village, planted the standard of the cross, and raised the arms of the king. The cross was blessed with all the ceremonies of the Church, by the superior of the missions; and while being raised, the *Vexilla* was chanted by the assembled Frenchmen, to the great delight of the savages. The shield of France was suspended from a cedar post above the cross, while they chanted the *Exaudiat*, and prayers were offered for the sacred person of His Majesty.

"St. Lusson formally took possession of the lands; after which guns were fired, and other manifestations of joy exhibited.

"Father Allouez was present, mindful of the interests of his divine as well as temporal master. He pronounced the following panegyric on the king, which is worthy of being preserved:

"'It is a most important affair that calls us together. Cast your eyes on that cross which is high above your heads. It is there where the Son of God was willing to be attached and to die, in order to satisfy His eternal Father for your sins. He is the master of our lives, and also of heaven, and earth, and hell. It is He of whom I have often spoken, and whose name and word I have borne into these distant lands.

"'But, at the same time, look upon that other column, to which are attached the arms of that great chief of France whom we call king. He lives beyond the sea. He is the chief of chiefs, and has not his like in the world. All the chiefs of whom you have heard are but children compared with him. He is like a great tree, while they are mere shrubs which we tread upon. You know Onontio (the governor-general), the renowned chief of Quebec. You know that he is the terror of the Iroquois, and that his name is sufficient to make them tremble, since he has desolated their lands, and carried fire among their settlements. There are beyond the sea, ten thousand Onontios like him, who are but warriors of the great chief, our king, of whom I speak. When he says, "I go to war," everybody obeys, and these ten thousand chiefs raise bands of warriors both for the land and the sea. Some embark in ships, like those you have seen at Quebec. Your canoes will hold but four or five men, twelve at the utmost. Our vessels carry four or five hundred, and even a thousand.

"'Another portion go to war on land, but in such numbers that when arranged in double ranks, they would reach to Mississaquenk, which is twenty leagues from here. When he attacks, he is more fearful than thunder. The earth trembles, and the air and sea are on fire from the discharges of his cannon. He has been seen in the midst of his squadron covered with the blood of his enemies; so many of whom has he put to the sword, that he does not number their scalps, but merely the rivers of blood which he causes to flow. He carries such a number of captives with him that he does not value them, but lets them go when they please, to show that he does not fear them. Nobody dare make war on him. All nations beyond the sea have sued for peace with great submission. They come from every quarter of the globe to listen to him, and to admire him. It is he who decides upon the affairs of the world.

"'What shall I say of his riches? You think yourselves rich when you have ten or twelve sacks of corn, and hatchets, and kettles, and other things of the kind. He has more cities than you have men, which are scattered over a space of more than five hundred leagues. In each city there are hatchets enough to cut all your wood, kettles enough to cook all your caribou, and sugar enough to fill all your wigwams. His house extends farther than from here to the Saut, is higher than the tallest of your trees, and contains more people than the largest of your settlements ever contained.'

"The same year Marquette removed to St. Ignace, north of Mackinac. Here he built a chapel and gathered about him the wandering Hurons. Marquette and Dablon made numerous excursions to the tribes which dwelt in the territory now embraced in northern Illinois and eastern Wisconsin.

"Marquette, like Allouez, had heard marvelous accounts of the region beyond the great lake, and longed to explore it; but it was not until the year 1673 that he was enabled to carry his project into execution. His route lay up the Fox river through Lake Winnebago, and thence down the Wisconsin into the Mississippi. In this expedition he was accompanied by Joylet, a courtier of France. They descended the mighty current as far as the Arkansas, and then turned back. They represented that they were hospitably entertained by the Illinois, who dwelt upon its banks, while by other tribes they were repulsed.

"The relation of this voyage of Marquette was not published until some time after his death, and by some was considered fabulous, but Bancroft is disposed to adopt it as worthy of entire credence.

"Late in the season, the voyageurs reached Chicago. Joylet hastened to Quebec to announce the result of their discoveries, while Marquette remained to plant the standard of the Cross among the Miamis.

"The manner of his death is thus narrated by Bancroft. 'In sailing from Chicago to Mackinac during the following spring, he entered a little river in Michigan. Erecting an altar, he said mass after the rites of the Catholic Church; then begging the men who conducted his canoe to leave him alone for half an hour—

'In the darkling wood,
Amid the cool and silence, he knelt down
And offered to the Mightiest solemn thanks
And supplication.'

"'At the end of half an hour they went to seek him, and he was no more. The good missionary, discoverer of a world, had fallen asleep on the margin of a stream that bears his name. Near the mouth, the voyageurs dug his grave in the sand.'

"This event happened May 18th, 1675.

"Allouez died soon after, in the midst of his labors among the Miamis.

"Allouez, Marquette, and Jogues were remarkable men; and had their lots been cast in a different sphere, they would have left a more durable impress upon the age in which they lived. Their efforts to win the tribes of the Northwest to the standard of the Cross, prosecuted with great zeal, and under circumstances of privation and suffering, may be regarded as abortive.

"There is something impressive in the rites of the Catholic Church, something in its mysteries calculated to overawe the wild men of the woods. So long as the missionary was in their midst and superintended their labors, they yielded to his guidance and adopted his recommendations, so far at least as conduced to their comfort; but when he withdrew, with equal facility they glided into their former habits. The superstructure, raised with so much care, fell to the ground the moment the sustaining hand was withdrawn.

"The effect of the contact of the two races has been to afford the Indian additional incentives to vice, while his intellectual and moral elevation has been little advanced; and at this day, it cannot be said that he stands higher in the scale of civilization than when first known by the white man."

## CHAPTER II.

Count Frontenac appointed Governor-General of New France—Fort Frontenac built—La Salle appointed Commandant—Resigns his command—Crosses Lake Ontario—Ascends the Niagara river—Builds the Griffin—Traverses lakes and rivers to Michilimackinac—Indian villages on the Detroit—Storm on Lake Huron—Michilimackinac—Signification of the name—Murder of two French traders—Arrest of the murderers—Their trial and execution.

FREQUENT changes occurred in the administration of the colonial affairs of New France, from the death of Champlain, in 1635, to the year 1672, when the Count de Frontenac was appointed governor-general. He was the god-son of Louis XIII., and was honored with his name.

Brave, judicious, and energetic, Frontenac was well qualified to manage the affairs of this new province. His first efforts were directed to the extension of the French interests in the region of the great lakes. Under his guidance and encouragement, the posts at Michilimackinac and Saut Ste. Marie were established, former explorations perfected, and conciliatory treaties made with the immense hordes of Indians who roamed through that far-off wilderness.

The route by which the Jesuits and traders penetrated into these wilds was by way of the Ottawa river, with its numerous rapids, and consequent toilsome portages, as far as Little River. Ascending this stream, they crossed numerous small lakes to Lake Nepissing, thence down the French river to Georgian Bay, which forms the eastern portion of Lake Huron. Birch canoes, so light as to be carried over the portages on the shoulders of one or two men, were their ships; while their stores, and munitions of war, consisted only of such articles as could be transported in like manner.

While Mesnard, Allouez, Marquette, and others were thus exploring the far Northwest, La Salle, with another band of adventurers, ascended the St. Lawrence to Lake Ontario. Near the outlet of the lake, on the northern shore, they established a trading-post to which they gave the name of Fort Frontenac, in honor of the governor-general.

Robert, Chevalier de la Salle, was appointed commandant. He was a man of genius, enterprise, undoubted talent, and indomitable perseverance, and the originator of the plan for a chain of fortifications afterward established on the water-line in the Northwest. Ambitious to complete the exploration of the Mississippi which had been begun by Marquette, and unwilling to undertake the voyage in the frail canoes hitherto employed, he formed the design of building a vessel suitable for his purpose. Accordingly, he resigned his command at Fort Frontenac, traversed the length of Lake Ontario, ascended the Niagara river to the great cataract, where he "made the portage." Two leagues above the great fall he erected a rude fortification, and commenced his work, undaunted by the numerous difficulties that surrounded him. Late in the autumn of 1678 the keel of the vessel was laid, and on the 7th of August, 1679, she set sail on the first voyage which had ever been made by Europeans upon that inland sea, amid the sound of *Te Deums* and the discharge of arquebuses.

The vessel was called the *Griffin*, and the image of that mythological animal was carved upon her prow. She was of sixty tons burden, and carried five guns. La Salle was her commander, and Louis Hennepin, the missionary, ardently zealous in the pursuit of new discoveries, was the journalist of the expedition. The crew consisted of fur-traders belonging to the Canadian colonies. Ignorant of the depth of the water, they sounded frequently while dashing along over Lake Erie's foam-crested waves. On the 10th of August they reached the islands which are grouped at the entrance of Detroit river, where they anchored.

Hennepin says of these islands: "They are the finest in the world. The strait (détroit) is finer than Niagara, being one league broad, excepting that part which forms the lake that we have called St. Clair."

Ascending the river, the explorers found along its banks several Indian villages, belonging to different tribes who were at peace with each other. A large village of the Hurons, called *Teuchsagrondie*, stood on the present site of Detroit. These villages had been visited by the Jesuit missionaries, and the *coureurs des bois*, but no settlement had yet been attempted.

On Lake Huron, La Salle's vessel encountered a violent storm, and was in imminent danger of shipwreck. The pilot was a skillful and experienced seaman. While the rest were saying their prayers and preparing for death, he stood at the rudder, "cursing La Salle, who had brought him hither to perish in a dirty lake, and lose the glory he had acquired by his long and prosperous navigation of the ocean."

At length the storm abated, and the following day the Griffin lay anchored in a little cove opposite the island of Michilimackinac, sheltered on the north by a point of the peninsula on which stood a village of the Hurons. The word Michilimackinac* (great turtle) is a most

* Schoolcraft says that the present Indian signification of the name of this island is "Place of the Dancing Spirits," and that the popular etymology, which derives the word from "big turtle," dates still farther back, and is founded on the fact that the *michi* were turtle spirits.

significant name for this island. It is nearly round, and rises high above the water, at first view appearing not unlike a gigantic specimen of the animal whose name it bears. The French gave the same appellation to all the country in the immediate vicinity, both on the upper and lower peninsula.

Father Hennepin says: "Michilimackinac is a neck of land to the north of the strait through which the lake of the Illinois discharges itself into Lake Huron. We lay between two different nations of the savages; those who inhabit the point of Michilimackinac are called Hurons, and the others, who are about three or four leagues more northward, are Outawas."

Describing the habits of the savages, he says: "They sow Indian corn, which is their ordinary food, for they have nothing else to live upon, except the fish they take from the lakes. They boil their fish with their *sagamittee*, a kind of broth made of water and the flour of corn, which they beat in a mortar made of the trunk of a tree, which they make hollow by fire."

In 1683 two French traders, Jacques le Maire and Colin Berthot, left Saut Ste. Marie with a large quantity of merchandise, which they were carrying to Kiaonan, an Indian village and trading-post on the shore of Lake Superior. They were murdered on the way by three Indians, belonging to two different tribes, who secreted their bodies and the merchandise which they had in their custody.

As soon as a knowledge of the affair reached M. du Lhut, commandant at Michilimackinac, he at once set about bringing the offenders to justice. Almost alone, in the far-off wilderness, with but a handful of Frenchmen in the whole region, at the mercy of countless hordes of savages, the daring intrepidity exhibited by M. du Lhut and M. Péré has scarcely a parallel in the history of the settlement of this country.

The following letter from M. du Lhut to Count Frontenac, governor-general of Canada, gives a minute and interesting account of the occurrence:

"MICHILIMACKINAC, April 12, 1684.

"MONSIEUR:—I did myself the honor to write to you in September and October of last year, giving an account of a murder committed by the children of Achiganaga. Allow me now to inform you of the means I used to avenge the death of the two assassinated Frenchmen of whom I spoke.

"To follow the affair step by step, be pleased to know, sir, that on the 24th of October last, I was told that Folle-Avoine, accomplice in the murder and robbery of the two Frenchmen, had arrived at Saut Ste. Marie, with fifteen families of the Sauteurs, who had fled from Chaouamigon, on account of an attack which they, together with the people of the land, made last spring upon the Nadouecioux.

"He believed himself safe at the Saut, on account of the number of allies and relatives he had there. Rev. Father Albanet informed me that the French at the Saut, being only twelve in number, had not arrested him, believing themselves too weak to contend with such numbers, especially as the Sauteurs had declared that they would not allow the French to redden the land of their fathers with the blood of their brothers.

"On receiving this information, I immediately resolved to take with me six Frenchmen, and embark at the dawn of the next day for the Saut Ste. Marie, and, if possible, obtain possession of the murderer. I made known my design to the Rev. Father Enialran; and at my request, as he had some business to arrange with Rev. Father Albanet, he placed himself in my canoe.

"Having arrived within a league of the village of the Saut, the Rev. Father, the Chevalier de Fourcille, Cardonniere and I, disembarked. I caused the canoe, in which were Baribaud, Le Mere, La Fortune, and Maçons, to proceed, while we went across the wood to the house of the Rev. Father, fearing that the savages, seeing me, might suspect the object of my visit, and cause Folle-Avoine to escape.

"Finally, to cut the matter short, I arrested him, and caused him to be guarded day and night by six Frenchmen.

"I then called a council, at which I requested all the savages of the place to be present, where I repeated what I had often said to the Hurons and Ottawas since the departure of M. Péré, giving them the message you ordered me, sir, that in case there should be among them any spirits so evil-disposed as to follow the example of those who have murdered the French on Lake Superior and Lake Michigan, they must separate the guilty from the innocent, as I did not wish the whole nation to suffer, unless they protected the guilty.

"I informed them that I expected those present to declare themselves; that if there were any factious spirits who intended to shield Folle-Avoine, I might know them, and they would see that I did not fear them enough to prevent me from doing my duty.

"The savages held several councils to which I was invited; but their only object seemed to be to exculpate the prisoner, in order that I might release him. All united in accusing Achiganaga and his children, assuring themselves with the belief that M. Péré, with his detachment, would not be able to arrest them, and wishing to persuade me that they apprehended that all the Frenchmen might be killed.

"I answered them, in respect to Folle-Avoine, that I was not obliged to believe a man whom I looked upon as having helped to shed the blood of my brothers; that meanwhile, in consequence of the submission to the orders of Onontio, their father, which they manifested, I should determine nothing, until I might be better informed of the facts; and, moreover, if I had no more convincing proof against him than that which was already known to me, I would give him back to them. If, on the contrary, it was true that he was of the number of the assassins, I would see in what way I would dispose of him. As to the anticipated death of M. Péré, as well as of the other Frenchmen, that would not embarrass me, since I believed neither the allies nor the nation of Achiganaga would wish to have a war with us to sustain an action so dark as that of which we were speaking. So, having only to attack a few murderers, or at most those of their own family, I was certain that the French would have them, dead or alive. This was all the answer they had from me during the three days that the councils lasted; after which I embarked, at ten o'clock in the morning, sustained by only twelve Frenchmen, to show a few seditious persons, who boasted of taking the prisoner away from me, that the French did not fear them.

"I received accounts daily of the numbers of savages that Achiganaga drew from his nation to Kiaonan, under pretext of going to war in the spring against the Nadouecioux, to avenge the death of one of his relatives, son of Ouenaus, but really to protect himself against us, in case we should become convinced that his children had killed the Frenchmen. This precaution placed me between hope and fear respecting the expedition which M. Péré had undertaken.

"On the 24th of November he came across the wood, at ten o'clock at night, to tell me that he had arrested Achiganaga and four of his children. He said it was true that they were not all guilty of the murder, but he had thought proper, in this affair, to follow the custom of the savages, which is, to seize all the relatives. Folle-Avoine, whom I had arrested, he considered the most guilty, being without doubt the originator of the mischief.

"I immediately gave orders that Folle-Avoine should be more closely confined, and not be allowed to speak to any one; for I had also learned that he had a brother, sister, and uncle in the village of the Kiskakons.

"M. Péré informed me that he had released the youngest son of Achiganaga, aged about thirteen or fourteen years, that he might make known to their nation, and to the Sauteurs who were at Nockè and in the neighborhood, the reason why the French had arrested his father and brothers. M. Péré bade him assure the savages that 'if any one wished to complain of what he had done, he would wait for them with a firm step;' for he considered himself in a condition to set them at defiance, having found at Kiaonan eighteen Frenchmen who had wintered there. However, no one opposed his design.

"On the 25th, at break of day, M. Péré embarked at the Saut, with four good men whom I gave him, to go and meet the prisoners. He had left them four leagues from there, under a guard of twelve Frenchmen, and at two o'clock in the afternoon they arrived. I had prepared a room in my house for the prisoners, in which they were placed under a strong guard, and were not allowed to converse with any one.

"On the 26th, I commenced proceedings; and this, sir, is the course I pursued. I gave notice to all the chiefs and elders to appear at the council which I had appointed, and gave to Folle-Avoine the privilege of selecting two of his relatives to support his interests; and to the other prisoners I made the same offer.

"The council being assembled, I sent for Folle-Avoine to be interrogated, and caused his answers to be written; and afterwards they were read to him, and inquiry made whether they were not, word for word, what he had said. He was then removed from the council under a safe guard. I used the same form with the two eldest sons of Achiganaga; and as Folle-Avoine had indirectly charged the father with being accessory to the murder, I sent for him, and also for Folle-Avoine, and bringing them into the council, confronted the four. Folle-Avoine and the two sons of Achiganaga accused each other of committing the murder, without denying that they were participators in the crime. Achiganaga alone strongly maintained that he knew nothing of the design of Folle-Avoine, nor of his children, and called on them to say if he had counselled them to kill the Frenchmen. They answered 'No!'

"This confrontation, which the savages did not expect, surprised them; and seeing the prisoners had convicted themselves of the murder, the chiefs said: 'It is enough, you accuse yourselves; the French are masters of your bodies.'

"The next day I held another council, in which I said there could be no doubt that the Frenchmen had been robbed and murdered; that the murderers were known, and that they knew what the practice was among themselves on similar occasions. To all this they said nothing, which obliged me on the following day to hold another council in the cabin of Brochet, where, after having spoken, and seeing that they would make no decision, and that all my councils ended only in reducing tobacco to ashes, I told them that since they did not wish to decide, I should take the responsibility, and that the next day I would let them know the determination of the French and myself.

"It is proper, sir, you should know that I observed all these ceremonies only to see if they would feel it their duty to render to us the same justice that they do to each other, having had divers examples of similar cases in which, when the tribes of those who had committed the murder did not wish to go to war with the tribe aggrieved, the nearest relations of the murderers killed them themselves, that is to say, man for man.

"On the 29th of November I gathered together the French that were here, and after the interrogations and answers of the accused had been read to them, the guilt of all three appeared so evident, from their own confessions, that the vote was unanimous that all three should die. But, as the French, who remained at Kiaonan to pass the winter, had written to Father Enialran and to myself, to beg of us to treat the affair with all possible leniency, the savages declaring that if they made the prisoners die they would avenge themselves on the French.

"I told the gentlemen who were with me in council, that this being an affair without a precedent, I believed it was expedient, for the safety of all the French who would pass the winter in the Lake Superior country, to put to death only two, as the death of the third might bring about grievous consequences; while, on the contrary, the putting to death of man for man could give the savages no cause for complaint, since this is their own custom under the circumstances.

M. de la Tour, chief of the Fathers, who had served much, sustained my opinions by strong reasoning; and all the gentlemen whom I had called in council decided that two should be shot, namely, Folle-Avoine, and the elder of the two brothers, while the younger should be released, and hold his life as a gift from you, sir.

"I then returned to the cabin of Brochet with Messrs. Boisguillot, Péré, De Repentigny, De Manthet, De la Ferté, and Maçons, where were all the chiefs of the Outawas du Sable, Outawas Sinagos, Kiskakons, Sauteurs, Mississagués, D'Achiliny, a part of the Hurons, and Oumamens, chief of the Amikoys. I informed them of our decision, telling them, that, not being ignorant of the murder committed on the two Frenchmen, and knowing all the murderers, I was surprised that no one dared to decide for us, and cause justice to be done. Meanwhile, Onontio had lost his blood, it was yet warm, and it was necessary to have other blood to satisfy him.

"I then informed them that the Frenchmen having been killed by two different nations, one of each nation must die, and that the same death they had caused the

French to suffer, they must also suffer; therefore they must be shot; that, to the third prisoner, you, sir, would give his life, on condition that he would tell all his allies the great kindness you had done him. I told them that if I did not relax the rigor of our laws, I should put to death all six of those who had participated in the theft, and perhaps contributed to the murder by their wicked counsel, but for this time I hoped you would not condemn me for my mildness.

"This decision, to put the murderers to death, was a hard stroke to them all, for none had believed that I would dare undertake it.

"The Outawas du Sable, and the Outawas Sinagos, in order to have no trouble with you, sir, had appeared to blame their conduct, and not to care what became of them; but then, Falon Seleva, chief of the Outawas du Sable, after a long harangue, concluded that, if I dared, I would give them life.

"The chief of the Outawas Sinagos said that he had captured some of the Iroquois, and that M. Courcelle asked him to deliver them over to him, promising that they should have their life, and that I ought to do the same by the prisoners. The Sauteurs having left the Saut, had appointed Oumamens, chief of the Amikoys, to speak for them. He thanked me that I had satisfied myself with so little, praising the Frenchman for his good heart, which prompted him to release the father and three of his children. The other nations said nothing.

"The different sentiments expressed, made me reply to the first, that if the accused were prisoners of war, I should do myself the pleasure to give them their life; but, being murderers, it was necessary they should die, as an example to those who might have similar designs, and, by this fear, would be prevented from committing murder so easily, especially from taking the lives of Frenchmen. I told them they knew very well that I loved all men, but that I did not fear them enough to prevent me from executing your orders, which are, to cause those to die who kill the French; that, having become master of those who had killed your first children, if I did not cause them to be put to death, you would believe it was the fear I had of men; and that as soon as I should come into your presence, you would make me suffer the death which their crime deserved. Besides, I was not the author of their death, but only spoke the sentiments of all the elders.

"I also reminded them that this was but the fruit of their own teachings: they had taught their youth that to kill a Frenchman was not an affair of much importance, since one was acquitted for a captive or a pack of beaver; for, till now, no more troublesome consequences than these had befallen those who had murdered. But, had they taught their young men that murder was a wicked thing, and, if committed, the nation would abandon them, they would have been more wise, and the Frenchmen would still be alive.

"I then left the council, and asked the Rev. Fathers if they wished to baptize the prisoners, which they did.

"An hour after, I put myself at the head of forty-two Frenchmen, and in sight of more than four hundred savages, and within two hundred paces of their fort, I caused the two murderers to be shot.

"The impossibility of keeping them till spring, to send them to you, sir, made me hasten their death, being persuaded that in such cases prompt execution is necessary to calm all things, and not to give time to interested persons to take measures to get away the prisoners.

"When M. Péré made the arrest, those who had committed the murder confessed it; and when he asked them what they had done with our goods, they answered that they were almost all concealed. He immediately proceeded to the place of concealment, and was very much surprised, as were also the French who were with him, to find the goods in fifteen or twenty different places. By the carelessness of the savages, the tobacco and powder were entirely destroyed, having been placed in the pinery, under the roots of the trees, and being soaked in the water caused by ten or twelve days' continued rain, which inundated all the lower country. The season for snow and ice having come, they had all the trouble in the world to get out the bales of cloth. They then went to see the bodies, but could not remove them, these miserable wretches having thrown them into a marsh, and thrust them down into holes which they had made. Not satisfied with that, they had also piled branches of trees upon the bodies, to prevent them from floating when the water should rise in the spring; hoping that, by this precaution, the French would find no trace of those who were killed, but would believe them drowned, by being upset, as they reported that they had found in the lake, on the other side of the Portage, a boat with the sides all broken in, which they believed to be a French boat.

"Those goods which the French were able to secure, they took to Kiaonan, where were a number of Frenchmen, who had gone there to pass the winter, and who knew nothing of the death of Colin Berthot and Jacques le Maire, until M. Péré arrived. The ten who formed M. Péré's detachment, having conferred together concerning the measures they should take to prevent a total loss, decided to sell the goods to the highest bidder.

The sale was made for 1100 *livres*, which amount was to be paid in beavers, to M. de la Chesnaye, to whom I send the names of the purchasers.

"The savages who were present when Achiganaga and his children were arrested, wished to dance the calumet to M. Péré, and give him captives to satisfy him for the murder committed on the two Frenchmen; but he knew their intention, and would not accept their offer. He told them neither a hundred captives nor a hundred packs of beaver would give back the blood of his brothers; that the murderers must be given up to me, and I would see what I would do.

"I caused M. Péré to repeat these things in the council, that in future the savages need not think by presents to save those who commit similar deeds. Besides, sir, M. Péré showed plainly, by his conduct in investigating this affair, that he is not so strongly inclined to favor the savages as was reported. Indeed I do not know any one whom they fear more, yet who flatters them less, or knows them better.

"The criminals being in two different places, M. Péré being himself obliged to keep four of them, sent Messrs. de Repentigny, Manthet, and six other Frenchmen, to arrest the two who were among their people eight leagues in the woods, which they did promptly and vigorously. Among others. M. de Repentigny and M.

de Manthet showed that they feared nothing when their honor called them.

"M. de la Chevrotière has also served well in person and by his advice, having indicated the place where the prisoners were. Achiganaga, who had adopted him as a son, had told him where he should hunt during the winter.

"Two days after the murderers were shot, the Kiskakons, Outawas du Sable, and the Outawas Sinagos held a council, in which they gave me six strings of wampum, each nation two, 'to cover the dead Frenchmen and dry up their blood, that the earth might be beautiful in future.'

"An hour afterwards, they made the same presents to Achiganaga, and to the friends of Folle-Avoine, who were still here.

"The next day I had a great festival of corn and tobacco in the cabin of Brochet, in order 'to take away the sickness of heart that he had, because I pronounced the sentence of death on two savages in his house, without even speaking to him about it.'

"To this feast, all the chiefs and elders of the nation before-mentioned were invited. The Hurons gave me three strings of wampum for the same reason that the others were given. They also gave three for the Sauteurs and the Folle-Avoines.

"It still remained for me to give to Achiganaga and his three children the means to return to their family, which they could not do without my assistance. Their home, from which they were taken, was nearly twenty-six leagues from here. Knowing their necessity, I told them you would not be satisfied with giving them life. You wished also to preserve it, by giving them all that was necessary to prevent them from dying with hunger and cold by the way, and that your gift was made by my hands. I gave them blankets and shirts, guns and ammunition, tobacco, meat, hatchets, knives, twine to make nets for beavers, and two bags of corn, to supply them till they could kill game.

"They departed two days after, the most contented creatures in the world; but God was not, for when only two days' journey from here, the old Achiganaga fell sick of the quinsy and died, and his children returned. When the news of his death arrived, the greater part of the savages of this place attributed his death to the French, saying we had caused him to die. I let them talk, and laughed at them.

"It is only about two months since the children of Achiganaga returned to Kiaonan. I gave them letters to the French there, requesting them to say nothing to the savages about the death of their companions, having taken the satisfaction that I believed to be just.

"The Sauteurs gave them necklaces, to remind them that they should take good care to avoid agitating the subject of the death of their brother; and in case any should have a wicked design, the necklaces, of which they were the bearers, would deter them from its execution.

"As for me, I doubt not this example will make them wiser, and that it may produce good results."

## CHAPTER III.

Count Frontenac removed from office—Succeeded by M. le Barre—Le Barre recalled, and De Nonville appointed—M. du Lhut ordered to establish a fort on the Detroit—Count Frontenac reappointed to the government of Canada—Attempts a reconciliation with the Illinois—Invasion of Canada by the English in 1690—Attack on Montreal—Unsuccessful expedition against Quebec—Frontenac invades the country of the Iroquois—M. la Motte Cadillac appointed commandant at Michilimackinac—Remonstrates against the prohibition of the sale of brandy to the Indians—General account of the country, its condition, and inhabitants.

A MAN of Count Frontenac's abilities could not long occupy an exalted position without making enemies; and so successful were his enemies in their intrigues, that they accomplished their design of causing his removal from the government of Canada, in the summer of 1684.

M. de la Barre, his successor, arrived at Quebec the same season. He was entirely unacquainted with the Indian character, and commenced his administration by attempting to overcome the Five Nations by force of arms. The consequences were most disastrous to the French; and in 1685 La Barre was recalled, and the Marquis de Nonville appointed in his place.

In 1686 M. du Lhut, who still commanded at Michilimackinac, was succeeded by M. Perot, and received, through M. Durantaye, special commissioner, the following orders concerning his future movements:

LETTER TO M. DU LHUT.

"MONTREAL, 6th June, 1686.

"MONSIEUR:—Although I have ordered you to come to me this autumn, that I might confer with you concerning many things that may not be written, yet Rev. Father Anjolran having come here, and being obliged to return to Michilimackinac as soon as the restitution of prisoners shall have been made, your presence is much more necessary to the Outawas than to me. Therefore, I now direct you to remain, and unite with M. de la Durantaye, who is to be at Michilimackinac, in the execution of the orders which I send him, for the safety of our allies and friends.

"You will see by the letter which I have written to M. Durantaye, that I wish you to establish a post on the Detroit, near Lake Erie, with a garrison of fifty men. I desire you to choose an advantageous place to secure the passage, which may protect our savages who go to the chase, and serve them as an asylum against their enemies and ours.

"You will do and say nothing to the Iroquois, unless they undertake something against us and our allies. You will also see that my intention is, that you go to this new post as soon as possible, with twenty men only, whom you will establish under the command of your lieutenant. You will select such a man for this station as shall best suit you, one whom you consider most suitable for the command.

"After having given all the orders that you may judge necessary for the safety of this post, and having well secured obedience from the soldiers, you will return to Michilimackinac, there to await Rev. Father Anjolran, by whom I will communicate what I wish of you there. You will then return to the said post, with thirty other men, whom you will receive from M. Durantaye, in order to fully establish the position. You will take care that each provide himself with provisions sufficient for his subsistence at the said post, where, I doubt not, you may trade for peltries; therefore your men will not do ill to carry some goods there also.

"I strongly recommend you to maintain a good understanding with M. Durantaye, without which our designs will come to nothing, and the service of the king and the public will suffer much. The post to which I send you is of much more importance, as I expect it will bring you in contact with the Illinois, to whom you will make known those things of which you will be informed by Rev. Father Anjolran. Consider nothing of so much importance as the proper execution of all which I now command you, and which I shall make known to you by the Rev. Father on his return to Michilimackinac.

"I send you the necessary commission for the command of this post, also one for your lieutenant. Concerning your own interests I say nothing; but you may expect that I will do with pleasure all that will be for your advantage.

"Allow me to repeat to you once more, that you cannot use too much diligence to succeed in all that I shall require of you for the service of the king. If you can so arrange your affairs that your brother can be near you in the spring, I shall be very glad. He is an intelligent lad, and might be a great assistance to you; he might also be very serviceable to us.

"I beg you to avoid, in conversation, any allusion to our designs."*

In obedience to these instructions, M. du Lhut proceeded to the entrance of the strait from Lake Huron, where he erected a fortified trading-post, which he named Fort St. Joseph. This fort was abandoned in 1688, only two years after it was built. It stood on the present site of Fort Gratiot.

* "This letter is without signature, but every thing causes us to think that it was from the governor-general."—*Note on the MS.*

Meanwhile, affairs in Canada waxed worse and worse. The English traders, who had become quite numerous in the region of the Iroquois, instigated that powerful nation, or rather confederacy of nations, to an attack upon the French settlements in Canada. An open war ensued. In almost every skirmish—for the Indians seldom fight open battles—the French were the most severe sufferers.

The Far Indians, as those in the vicinity of the great lakes were called, began to manifest dissatisfaction and distrust of the French. In this critical state of affairs, M. de Nonville was recalled, and Count de Frontenac reappointed governor-general. He arrived at Quebec October 15th, 1689, to the great joy of the colonists.

"The arrival of Frontenac," says the McDougall MS., "was hailed by the French as the dawn of a deliverance from their calamities. The wise policy pursued by him during his former administration was now apparent to every one. A more judicious selection could not have been made in the present desperate situation of affairs.

"New and unforeseen troubles began to arise. The abdication of James II. involved France in a war with England. The example set in Europe of forming national alliances was greatly improved in America; for, while the English colonies had become the allies of the

Five Nations, they, in turn, became the allies of the Far Indians.

"Count Frontenac first attempted to bring about a reconciliation with the Illinois. For this purpose, he sent ambassadors to their country to inform them 'that their old friend Frontenac had returned; that he had brought back Tawerahet, the Cayuga sachem, and twelve of their tribe, who had been sent to France by De Nonville; that he was sorry the tomahawk had been dug up during his absence; and that he was desirous of planting the tree of peace, and burying the hatchet under its branches.'

"The savages, encouraged by the English, and furnished with guns and ammunition, instead of listening to these propositions, assumed, if possible, an aspect more terrific than ever; and Frontenac soon found that he had to contend, not only with the English colonies and Iroquois, but with the Ottawas, Hurons, Miamis, Illinois, Pottawatomies, and several other tribes of western Indians.

"The good old governor, now in the sixty-eighth year of his age, did not once suffer his fortitude to forsake him. His mental and physical abilities were undiminished; and by his indefatigable exertions, several of the outposts, which had been partially demolished and abandoned, were rebuilt.

"Early in 1690, an invasion of Canada was planned by the New England and New York colonies, in conjunction with their allies. The New York troops and Indians were to march by land and attack Montreal, while the New England forces were to proceed by water and storm Quebec.

"Accordingly the land forces, under the command of Major Schuyler, left Albany about midsummer. Having arrived at Chambly, they were discovered by a Frenchman, who proceeded with all possible speed to Montreal with the intelligence, so that a day or two was allowed to prepare for the invaders. Monsieur Callieres was commandant at Montreal, and, fortunately, the governor himself was there at that time.

"The attack was commenced on the militia, which gave way; but as soon as the regulars were brought into action the English were repulsed at every point, and finally dispersed, not, however, without the loss of three hundred men.

"On receiving intelligence that a large armament was in the St. Lawrence, Frontenac, with three hundred troops, repaired forthwith to Quebec; and by rowing night and day, arrived there a day or two before the attack was made. This fleet, consisting of thirty-four sail and two thousand men, commanded by Sir William Phipps, arrived on the 7th of October. The town contained but few troops, and would have surrendered at discretion, had an attack been made at once; but with the same imbecility which prevented a co-operation with Major Schuyler, Sir William continued to disgrace the expedition. He accordingly came to anchor, and lay in the bay five days, and did nothing but send a flag on the fourth day to Frontenac, with an insulting letter, requiring an unconditional surrender.

"The next day it was discovered that Sir William was landing twelve or fifteen hundred men four miles below the town. The French and Indians repaired to a wood through which the English must pass, and concealed themselves. The unsuspecting invaders had proceeded part way through the wood, when suddenly they were assailed in every direction. They fled precipitately, in the utmost confusion, leaving nearly four hundred dead on the spot. The total loss of the French and Indians was only sixteen!

"On the following day, Sir William landed four pieces of artillery, with one thousand men, to force the wood, while he commenced bombarding the town. These were again met and completely repulsed, with the loss of between three and four hundred of the enemy and all their artillery, while the loss of the French was but forty. Sir William, having kept up the fire for twenty-four hours, raised the siege, proceeded down the

St. Lawrence, and arrived at Boston on the 13th of November.

"The savages continued their incursions all along the St. Lawrence, laying waste plantations, and carrying off many scalps. The farmers could not cultivate their land, provisions became scarce, and the inhabitants were obliged to feed the soldiers, while their own children were famishing.

"In the summer of 1693, Frontenac invaded the country of the Iroquois, destroyed three castles, and, two years afterward, rebuilt Fort Cadaraqui. The following year, 1696, he destroyed a strong fort at Onondaga, erected by the English about six years previously, together with several Indian villages. He also made a number of prisoners.

"Thus the war was continued, with varied success, until the peace of Ryswick restored order in Europe, which soon extended to America."

During this eventful period in the history of New France, while many of the French trading-posts were abandoned, Saut Ste. Marie and Michilimackinac, though suffering much from constant anxiety and privation, withstood the tide of war, and maintained their position. M. Perot, commandant at Michilimackinac during the first years of the war, was a man of great ability; yet he often found his powers fully taxed in maintaining order and subordination amid the discordant elements of his little garrison, consisting of soldiers, fur-traders, and *coureurs des bois*, deprived of their former exciting occupations, and surrounded as they were with every possible discouragement. The disaffection of many of their Indian allies, and the frequent incursions of the hostile Iroquois, almost destroyed the fur-trade, while nearly all intercourse with Quebec and Montreal was cut off. Yet the heroic commandant remained firm at his post—though at one time, for many months, the fish, which were abundant in the waters almost beneath their feet, constituted the only food of the garrison.

About the year 1691, M. de la Porte Louvigny was appointed commandant in place of M. Perot, and was himself superseded by M. de la Motte Cadillac in 1696.

Since the year 1684 the Iroquois had kept up an almost continual state of warfare with the French and their allies; and Count Frontenac found there was no way to terminate this harassing state of affairs, except by treating the prisoners of war according to the Indian customs, and M. de la Motte Cadillac received orders accordingly.

Representations of the bad effects produced upon the Indians by the sale of intoxicating drinks had been repeatedly made to Louis XIV. In 1694 the king and bishops began seriously to question the propriety of allowing brandy and other intoxicating drinks to be transported to Michilimackinac as an article of traffic. After much discussion, the subject was finally referred to the *Sorbonne* for decision. Upon mature deliberation, this august body decided the question in the negative, and the king immediately issued an edict forbidding the transportation of brandy to Michilimackinac as an article of traffic.

The French at that post submitted to this prohibition with a very bad grace, and the following letter from M. de la Motte Cadillac gives his view of the subject. It also contains an interesting history of the condition of the fort and its surroundings, with an account of his obedience to the barbarous but perhaps necessary orders of Count Frontenac. The letter appears to have been written to a personal friend, at Quebec.

"FORT BUADE, MICHILIMACKINAC, August 3, 1695.

"MONSIEUR:—You already know, without doubt, that Count Frontenac appointed me, last year, to the command of this country, in the place of M. Louvigny; and that the convoy which I conducted revolted, the season being bad, and very far advanced.

"My departure was on the 24th of September, and I could only go twenty-five leagues in twelve days, on account of the continued rains and contrary winds that prevailed. I did all I could to encourage the voyageurs to proceed on the journey, but to no purpose; and, not knowing what else to do, I took the resolution to send them back, in good condition—foreseeing that they would not fail to go, even without my permission. I was not sorry afterward that I resolved upon this course, though the remainder of the journey seemed frightful, on account of the quantities of floating ice in the large lakes which we must cross. However, I decided, without hesitation, to accomplish the journey, or perish by the way. Accordingly, I made choice of five of the most vigorous men in the convoy, and two savages; and taking only sufficient food for two months, I continued my journey, and at length reached my destination.

"I immediately found myself in circumstances of great embarrassment, in consequence of the departure of the convoy that goes down to Montreal yearly, and by the arrival of the one that comes from that place. This post is the rendezvous of the chiefs of all the nations in the surrounding country, and I was obliged to be in their councils to decide all their different propositions. These circumstances caused me so great heaviness, that I sought relief by fully informing Count Frontenac of affairs here, and you, without doubt, have received better information from him than I could give, whatever care I might devote to the subject.

"As there was a cessation of hostilities, on propositions of peace made by the Iroquois, with much apparent submission, it was necessary to make great efforts to induce all these nations to recommence the war, according to the orders I had received. Although there went out from here, and from the villages depending upon this post, about eight or nine hundred men, in different parties, they only brought in fifty-six scalps, and made four prisoners, whom we burned, according to their custom, notwithstanding all the assurances the victims could give that a treaty of peace had already been made at Montreal.

"As the Iroquois are not to be trusted, our allies were not disposed to believe the assurances of the prisoners, and finally subjected them to the usual treatment of those who fall alive into the hands of their enemies. There are several parties which have not yet returned; if they bring any prisoners to me, I can assure you their fate will be no sweeter than that of the others.

"From the orders he gave me, I am persuaded that the Count will prosecute the war with greater energy than ever before. Nor do I believe that in future he will be in a mood to listen to any propositions from the Iroquois, who have at last yielded to the powerful efforts made by the English to dissuade them from completing the treaty of peace for which they had been so very solicitous.

"I am fully persuaded of the necessity of taking Manathé. As long as that place stands, we shall never be masters of these nations. Experience has taught me, better than I had before known, that, so long as Manathé stands, occasions will always be found for its people to annoy us.

"In regard to the decision made by the court, concerning the transportation of liquors to this place, I am far from daring to disapprove of it; but nothing can induce me to be entirely silent on a subject involving so deeply the interest of the king.

"It is a great mistake, if people have an idea that this place is deserted; if it be possible that any are in this belief, I think it my duty to correct the erroneous impression. It is very important that you should know, in case you are not already informed, that this village is one of the largest in all Canada. There is a fine fort of pickets, and sixty houses, that form a street in a straight line. There is a garrison of well-disciplined, chosen soldiers, consisting of about two hundred men, the best-formed and most athletic to be found in this New World; besides many other persons who are residents here during two or three months in the year. This being an indubitable fact, it seems to me that this place should not be deprived of the privilege which His Majesty has accorded to all the other places and villages in Canada—the privilege of furnishing themselves with the necessary drinks for their use. If there are but few places which should enjoy this liberty, this would undoubtedly be one, as it is exposed to all kinds of fatigue. The situation of the place, and the food also, require it.

"The houses are arranged along the shore of this great Lake Huron, and fish and smoked meat constitute the principal food of the inhabitants, *so that a drink of brandy, after the repast, seems necessary to cook the bilious meats, and the crudities which they leave in the stomach.* The air is penetrating and corrosive, and without the brandy that they use in the morning, sickness would be much more frequent.

"The villages of the savages, in which there are six or seven thousand souls, are about a pistol-shot distant from ours. All the lands are cleared for about three leagues around their village, and perfectly well cultivated. They produce a sufficient quantity of Indian corn for the use of both the French and savage inhabitants. The question is, then, what reason can there be for this prohibition of intoxicating drinks, in regard to the French who are here now, and who only go and come once a year? Are they not subjects of the king, even as others? In what country, then, or in what land, until now, have they taken from the French the right to use brandy, provided they did not become disorderly? And if, by chance, some should become so, the commandants know how to apply the remedy. They can imprison, fetter, and chastise disorderly persons here as well as elsewhere.

"Now what reason can one assign that the savages should not drink brandy bought with their own money as well as we? Is it prohibited to prevent them from becoming intoxicated? or is it because the use of brandy reduces them to extreme misery—placing it out of their power to make war, by depriving them of clothing and arms? If such representations in regard to the Indians have been made to the Count, they are very false, as every one knows who is acquainted with the ways of the savages.

"It is an undeniable fact, that the law strictly forbids any one to trade with the savages for their arms, under pain of a large pecuniary fine. As for their clothing, can any one assert that clothing is necessary for them when they go to war, since everybody knows that it is the custom of all the nations here, when they 'go to eat their enemy on his own land,'* they go naked, and paint

* "When the business is to declare war, in form, between two or three nations, the manner of expressing it is, to 'hang the kettle over the fire;' which has its origin, without doubt, in the barbarous custom of

themselves black and red from head to foot, if they are rich enough to do it.

"It is the custom, when the moment comes for their departure on warlike expeditions, for each warrior to dispose of all his clothing, making presents of the different articles to those who remain at home; and on their return, while they are singing their songs of war, of prowess, and of victory, it is permitted to each of them to gather all that belongs to him, such as guns, bows and arrows, kettles, and even all they can seize of the spoils of their enemies, which consist only of such articles as I have mentioned.

"It is bad faith to represent to the Count that the sale of brandy reduces the savage to a state of nudity, and by that means places it out of his power to make war; since he never goes to war in any other condition.

"It is certain that the bravest of their warriors have never used more than half a pound of powder, and a pound of balls, in one battle. Their manner is to fire

eating their prisoners, and those they have killed, after boiling them. They likewise say, simply, that 'they are going to eat such a nation,' which signifies that they are going to make war against them in the most destructive and outrageous manner; and indeed they seldom do otherwise. When they intend to engage an ally in the quarrel, they send him a porcelain or wampum, which is a large shell, in order to invite him to drink the blood, or, as the terms made use of signify, the broth of the flesh of their enemies."—*Charlevoix.*

three or four times, and when they have the advantage of their enemy, they rush upon him. They are very strong and quick, and, as they never rally, their battles are soon ended.

"Finally, this prohibiting the transportation of brandy to this place, has much discouraged the Frenchmen who are here, from trading in future. Ceasing to sell liquor to the savages has caused a universal commotion among all the nations, as will be seen by what took place here on the 21st of last March. All the chiefs, and a large number of the inhabitants of all the surrounding villages, assembled here, and addressed me as follows:

"'O chief, what evil have thy children done to thee, that thou shouldst treat them so badly? Those that came before thee were not so severe upon us. It is not to quarrel with thee that we came here, it is only to know for what reason thou wishest to prevent us from drinking brandy. Thou shouldst look upon us as thy friends, and the brothers of the French, or else as thy enemies. If we are thy friends, leave us the liberty of drinking; our beaver is worth thy brandy, and the Master of Life gave us both, to make us happy. If thou wish to treat us as thy enemies, or as thy slaves, do not be angry if we carry our beaver to Orange, or Corland, where they will give us brandy, as much as we want.'

"This speech did not fail to embarrass me, and I thought best to make them the following answer:

"'My children, I am a good father; I have a very tender heart, and I hear from afar the cries of my children. I do not wish to wrong you, still less to treat you as my enemies, or my slaves. Do not be angry if you have no brandy this year. The reason for it is, that the trees which produce it on the other side of the great water, have frozen this year, and the vessels only brought a very little, so that the French could scarcely have what they wanted for themselves. The frost that destroyed your corn this year, has also destroyed the fruit from which they make the liquor; it is to be hoped that next year you will not lack. Take courage, do not be disheartened; Onontio will send you a sufficient quantity to rejoice you.'

"They replied that they wished me to write to the governor-general, which I promised. Meanwhile, to show you that this people care only for the present, and never regard the future, I ought to tell you that on the 4th of July, twenty Hurons departed from here without the knowledge of any one, and have gone to the Iroquois to make negotiations of peace, in order to facilitate the passage to the English, where they can trade and get brandy.

"This is the effect produced by the bad counsel given

to the Count; and, indeed, there is nothing more provoking than to witness the manifestation of a wish to take from a people not yet civilized, the rights they have enjoyed ever since they have known the French.

"It seems very strange that they should pretend that the savages would ruin themselves by drinking. The savage himself asks why they do not leave him in his beggary, his liberty, and his idleness; he was born in it, and he wishes to die in it—it is a life to which he has been accustomed since Adam. Do they wish him to build palaces, and ornament them with beautiful furniture? He would not exchange his wigwam, and the mat on which he camps like a monkey, for the *Louvre!*

"An attempt to overthrow the present state of affairs in this country, would only result in the ruin of commerce and the destruction of the colony.

"Perhaps it will be said that the sale of brandy makes the labors of the missionaries unfruitful. It is necessary to examine this proposition. If the missionaries labor only for the extension of commerce, pursuing the course they have hitherto, I agree to it; but, if it is the use of brandy that hinders the advancement of the cause of God, I deny it; for it is a fact which no one can deny, that there are a great number among the savages who never drink brandy, yet who are not, for that, better Christians.

"All the Sioux, the most numerous of all the tribes

who inhabit the region along the shore of Lake Superior, do not even like the smell of brandy—are they more advanced in religion for that? They do not wish to hear the subject mentioned, and when the missionaries address them, they only laugh at the foolishness of preaching. Yet these priests boldly fling before the eyes of the Europeans, whole volumes filled with glowing descriptions of the conversion of souls by thousands, in this country, causing the poor missionaries from Europe to run to martyrdom, as flies to sugar and honey.

"I am an eye-witness to all that passes here, yet I do not believe I shall ever be in humor to write on this point."

Count Frontenac, who had devoted the best portion of his life to the service of New France; the friend and adviser of the struggling colonists; the guide and controller of those rash, enthusiastic adventurers, whose zeal in prosecuting distant explorations seemed unquenchable; the safe director of the intricate workings of colonial home-policy, and the successful general, having conducted his country through a most perilous and distressing war, lived only to conclude a peace with his savage neighbors, and died, in 1699, in the seventy-eighth year of his age. His death was universally lamented.

"At the age of fifteen," says a note in the Cass MSS., "Count Frontenac signalized himself in Holland, where he served his apprenticeship of arms. He was recalled to France for the service of the king. He commanded the regiment of Normandie, and in the several battles which were fought in Germany and Italy, he merited, by his valor and his talents, to be successively promoted as master and marshal of the camp, and even to command a separate corps of the army.

"When the Venetians sent to ask aid of Louis XIV., this prince consulted Marshal Turenne on the choice of a commanding officer for the troops of the Republic, and M. de Frontenac was the one designated by the great captain.

"In Canada, he justified his reappointment to its government, by subduing the Iroquois, and by repulsing the English. When the English envoys demanded of him the surrender of Quebec, giving him a certain time in which to decide, placing his watch in his hand to mark the time, his haughty answer was, 'My reply is from the mouth of my cannon;' notwithstanding Quebec was almost without ammunition and food.

"M. de Frontenac had his arm broken at Orbitelle. His grandfather was one of the most distinguished of the French nobility, and all his connections and family alliances were sufficient recommendations for any ordinary man; but the Count added to all these illustrious names the glory of his own services."

M. de Callieres succeeded Count Frontenac in the government of Canada. He occupied the post of governor-general until early in the summer of 1703, when he died suddenly. The Marquis de Vaudreuil was appointed his successor.

## CHAPTER IV.

The peace of Ryswick—France retains her possessions in America—Commercial rivalry between the French and English—Cadillac's management of the Indians—Their attachment to the French—Upper Nations send envoys to Montreal in 1700—Written treaty made and signed by the governor-general and envoys—Importance of a fort on the Detroit—M. la Motte Cadillac goes to France—Recital of his plans to Count Pontchartrain—Project approved by the king—Cadillac appointed commandant—Returns to Canada—Leaves La Chine for Detroit—Establishes Fort Pontchartrain in 1701—Company of the colony organized.

THE peace of Ryswick, ratified Sept. 11th, 1697, allowed France to retain all the places of which she had possession at the beginning of the war, but it did not quiet the restless spirit of the English colonists. They were not willing to pursue the same conciliatory course which had given the French an almost unbounded influence over the savages, yet were exceedingly jealous of that power which thus retained the profits of the fur-trade. This commercial rivalry, and strife for domination, kept the French and English colonies, even during the brief peace, in a state of inimical excitement.

By the prudent management of M. de la Motte Cadillac, who was commandant at Michilimackinac from 1695 to 1699, permanent treaties of peace had been made with the tribes in that distant region, and they had become strongly attached to the French. In July, 1700, four of these "upper nations" sent envoys to Montreal "to weep for the French who had died in the war." The governor-general took advantage of this visit, and of the conciliatory spirit recently manifested by the Iroquois, to make a written treaty with the Five Nations, and these allies from the Northwest. All the preliminaries were amicably settled, and the treaty was signed by each nation, with its own to-tem, or symbols.

The sad experiences of the recent war with England and the Iroquois, and the evident disaffection which still existed, though restrained by the treaties from absolute outbreak, rendered more than ever apparent to the French, the importance of a fort on the Detroit, which should command this channel of communication with the great lakes, thus preventing the English from having access to the Far Indians. The attempt of M. du Lhut had failed, and M. de la Motte Cadillac, fearing that a written petition would meet with a repulse, proceeded in person to Versailles, and presented the subject to the consideration of Count Pontchartrain, the colonial minister. The count received the self-appointed envoy with great kindness, and listened attentively to the plan of his proposed enterprise. The following conversation then ensued, which Cadillac afterward committed to writing.

*Count.* "What reasons have you for wishing to establish a fort on the Detroit?

*La Motte.* "I have many; the first, and perhaps most important object, would be to make it a permanent post, not subject to frequent changes as are many of the others. To effect this, it is only necessary to have a good number of the French, soldiers and traders, and to draw around it the tribes of friendly Indians, in order effectually to conquer the Iroquois, who, from all time, have ruined the colonies, and prevented the advancement of civilization.

*Count.* "That would be well, if what you propose could be executed without great difficulty; but it seems to me that, instead of fortifying the colony by this establishment, you will only weaken it.

*La Motte.* "That would be true, if the Iroquois were the friends of the French inhabitants, but they are the enemies. The forces of the French are too much scattered; they live too far apart. It is absolutely necessary to draw them together, because when it is desirable to attack the Iroquois in their villages, the French must make great movements, and march in large numbers, which causes the king very heavy expenses. Often, the result of such a march consists in killing four or five unhappy wretches, because great movements cannot be made without noise, and without the savages knowing it. They retire into the woods when their forces are inferior, and by this means render useless the expense and preparation of the French.

*Count.* "I see that you are right, since the great enterprises which have been undertaken in Canada, and even the general movements of the whole colony have been unsuccessful, having done no other harm to the Iroquois than merely pillaging their grain, which they had left to pursue the chase along the Detroit; and their game has furnished them subsistence till the following harvest. I see that you will tell me, if Detroit were fortified with a good number of French and savages, they would deprive the Iroquois of the resources of the chase; and by the continual incursions they would make upon them, on account of the proximity of the post, the Iroquois would be reduced to the last extremity, and often perish with hunger.

*La Motte.* "Sir, your penetration has anticipated my speech; I am persuaded that when you have heard the other reasons for this establishment, you will be still more deeply convinced of the necessity for it. It is incontestable that all the waters of the great lakes pass through this strait, and this is the only practicable path by which the English can carry on their trade with the savage nations, which have correspondence with the French. The English use every possible means to obtain trade, but, if that post were fortified in form, the English would entirely abandon the hope of depriving us of its advantages.

*Count.* "I understand what you intend; your design is good. You would deprive the enemies of the state, of the means of prosecuting the fur-trade in that country; but how will you prevent the savages from going to them, if they wish, and if they are drawn by the advantageous price of goods?

*La Motte.* "I confess that is a great attraction for them; but experience shows us that although the savages in the neighborhood of Quebec, Three Rivers, and Montreal, are perfectly well informed that their furs sell better with the English, and that they can obtain goods at a lower price, yet they make all their trade with us. There are many reasons for this. One is, that each savage, one with another, kills, per year, only fifty or sixty beavers, and as he is neighbor to the Frenchman, frequently borrows of him, paying in proportion to his returns by the chase. With the little that remains to him, he is compelled to make purchases for his family. Thus he finds himself unable to go to the English, because his remaining goods are not worth the trouble of carrying so far, not being sufficient to pay him for the expense of his journey. Another reason is, that in frequenting the French he receives many caresses; they are too cunning to allow his furs to escape, especially when they succeed in making him eat and drink with them.

"The *will* to go to the English still exists among the savages, but they are skillfully reduced to the impossibility of its execution. If Detroit is not established, sir, we shall soon see all the savages of the country going to the English, or inviting them to come and establish themselves in the Indian country.

*Count.* "Have you not still other reasons?

*La Motte.* "One cannot deny that our savages have hitherto hunted north of Lake St. Clair, but by this establishment, they would pursue the chase as far as two hundred leagues south of Lake Erie, toward the sea. Consequently, those furs that make the greater part of the trade of the English by means of their savages, would be conveyed by ours into the French colony, and make a very considerable increase in its commerce.

*Count.* "What furs are there in that country?

*La Motte.* "The skins of the stag, deer, elk, roebuck, black bear, and buffalo, with wolf, otter, wildcat, beaver, and other small furs.

*Count.* "Are those larger skins worth money, and do the traders find sale for them? Could we not find means to occupy the savages in the pursuit of these animals, and cause them to abandon that of the beaver, which is now prohibited merchandise? The vast accumulation of beaver fur is becoming burdensome to France.

*La Motte.* "Those skins are actually in favor; the skins of the deer and the stag are worth sixteen francs a-piece; those of the elk, twenty francs; the black bear, ten francs; the roebuck, five francs, and the rest in proportion; therefore it is certain that we could easily occupy the savages in this pursuit, provided we furnish them with goods to the value of their peltry. This would be an unfailing means of making sale for the beaver in the kingdom, since, instead of one hundred and thirty thousand now received every year at the storehouse in Quebec, there would be but about seventy thousand, which would be a large yearly diminution. I do not include the inferior beaver of Canada.

*Count.* "You have given many excellent reasons, the means of humbling the Iroquois, and causing them to respect the French; the exclusion of the English commerce and consequent French domination, and their increased profit by trading for different furs. It is absolutely necessary to establish this post.

"If the king approves this project, I will give you two hundred chosen men, of different trades, with six companies of soldiers, in order that the place may be in a condition to hold the Iroquois in subjection in time of peace, and to destroy them if they wish for war; and particularly that our allies may be secure under this protection. Therefore, prepare yourself to return to Canada, and commence the establishment of Detroit.

*La Motte.* "I will go, since you command me, but I shall find many difficulties to overcome in the accomplishment of this enterprise, as the Jesuits of that country are, personally, my enemies.

*Count.* "Only go, do not place yourself in difficulty; vigorously prosecute this affair, and if you find obstacles which prevent your success, you have only to return and render me an account of them."

After some time, M. de la Motte Cadillac was again summoned into the presence of Count Pontchartrain, who remarked:

"The king has examined your project, and has given me orders to send you back, without delay, to take prompt possession of Detroit, wishing you to command there until further orders. You will, therefore, depart immediately for Rochefort, whence you will embark.

"Pardon me, sir," replied La Motte, "but I beg you will take into consideration the expense of the two painful voyages I have already made, which have exhausted my own purse and the liberality of my friends; also, the expenditures I shall be obliged to make in perfecting this establishment."

"I will take care of you; only pursue such a course as will insure you success," said the count.

"Provided I am supported by the honor of your protection, I am sure of perfecting this work," was La Motte's enthusiastic rejoinder.

Count Pontchartrain then presented him with a commission as commandant, and a grant from his majesty, Louis XIV., of a tract of land, fifteen acres square, "wherever on the Detroit the new fort should be established."

M. Cadillac arrived at Quebec on the 8th of March, 1701; thence he proceeded to Montreal, where he was occupied until June in making the necessary preparations for his expedition. He left La Chine on the 5th of June, with fifty soldiers, and fifty Canadian traders and artisans. His officers were M. de Tonti as captain, and Messrs. Dugué and Chacornacle as lieutenants. A Récollet priest accompanied the troops as chaplain, and a Jesuit went as missionary to the Indians. In compliance with the orders of the governor-general, he took the old route by the Ottawa river, and arrived at Detroit on the 24th of July, 1701.

The fortification erected by M. de Cadillac was nothing more than a strong stockade of wooden pickets.

The space inclosed was nearly square, with wooden bastions at each angle, only two of which seem to have been serviceable, according to M. d'Aigrement, who says—"there are two bastions, so small and of such irregular figure as to be of little use."* Within this inclosure, which was dignified with the name of Fort Pontchartrain, M. de la Motte caused a few log huts to be erected, the roofs of which were thatched with grass. Such was Detroit in 1701.

As the principal object in the establishment of this post, as well as Forts Frontenac, Michilimackinac, and Saut Ste. Marie, was to secure to France the immense fur-trade of the great Northwest, of necessity one of the first acts of the colonial executive at Quebec must have been to make such arrangements as would best promote the interests of the government, and at the same time most effectually guard against oppression on the one part, and disaffection on the other, among the officers, subordinates, and traders, occupying points so remote from the capital.

The most natural, and probably the most effectual method of accomplishing these objects, would be the

* The first fort erected at Detroit inclosed the portion of ground extending from where the house of Mr. Joseph Campau now stands, on Jefferson Avenue, to a few feet below Shelby-street, and thence to Woodbridge-street, which was then very near the margin of the river.

organization of the traders, occupying any such post, into a company with certain privileges and restrictions. In accordance with this universal business principle, a company was formed by the merchants interested in the trade at Fort Frontenac and Fort Pontchartrain, known as the "Company of the Colony of Canada," and the following contract was duly confirmed at Quebec, October 31st, 1701:

"COMPANY OF THE COLONY OF CANADA.

"*Contract made with the Company of the Colony of Canada concerning Fort Frontenac and Detroit, to enable said Company to traffic for beaver and other peltries, in conformity to the agreement made in a convention held at Quebec, October 31st*, 1701.

"Before the royal notaries, at Quebec, in New France, appeared M. le Chevalier Callieres, lieutenant-governor for the king in this country of New France, and Monsieur Champigny, administrator of justice, police, and revenue of the said country, who testify that, in consequence of orders which they have this year received from his majesty, to intrust to the Company of the Colony of this said country the posts of Detroit and Fort Frontenac, there was held at the Chateau St. Louis, in this city, on the eighth of the present month, a general assembly of all the inhabitants of this country who have a deliberative voice in the said company, that all the arrangements might be made in their presence, if the company should decide to accept the said posts of Detroit and Fort Frontenac.

"There were present at this assembly the seven directors-general of the said company, the governors of Montreal and Three Rivers, many civil and military officers, and the merchants and other inhabitants interested in the company.

"After mature deliberation, the result was declared to be the acceptance of these posts by the company, for the purposes of trade in beaver and other peltries, to the entire exclusion of all private individuals, who are now, or may hereafter become, residents of that country; and that the act of said acceptance shall be passed between the governor-general and intendant, and the directors-general of the said company.

"In consequence of said decision, the following articles of agreement have been made between the governor-general and intendant on the one part, and Messrs. d'Auteuil, procureur-general of the king in the sovereign council of this country, Lotbinieres, lieutenant-general of this city of Quebec, Irazeur, Gobin, Macart, and Pierre, gentlemen, merchants of this city of Quebec, all directors-general of the said company, on the other part.

"Be it known, that the governor-general and intendant, in consequence of the express orders which they have this year received from the king, do, by these presents and acceptances, in the name of His Majesty, cede and convey to the directors of the said Company of the Colony the said posts of Detroit and Fort Frontenac, giving into the possession of the said Company of the Colony, from this day forth, the said posts in the state in which they now are, for their use, to traffic in furs, to the exclusion of all other inhabitants of said country, so long as it shall please His Majesty.

"It shall be the duty of the said company to complete the construction of the fort at Detroit, and the buildings properly belonging thereto; and the company shall in future keep said fort and buildings in good repair, that they may be maintained and rendered in the same state in which they are now, and better, if possible, whenever His Majesty shall judge proper to receive them, if in the course of time he so order.

"The Company of the Colony is also to take charge of the goods which have been sent to the said place, obeying the conditions that have been agreed upon—Messrs. Radisson and Arnault to be overseers of the storehouse of the said goods which the intendant has placed in the hands of the directors of the company. They are also to have charge of the other advances made by the king for this establishment, and to make payment for the said goods, and advances to the intendant from the first bills which shall be returned from Detroit; and in case said bills should not be sufficient, on the first of October, 1702, the said overseers shall give bills of exchange for the remainder, which shall be drawn upon the directors and commissioners of said company in Paris, payable to the securities and overseers of the storehouses, for the purpose of liquidating the claims against the said company, conformably to the agreement made with the said lord-lieutenant.

"The intendant shall deduct from the amount due, six thousand livres, French money, being the gift ordered by His Majesty for the support of honest families in this country who may need assistance.

"The payment of the said sum of six thousand livres shall be made by the said company every year, on the said first of October, so long as it shall enjoy the commerce of the said post of Detroit.

"It is also agreed that the king shall support, at his expense, the garrison which the governor shall order for the protection of the said fort of Detroit, and that the commandant and one other officer only, shall be maintained by the company.

"The said commandant and soldiers shall not make any trade for furs with the savages nor French, directly nor indirectly, under any pretext whatever, under pain of confiscation of the said furs, and other punishment prescribed by the king.

"Moreover, the said company binds itself to cause to be conveyed from Montreal to Detroit, at its own expense, the provisions and other articles which His Majesty shall furnish to the said garrison, with the help of fifteen livres per hundred weight, which the intendant shall cause to be paid from the treasury of His Majesty to the company.

"In regard to Fort Frontenac, it will remain as it now is, fully and entirely at the disposal of His Majesty, unless the company can advance some better claim than that of placing deputies there to make commerce in furs for their profit, to the exclusion of all others.

"Until His Majesty's orders shall be received, the deputies shall be lodged, and their goods stored, in the storehouses of the fort, as the magazine guard and the goods of the king have been heretofore.

There shall be made an inventory of all the effects which shall be found at the said fort, for the commerce of the said place, after the return of the last convoy for this year, which effects shall remain for the company, who shall be bound to pay for them at the price expressed in the invoice and statement which is in the hands of the intendant. The said amount to be paid during the year 1702, from the returns of the commerce; and in case that the said returns shall not be sufficient, the balance shall be paid in bills of exchange, which shall be drawn upon the said commissioners of the said company, and its director in Paris.

"The said company shall be required to pay the sum of seven livres and ten sous, French money, per hundred weight, for the transportation of effects from Montreal to the said fort; and the said company enjoying, as hereinbefore stated, the privilege of trading for furs at the said place of Fort Frontenac, exclusive of all others, will be required to transport to the said Fort Frontenac the articles necessary for the subsistence of the garrison of the said place, conformably to the orders of the king, contained in his dispatches of the present year. The commandant, officers, and soldiers which the governor-general shall hold there in garrison, shall make no trade, directly or indirectly, on pain of confiscation of their furs, and other punishments prescribed by the laws of the king, until the agreement be revoked.

"Executed and conveyed at Quebec, Chateau St. Louis, in the forenoon of the thirty-first day of October, 1701, the said gentlemen interested and the notaries having signed at the time, the agreements remaining in the office of M. de Chamblon, one of the notaries."

## CHAPTER V.

Difficulty between the Jesuits and Franciscans—Character of M. Cadillac—Letter to Count Pontchartrain—Account of religious affairs—Removal of the savages to Detroit—Hurons—Miamis—Messages from the Outawa-Sinagos and Kiskakons—Necessity of presents to the savages—Trade in buffalo-skins—Mulberry-trees on Grand river—Fine harvest at Detroit—Indian chiefs wish to visit France—Plan to form a company of Indian soldiers—Establishment of a seminary for the savages—Settlement by the Canadians—Cadillac complains of the large number of "permits"—Massacre of the Miamis by the Sioux—Other Indian difficulties arising from the "permits."

The directors of the "Company of the Colony" were Jesuits, and it was by their solicitation, aided by the united petition of the Jesuit missionaries already established in different portions of the Northwest, that they succeeded in obtaining from the governor-general the appointment of Father Vaillant to accompany M. de la Motte Cadillac, and establish himself as missionary at Detroit.

M. Cadillac was a zealous Catholic, as his correspondence abundantly testifies; but he was a Franciscan, and a cordial hater of the Jesuits. This fact was undoubtedly well known, as he did not hesitate to speak his sentiments in his official letters, and in his private correspondence; and a disposition to thwart his plans and purposes was soon manifested by that powerful and completely organized body. Many of the difficulties which subsequently arose in the colony, are clearly traceable to these personal dislikes.

M. de la Motte Cadillac was a bold, ambitious, enthusiastic man; somewhat visionary in his plans, prompt in action, fearless in speech, and of that decided cast of mind that always gives its possessor many enemies. Yet he was kind-hearted; and, if the decision of a superior court is any evidence, more frequently right than wrong in the course he pursued in the management of the affairs of the colony.

A man's writings usually contain the impress of his mind, at least in a sufficient degree to enable one to judge quite correctly of his habits of thought, and thence to infer, with some certainty, his general course of conduct. The voluminous MSS. of M. la Motte are deeply interesting. They give the reader a more correct idea of the man as he was, than any mere individual opinion could do, while a life-like picture of those early scenes is here preserved, which would otherwise have been lost in oblivion.

The following letter, addressed to Count Pontchartrain, shows the state of the colony two years after its settlement, and details the plans of the zealous commandant for its future welfare:

"Fort Pontchartrain, Aug. 31, 1703.

"Monseigneur:—I had the honor to write you, last year, a full account of all the affairs of this post; and I write you again, not knowing what arrangements you may have made concerning it.

"Doubtless you have noticed the regulations which were made by M. le Chevalier de Callieres, between Rev. Father Bouvert and myself, while I was at Quebec, and have supposed that all its stipulations were fulfilled on both sides.

"These regulations prove, with evidence, the opposition which the Jesuits in this country have raised against the settlement of the savages at this post; and I did hope that they would keep the promises which they made by public compact.

"You had the kindness to write me that the king wishes the savages to be served by the Father Jesuits; and that the Superior of Quebec would give me those who would enter into my plans better than did Father Vaillant.

"One would suppose that your orders would have sufficed to engage the services of the Superior in providing for this mission immediately; especially when you had so kindly favored him by permitting Father Vaillant to remain in this country after opposing, as he did, the intentions of His Majesty.

"The regulations of M. Callieres seem also to require him to provide for the missions, as it is clearly expressed there. Yet you will see that till now, the Jesuits have done nothing towards executing the intentions of His Majesty, though you have plainly expressed them to M. de Callieres and the Superior of Quebec, and have also been pleased to inform me of them.

"I do not know whether you have been informed that, in consequence of these regulations, the Company of the Colony have agreed to pay to the missionaries on the Detroit, the yearly sum of eight hundred francs each, and furnish them with necessary food and clothing, to be transported to their stations at the expense of the company; lodging them in the villages of the savages until more commodious houses can be erected for them.

"I am satisfied, on my part, in regard to the measures they have taken; and the company seems to be satisfied on its own part, having this spring, in conformity to the regulations, sent an express canoe for Father Marest, Superior of Michilimackinac. He pretended to have very important reasons for not coming here; and the company incurred the expense of the voyage to no purpose, as they had before done for Father Vaillant.

"You wished me to be a friend of the Jesuits, and to

have no trouble with them. After much reflection, I have found only three ways in which this can be accomplished: the first is, to let them do as they please; the second, to do whatever they desire; and the third, to say nothing of what they do.

"If I let the Jesuits do what they please, the savages will not establish themselves at Detroit; nor would any of them ever have settled here. If I do what they would desire, it will be necessary to have this post abandoned; and if I say nothing of what they do, it will only be necessary for me to pursue my present course. Notwithstanding this last essential point, I cannot yet engage them to be my friends.

"It is for you, my lord, to say whether you wish me to continue to induce the savages to establish themselves here, that this post may be preserved and sustained with *eclat*. If these are your sentiments, as I believe they are, perhaps I am the proper person to carry your plans into execution. But, I dare say to you, that the opinions of the Jesuits in this country are totally opposed to yours, at least on this point.

"All these things have not prevented the Sauteurs and Mississagués from coming here again this year, to build a village on this river. By my advice, these two nations have united into one. I judged this proper, thinking their union would be better for themselves, and for us, if any rupture should occur between these colonies and their enemies.

"Thirty Hurons of Michilimackinac arrived here on the 28th of June, to unite themselves with those already established here. There remain only about twenty-five at Michilimackinac. Father Carheil, who is missionary there, remains always firm. I hope, this fall, to pluck out the last feather of his wing, and I am persuaded that this obstinate old priest will die in his parish, without having a single parishioner to bury him.

"Several small bands of the Miamis have established themselves here, and also a few of the Nepisserinieux; some have joined the Hurons, and others the Outawas, and the Oppenagos, or Loups.

"The remainder of the Outawa-Sinagos, who are still at Michilimackinac, have sent me a necklace, in secret, to tell me they will come to join their brothers at Detroit, after they have gathered in their harvest. Six wigwams of Kiskakons have sent me the same message. I have replied, by necklaces, that I was going to mark out the land where they could make their fields.

"This proceeding on the part of the savages, shows how much the Jesuits intimidate them, by causing the apprehension to creep into their minds that some bad trick will be played upon them if they come here.

"When it pleases you that I should make an entire reunion of our allies at this place, it will be very easy to accomplish it; though on account of the extraordinary war of Canada, it will now be necessary to have about six thousand francs placed at my disposal, to be employed as I judge expedient, for the success of this enterprise; and of which I will give an exact account to M. de Callieres, and M. Beauharnais, the intendant.

"I have already had the honor to write you concerning the presents and necklaces which we give the savages. These are especially given to induce their *transmigration*, and are, to them, pledges of our fidelity to the promises we make them; and are titles which give them the right to possess, or abandon, as contracts do among civilized people.

"You know that, to this day, the company have not contributed a farthing for gifts, to put the savages in motion. It is true that they have placed in my hands a considerable stock of goods, to give an appearance of prosperity to this establishment, without cost to the king; and I believe they have reason to be satisfied with my management, since it is certain that they have rather gained than lost. I am better informed concerning this than any one else; at any rate, if they complain of the expenses which it has been, or may be, necessary to incur to sustain this post, I willingly pledge myself to indemnify them, and to urge on affairs here as your Highness may desire.

"If you doubt it, I will, whenever you please, give you such proof, that I dare flatter myself you will fully believe my statement.

"If this portion of the country had not been excluded from commerce, it would have fortified itself.

"I think the shortest way by which I could inspire you with confidence, would be by actual service. Have the kindness to employ me in some enterprise, and sustain me with the honor of your protection; and if, in spite of all the malice and trickery of my enemies, I do not succeed, never use me again.

"My enemies are continually attempting to overthrow my plans, or at least to produce vexatious delays, by presenting numerous arguments against them, representing the obstacles to be insurmountable, while I am employed in proving the fallacy of their objections.

"I do not know that the trade in buffalo-skins could be sustained, on account of the contempt in which they are held by the company. They do not pay the savages for them more than six francs a-piece. This does not please the hunters, because a package of hides, weighing two hundred and fifty or three hundred pounds, must be transported from three to four leagues inland, which they find too much labor. They therefore prefer to employ themselves in hunting beavers and other animals, whose skins are lighter and easier to transport.

"If the company does not increase the price of buffalo-skins, I think the savages will follow this chase only at a time when they can obtain no other furs.

"We have found a mine of copper on Lake Huron, of which I send you a specimen, which seems to me very pure. I have sent as much to M. de Callieres, and to the directors of the company, in order that they may take measures to know if it is sufficiently abundant to induce them to make an enterprise of it. The conveniences would be great, as the boats, and even the vessels could go to the places where it is, not being very far distant from this post.

"If you will permit me to explore the mines in the neighborhood of the lakes and rivers, I will *devote* myself to the exploration, visiting the different localities in person, that you may be more certainly informed of the facts. I am not able to incur the expense, but will only ask permission to choose for this enterprise twelve capable men, in Canada, who shall have the liberty to carry goods to the amount of four hundred francs each, and no more, into the places which they shall visit. In conforming myself to your wishes, I will close the mouth of all my enemies. By this means, perhaps, there will remain to the envious, only the vexation of seeing me succeed.

"In any case, this attempt will cost nothing to the king, nor to the public; consequently, they will have little ground of complaint.

"The Grand river, so called, on Lake Erie, near the farther extremity, is about fifteen leagues from here; and along its shores, and extending into the depths of its forests, are great numbers of mulberry-trees; the land is also perfectly good. If you will have the kindness to grant me six leagues on each side of the river, and as much in the forest, in title of marquisate, with the rights of hunting, fishing, and trade, I will undertake the cultivation of silk, by having people come from France who understand the business, and who will bring with them the necessary quantity of silkworms. Should you grant me this kindness, I will take measures to have them come by the first vessels, in order that they may arrive here before winter.

"As to trade, I will not make any till after the lease of the company expires.

"We have made a fine harvest this year, and have abundant supplies for a garrison of one hundred and fifty men, but I do not believe we shall be at that trouble, on account of the objections that are made to giving me soldiers.

"I have contented myself with asking for only fifty effective men; they left me but twenty-five, and I do not know as they will grant me even the additional twenty-five. I beg you to order M. de Callieres to grant me fifty more next year, that this garrison may be composed of one hundred effective men.

"This post should be equal to all emergencies, not only on account of our enemies, but also on account of our allies, whom it is necessary to hold in abeyance. It would be still better if you would send me some troops from France.

"The principal chief of the Hurons, who is very absolute in his nation, told me to write to you that he would be very glad to go to France, to assure His Majesty of his fidelity, and of his earnest desire to engage in the French service. He proposes to form a company of fifty men, of his nation, provided the French will make him captain, and give him a lieutenant and ensign. He also requires that we should pay him and his soldiers, by the month, the same wages that the officers and soldiers of the army are paid in this country.

"There is another chief, of the same nation, who obligates himself to do the same thing. They beg of you also to give them a passage on a vessel, to visit the king. I believe they intend to have a hunting expedition for the purpose of obtaining furs for a present to yourself, as an expression of their good-will.

"The principal chief of the Outawas, who is one of the noblest looking men I have seen among all these nations, and who is Frenchified in his habits, requested me to write you, that he also is anxious to visit you, but his age will not permit him to take so long a journey. However, he will send his nephew, with another friend, to France, to offer his services to the king. If His Majesty wishes to incur the expense, I think it will be the best means by which to secure the entire subjection of these two nations.

"I think it would be necessary to spare these Indian soldiers a little in the beginning, and only oblige them to do military duty once a month, when they would be reviewed with the other troops. It might even be expedient to release them entirely from military duty for three months during the winter, when they are engaged in hunting; but it would be necessary to be very exact in paying these companies every month.

"The chiefs who propose to form these companies, wish to have standards and clothes like the other soldiers; and they hope you will also furnish them with arms. They have assured me that they would obey me in all things pertaining to the service of the king, and have also promised obedience to all others who are commissioned by him. I have fully explained to them how they must behave as soldiers, and especially that they would be expected to exercise a spirit of subordination. They expressed themselves satisfied with all my instructions.

"None need be astonished at their ready acquiescence, for all men, in whatever state they are born, lack neither vanity nor ambition; and there are always enough who are anxious to make themselves esteemed and renowned among their fellow-men.

"The chief of the Hurons is already so inflated by this proposition, that he has requested M. de Callieres to cause him to live in French fashion. I received an order, when in Quebec, to build him a house of oak, forty feet long, and twenty-four feet wide. This house is delightfully situated on the margin of the river; it stands on a little eminence, and overlooks the village of the Hurons. His example has induced the chief of the Outawas to go to Montreal, to ask the same favor of M. de Callieres. He has not yet returned, but, without doubt, his request will be granted.

"You will perceive, by what I have written, that my plans seem to be working well. My opinion is, that these things are the most sure to render this people permanently subject to the king, and afterward to make them Christians. These projects will have a better effect than the preaching of the missionaries, since it is certain that they do not make any progress, and that all the good they do, is that which arises from the baptism of those children who die after having received it.

"Permit me to insist upon the great necessity there is for the establishment of a seminary at this place, for the instruction of the children of the savages with those of the French—instructing them in piety, and, at the same time, teaching them our language.

"The savages, being naturally proud, seeing their children placed among ours, would dress them in the same manner, and make their attendance at the seminary a point of honor. It is true that it would be necessary, at first, to allow these little savages great liberty, and only confine ourselves to the design of civilizing them, and rendering them capable of receiving instruction; and leave the rest to Him who made the heart.

"This expense would not be very great; I believe if His Majesty would grant a thousand crowns to the seminary at Quebec, that institution would commence this pious and holy work. Those gentlemen are so full of zeal for the service of God, and of charity for all that regards the subjects of the king in this colony, that we cannot help admiring them. All the country is under inexpressible obligations to them for the good education they give the youth, together with their good example and doctrine. It is these efforts which have produced very good subjects in the service of the Church in New France.

"I think you cannot commence this work too soon, and, if you object to it on account of the expenses which may arise afterward, I will pledge myself to raise, in this country, the amount necessary to continue to the savages this gratification, without any farther cost to the king.

"There is no reason to fear that savages will be wanting to do the hunting necessary to supply beaver and other furs. There are many nations in the vicinity of the lakes, and in the depths of the immense forests, who will never, perhaps, be reached by civilization, quite sufficient to kill all the animals whose furs are useful in trade.

"If these nations immediately around us are brought into subjection to the service of the king, in the manner I have proposed, it would not prevent them from doing their hunting at the proper time. These things will only bring them into a state to be Frenchified, and enable them to take arms in the service of the king, when he shall need them.

"One can easily perceive that if the savages were to-day upon the proposed footing, it would be of great advantage to the colony; since it is certain that, at the first beat of the drum, we could place under arms those savages who are disciplined, and their example would easily attract all the rest to follow them, and do like them. Thus, in the present war, these people, if united with us, would make incursions and terrible inundations upon the English colonies. Instead of that, they are divided among themselves, and are content to see us do, while we are only too happy if we can continue to hold them in that state.

"I foresee that there will be many objections to the plans which I have the honor to lay before you. I cannot prevent them, but can only assure you that the plans *shall* succeed if you wish.

"To come to the point, it will be necessary for you to send good orders, very decisive and exact, and to speak a little with the *great teeth.*

"If these plans were proposed by some one who has the protection of the Jesuits, they would have an excellent relish for them, and nothing would appear more easy to be put in execution. But, because I have not consulted them, or rather, because I have not been disposed to allow myself to be treated as a slave, as some of my predecessors were, who commanded in this country, they represent as impossible every thing that I propose. It seems to me, nevertheless, that if the Count would pay attention to these plans which I have the honor to present, and of which M. de la Touche is well-informed, it could be clearly seen whether I reason wisely or extravagantly.

"I will not repeat the different designs I have presented to the Count, I will only speak of Detroit. When I had the honor to present my memorial to you, remember, if you please, what trouble there was on account of the too great quantity of beaver, for which they could not find sale in France. The old traders complained that, on this account, they would not be able to sustain their lease. I mentioned this in my memorial, asking for the establishment of Detroit, and pledged myself to employ the savages in hunting other animals, such as the deer, the wild goat, the Canadian elk, the roebuck, the black bear, and the wolf, together with the lynx, otter, pecquans, and other small furs, for three years, without hunting the beaver, in order that they might, by this means, have time to sell a considerable quantity of the furs already amassed. I have so far executed what I promised, that there have been sent out from Detroit only about eight thousand beaver-skins in three years; and the surplus trade has been of large skins and small furs. The books of the company show that this fact is indisputable.

"The second design that I had in projecting this establishment, was not so much to have another post for commerce, as to afford a protection to commerce; since from this place we can go by canoe to all the nations that are around the lakes. It is a door by which one can go in and out, to trade with all our allies.

"I confess that to give success to this establishment, it will be necessary to make it a substantial post; to keep here a good garrison, to give the liberty to settle here, and not to allow any other establishment in the upper country.

"As several of the soldiers desire to establish themselves in this place, and for this purpose have asked of me grants of land, have the kindness to inform me if you wish me to comply with their request. They would take the confirmation of the grant from M. de Callieres and M. de Beauharnais.

"Do you wish the soldiers to marry here, when they shall be in a condition to support a family? I think it would be policy to settle a certain number of them every year.

"Be pleased also to inform me if you wish dwelling-places granted to the Canadians: there are several who persecute me continually for them.

"It is for you to speak decidedly on this point, for I cannot conceal from you that the company do not wish to do any thing about it. They pretend that this emigration would weaken the posts on this side of Quebec and Montreal. As for me, I do not believe that forty or fifty men, more or less, in those larger places, would make much difference, or prevent the execution of any of their projects, while at this post they would, without doubt, be a great assistance. Nothing can ever be accomplished here without more inhabitants. Our allies, who are already established here, and those who are on the way, would soon consider it a bad omen, and draw vexatious inferences concerning the faithfulness of our promises, as we have told them this should be a very considerable establishment.

"Perhaps you are already aware that there are no French settlements in this country, even to the habitation of M. Juchereau,* where there are not Jesuits. Detroit is the only exception. As they express so much earnest zeal in serving the missions, this fact shows the good-will they have toward me. As they trouble themselves so much with my affairs, I do not desire to see them here; yet they should choose for themselves, and make known their decision, that measures might be taken to have other missionaries come.

"It is proper that you should be informed that more than fifty years since, the Iroquois, by force of arms, drove away nearly all of the other Indian nations from

* M. Juchereau's was the most distant trading-post of the Northwest, and was, I think, at the western extremity of the country of the Illinois, beyond Lake Michigan.

this region to the farther extremity of Lake Superior—a country five hundred leagues north of this post, and frightfully barren and inhospitable. About thirty-two years ago, these exiled tribes collected themselves together at Michilimackinac, which is also an ungrateful land. There they were obliged to subsist principally upon fish, in the manner that I explained to you in a statement which I made when in France, and with which you had the kindness to tell me you were well satisfied.

"It seems that God has raised me as another Moses to go and deliver this people from captivity, or rather, as Caleb, to bring them back to the country of their fathers, to their ancient dwelling-place, of which there remained to them but a faint idea.

"Meanwhile, Montreal plays the part of Pharaoh; he cannot see this emigration without trembling, and he arms himself to destroy it. But I hope the Count, noticing that he is a ferocious beast without a guide, and without light, will smooth my path, and break through the impediments only to inundate and submerge those who have the rashness to desire the overthrow of a design so just.

"The people of Montreal do not know what they ask. They have broken the scepter of their first king, who is God himself. They wished to reject, and even stone

Him, who caused exquisite food to be rained upon the most ungrateful lands, and broke the rocks to satisfy their thirst.

"Of what do they complain, since the post of Detroit is established in an abandoned country, which has long remained in the possession of the Iroquois and the wolves?

"The Iroquois pursued the chase in all that region, and brought the beaver and small furs to the English. This is an indubitable fact, and one must be full of stubbornness to dispute it. I have, therefore, taken the right time to commence this establishment. The Iroquois have entirely withdrawn, or if any remain, they are intermingled with our allies. All the hunting is done by our savages, and all the trade returns to us. It is, then, a benefit to the kingdom of France, and a source of profit which we have torn from England.

"Individuals have complained that the Company of the Colony have the sole profit. I do not deny it; I leave them the liberty to clamor; I only wish that they may have eyes to distinguish that it is not the fault of the establishment, nor of him who planned it.

"I confess to some degree of boldness in coming to erect a trading-post for the company, in the midst of an ungoverned people. They now begin to have some first ideas of subordination, but these will soon be effaced, since the company have suddenly reduced them to the necessity of accepting whatever the commissioners feel disposed to give. The savages are also exposed to the insults of these commissioners of the company, who treat them according to their whim, or rather according to the brutal disposition which this kind of people usually possess.

"I wish to believe that the affairs of the kingdom have induced the Count to adopt the present system for a time, with the intention of uniting this post to His Majesty's domain, after the lease has expired. It is in this belief that I have devoted myself here to the service of the king. In managing our allies, I endeavor to make them understand that this second captivity, or rather this barbarous tyranny, will soon end. I do not know whether all our promises can induce them to be patient till that time. I fear that this kind of servitude will cause them to trade with the English, and form alliances with them. It will not be just to blame me if this should be the case.

"If this establishment is bad, it would be well for the Count to decide its fate at once. I have spoken my opinion about it; I have explained the circumstances of the case: you have been convinced of the necessity for erecting this fort, and its utility in the service of the king, the progress of religion, and the advancement of the colony. It only remains for me now to imitate the governor of the Holy City—take water and wash my hands of the affair.

"Had it been the pleasure of my lord to grant me the government of this colony, it would have been in my case as in all others. Cries and complaints would have been changed into congratulations and compliments; because those who envy me, and who, without cause, fear my advancement, have sufficient power to blacken all I do, with the desire to effect my removal; while, if they saw their hopes frustrated, they would follow the ordinary course of people, and applaud the very project against which they had inveighed.

"If you would yourself make the regulations for this post, instead of sending general orders to Canada, every thing would go much better; for, not being near the governor-general and intendant myself to urge my own claims, they always have some private reason for not granting me the protection which I ask of them. All this is done, in order to manage those who oppose me. It is not in my power to prevent this, whatever measures I may take.

"They continue to send out traders among our allies, under the plausible pretext of a continuation of the permits. The traders, finding themselves at greater liberty now than ever before, are guilty of conduct disgraceful to the French nation, and enormities are committed that deserve correction. These things cause great disaffection among our allies, which it will be difficult to remedy.

"Last year they sent M. Boudor, a Montreal merchant, into the country of the Sioux, to join Le Sueur. He succeeded so well in that journey that he transported thither twenty-five or thirty thousand pounds of merchandise, with which to trade in all the country of the Outawas. This proved to him an unfortunate investment, as he has been robbed of part of the goods by the Outagamies. I believed it necessary that you should be informed of this affair, that you might apply a remedy.

"The occasion of this robbery by one of our own allies was as follows: I speak with a full knowledge of the facts, as they occurred while I was at Michilimackinac. From time immemorial, our allies have been at war with the Sioux; and on my arrival at Michilimackinac, in conformity to the orders of M. Frontenac, the most able man who has ever come into Canada, I attempted to negotiate a truce between the Sioux and all our allies. Succeeding in this negotiation, I took the occasion to turn their arms against the Iroquois, with whom we were then at war; and soon after, I effected a treaty of peace between the Sioux, and the French and their allies, which lasted two years.

"At the end of that time, the Sioux came, in great numbers, to the villages of the Miamis, under pretense of ratifying the treaty. They were well received by the Miamis, and after spending several days in their villages departed, apparently perfectly satisfied with their good reception, as they certainly had every reason to be.

"The Miamis, believing them already far distant, slept quietly; but the Sioux, who had premeditated the attack, returned the same night to the principal village of the Miamis, where most of the tribe were congregated, and, taking them by surprise, slaughtered nearly three thousand, and put the rest to flight.

"This perfidy irritated all the nations. They came to Michilimackinac with their complaints, begging me to join with them and exterminate the Sioux. But the war we then had upon our hands did not permit me to listen to their proposition, so it became necessary for me to hold a great council, and play the orator in a long harangue. In conclusion, I advised them to 'weep their dead, and wrap them up, and leave them to sleep coldly till the day of vengeance should come;' telling them that we must sweep the land, on this side, of the Iroquois, as it was necessary to extinguish even their memory, after which the allied tribes could more easily avenge the atrocious deed that the Sioux had just committed upon them. In short, I managed them so well that the affair was settled in the manner that I proposed.

"But the twenty-five permits still existed, and the cupidity of the French induced them to go among the Sioux to trade for beaver. Our allies complained bitterly of this, saying it was gross injustice to them, as they had taken up arms in our quarrel against the Iroquois, while the French traders were carrying munitions of war to the Sioux, to enable them to kill the rest of our allies, as they had the Miamis. They begged me to remedy this, especially as the French were passing over their land and before their villages, which was a violation of their rights.

"I immediately informed M. Frontenac; and M. Champigny having read the communication and noticed the reasons that I gave, commanded that an ordinance be published at Montreal, forbidding the traders to go to the country of the Sioux for the purpose of traffic, under penalty of a thousand francs fine, the confiscation of their goods, and other arbitrary penalties, according to the opinion which I might give on the subject. This ordinance was sent to me at Michilimackinac, with orders to publish it there, and in all the other remote posts. This was faithfully executed.

"The same year I descended to Quebec, having asked

to be relieved. Since that time, in spite of this prohibition, the French have continued to trade with the Sioux, but not without being exposed to affronts and indignities from our allies themselves, which bring dishonor on the French name.

"All the nations, remembering the promise which I made to go with them against the Sioux as soon as the war with the Iroquois was ended, have now called on me to fulfill it. As the season furnished me a good excuse, I have made use of it; also telling them that to-day I was fighting against the English, and they must be patient a while longer.

"They replied, that, if I would not enter into their quarrel, they had one request to make, which they hoped I would grant, namely, to prevent the French, as I did at Michilimackinac, from going to the homes of the Sioux to carry them arms and munitions of war. They thought I ought to be the more determined in my orders, as they had recently had a combat with the Sioux, and had found among the slain the bodies of two Frenchmen, who had fought with the Sioux against our own allies.

"I have given my opinion on this subject to M. Callieres and M. Beauharnais, and explained to them clearly that it is important that we should not thus violate our promises, and that we cannot do so without exposing ourselves to the danger of losing the confidence of our allies. I do not consider it best any longer to allow the traders to carry on commerce with the Sioux, under any pretext whatever, especially as M. Boudor has just been robbed by the Fox nation, and M. Juchereau has given a thousand crowns, in goods, for the right of passage through the country of the allies to his habitation. They assert that they have a right to demand this, as he carries succor to their enemies—and I believe they reason correctly.

"The allies say that Le Sueur has gone to the homes of the Sioux on the Mississippi; that they are resolved to oppose him, and if he offers any resistance they will not be answerable for the consequences. It would be well, therefore, to give Le Sueur warning by the governor of Mississippi.

"All these disorders arise solely on account of the remote trading-posts, which are all useless, or rather very injurious, since they serve only as pretexts for obtaining permits. When these are obtained, instead of going directly to their several posts, they traffic for beaver and smaller furs along the great river of the Outawas, on the shores of Lakes Huron, Superior, and Michigan, and all through the country of the Outawas. It is thus they have been in the habit of doing, and still do. Messrs. de la Forest and De Tonti, and now Juchereau and Pascaud, who are associated with them, trade in all this country, even to the environs of Detroit.

"These things cause public jealousy, and give license to all the pranks of the lawless Canadians, who say, without ceremony, that it is only the circumspect and obedient who are dupes. In truth, they are not entirely wrong; for it is grievous to them to see the traders, with permits, skimming the very cream of the country, which had previously been given to themselves. I have written often on this subject, but a perfect silence has thus far been maintained in all my instructions from government.

"You know that the country of the Illinois has been granted to M. la Salle, with stipulations and conditions, by none of which, however, did he consider himself bound; and that post has only served to cause many disputes among His Majesty's traders, on account of the bad quality of beaver there. This is the reason that the Count has forbidden Messrs. la Forest and Tonti to establish themselves there, while, at the same time, he permits them to trade for small furs—which excites much surprise, since it is well known that there are no other furs than the skins of the buffalo and roebuck. Of these, however, they can find enough elsewhere, as they have always had the liberty of trading where they pleased, without any reproof.

"The Sauteurs, being friendly with the Sioux, wished to give passage through their country to M. Boudor and others, permitting them to carry arms and other munitions of war to this nation; but the other nations being opposed to it, differences have arisen between them, which have resulted in the robbery of M. Boudor. This has given occasion to the Sauteurs to make an attack upon the Sacs and Foxes, killing thirty or forty of them. So there is war among this people.

"I should have remedied all these disorders, and put an end to these differences, if I had not been here with my *bâton blanc*, with no instructions from the king to employ it in favor of the savages, to whom we never speak on subjects of importance with empty hands.

"Similar massacres have been committed formerly, but I have been able to settle all difficulties, because M. Frontenac sent me, every year, a considerable amount of goods, to be disposed of according to circumstances, the intendant taking certificates of the distributions as I made them.

"Since his death, the government has pursued a different course, sending me nothing to Detroit for such emergencies. I have written to the governor-general and intendant for such a fund, but they have not deigned to reply. There being, in all this region, no other establishment than this, of which M. Callieres has given me the general command, this authority will be but a shadow, if they continue the practice that they have commenced, which is to send special envoys to the homes of the nations with presents.

"These envoys cannot go without expense; or, at least, the government must permit those who go on such an embassy to load their canoes with goods for the purposes of trade. The effect is, that these persons have no other object than to obtain the greatest possible number of beaver, even employing the presents with which they are charged, for their own profit, having no person to inspect their conduct.

"It would be much more natural that all such commissions should be addressed directly to Detroit, and that every thing should pass through my hands, because I should order the chiefs of the nations to come here and settle all their disputes. In regard to the distribution and use which I should make of the presents that might be committed to my care, I would give my certificate for them, and the other officers, the missionaries, and even the agents, might give theirs—so there would be no abuses committed. Besides, who can be chosen to settle the quarrels of the savages, that knows their manners, their habits and inclinations, better than I, or in whom they have more confidence?

"Would it not be expedient for you to send me a

commission for the general command of this post, and of other remote ones, in order to put an end to the present system of injustice?

"The savages have just informed me that four loaded canoes have recently been sent into the north of Lake Superior, past a village of the Sauteurs; I do not know for what purpose, but probably, as usual, on some plausible pretext. The Sioux, to whom these canoes are probably sent, are a people of no value to us, as they are too far distant to be in any way advantageous to our commerce.

"As the convoy that comes from Montreal usually remains here only two or three days, I had written this letter thus far, in order not to delay it. I have frequently mentioned M. de Callieres, not knowing that he was dead, which I have just learned with sorrow. His death will be a loss to the colony, which had need of a person of such experience.

"Some time since I wrote to M. Callieres, not being aware of his death, requesting him to increase this garrison to fifty men, that it might be in a state of effectual defense in case of an attack. A sufficient number of men for this purpose seems peculiarly necessary at a post, that is liable to be deprived of all external aid. M. Vaudreuil, the present governor-general, has replied that he could not spare any soldiers, since many of them had died the past year, and some had deserted. Nine soldiers have also deserted from this post: however, they have requested permission to return. Some of them say that they took this course because they had been promised, on leaving Montreal, that after three years' service they should be discharged. In fact, M. de Callieres gave them his word for it in public. Others say that the cause of their desertion was, that they were overburdened with work; that they were required to do other than military service; and that they were vexed to see the profits of their labor returning to a company which treated them, in their need, as Turk treats Moor. There are yet others, who speak of promises to give them lands, and of allowing them to establish themselves here, and that, finding themselves deceived, they resolved to desert.

"It is very certain that when I left Montreal, Messrs. de Callieres and Champigny encouraged me to hope for an increased number of troops; therefore I thought best to refresh the memory of M. de Callieres in my letter. On that account, Messrs. Vaudreuil and Beauharnais allowed me to receive the deserters, supposing that the new ordinance against deserters had not been published.

"M. de Callieres had also granted my request that six families might be sent to settle here; but this has been refused me since his death, with the excuse that none have offered to go—although I am credibly informed that as many families as could be wished, would gladly come, if they had the liberty to do so. I had also asked for cattle. The company were very willing to bear the expense of their transportation, and the directors inform me they had borrowed two boats for conveying them—but M. Vaudreuil does not see fit to grant them.

"I do not know whether any one has written you that the directors made a new contract with me the past year, by which, in consideration of the care that I am to take of their interests at this post, preventing fraud and embezzlement on the part of the employees of the company, and, as far as is in my power, hindering others from trading in this vicinity, they pledge themselves to pay me the sum of two thousand francs a year, and to furnish subsistence to myself and family during the time of its tenure.

"Asking for myself only the continued honor of your protection, I am, with very profound respect, sir,

"Your very humble, and

"Very obedient servant,

"LA MOTTE CADILLAC.

"P. S.—M. de Tonti, who is at Quebec, informs me that M. Vaudreuil and M. Beauharnais have forbidden his writing to you at length concerning this post."

## CHAPTER VI.

Letter from M. Cadillac to M. la Touche—Complains of the Jesuits that they do not occupy their Mission at Detroit—Danger of opposing them—The "Company of the Colony" make a new contract with M. Cadillac—His account of the agreement—M. Cadillac detects two of the commissioners in fraud and embezzlement, and reports them to the Directors—Descends to Montreal, and is arrested on charges preferred by the Directors—Suit not decided till 1705—M. Tonti commands in his absence.

ACCOMPANYING M. la Motte's account of the condition of the establishment at Detroit was the following letter, addressed to Count Pontchartrain's first clerk, M. la Touche.

"August 31, 1703.

"MONSIEUR:—I gave to the minister a very exact account of all that concerns the fort at Detroit, and would have informed you likewise, if I had not feared to make a superfluous repetition, being well persuaded that he sends you all the information concerning the affairs of this colony.

"You will see, by the accompanying letter, which I have the honor to write him, the state of this establishment, the obstacles that are brought against it, and the means I take to overcome them.

"It appears evident that the Rev. Father Jesuits have asked of the court the privilege of preserving their missions at this post, and there were reasons for granting their request; yet, although the savages are established in sufficient numbers to have at least two missionaries, they have not succeeded in obtaining one.

"All things are arranged, as you will see by the copy of regulations that I send to M. de Pontchartrain, dated September 25th, 1702.

"The envoys from the colony who went to France last year, have doubtless informed you of the measures which the directors of the Company of the Colony have taken to induce these Fathers to come and establish themselves in this place, offering to give them eight hundred francs a year each, besides the compensation they have from the king, who sends, at his own expense, the necessary provisions for their subsistence. M. le Chevalier de Callieres had also gained the consent of their Superior at Quebec (if they had one) and of myself; but all that amounts to nothing at all. Father Marest, to whom the company sent an express canoe, has found reasons to excuse himself from coming to the mission which they had designed for him.

"You can see, by the councils held at this fort, and by the copies of the letters that I send to M. de Pontchartrain, what is the genius of this country; and if the Rev.

Fathers attempt to recognize any other Superior than one of themselves, I will take care to preserve the originals of any such papers, in case the Count should desire to see them. I showed the letters, which I send, to the governor-general last year, and he did not appear satisfied with their conduct. It was on that account that he made the present arrangement, which has been signified to them, but they do not pay any attention to it.

"Can any one believe that I would, without strong reasons, vex any of the Jesuits, or that I would take it into my head to attack this formidable society? I have not lived till now without knowing perfectly well how dangerous it is to cross their path. Is it not true that I have not imprudently nor inconsiderately attacked all the Jesuits in this country, but rather have been animated with zeal for the service of the king? I always had good ground for the differences that I had with them while I had the honor to command at Michilimackinac, on which all the distant posts then depended. The same is true since I have been at Detroit. I have decided to write all my reasons for my course, and, if they wish, they can give their own. They have never seemed to wish to have their course understood, that they might avoid a decision.

"Was I not right so to arrange my plans as to permit all kinds of workmen to labor in the vineyard of our

Lord? The Jesuits will say that the soul of the savage is their own domain; if so, they ought to cultivate it, and not leave it a prey to rapacious wolves. What pretext can they have to excuse themselves from doing their duty at this post? The service of God can be found here as well as elsewhere, and the service of the king agrees with it, because he wishes them to come. It is their duty to obey the commands of the governor-general. But this is the thesis of the missionaries of the society in this country: they say it is necessary that the orders of the king should be conformed to the will of God; and they pretend to have the right to decide what is the true wish of the king. As to their knowledge by which they make this decision, they say they have the true will of God.

"It is on this assumption that the Jesuits have clamored, and still continue to clamor, against the sale of brandy to the savages; and they seem to have satisfied the Count on this subject. Here is a passage from the sermon of Father Carheil, of the 25th of March, 1697: 'There is,' said he, 'neither divine nor human power, which can permit the sale of this drink.' Hence you perceive that this Father passes boldly on all matters of state, and will not even submit to the decision of the Pope.

"I do my best to make the Jesuits my friends, wishing truly to be theirs; but, if I dare say it, all impiety apart, it would be better to speak against God than against them, because, on the one side, a person might receive His pardon, but on the other, the offense, even though doubtful, is never forgiven in this world, and would not be in the other, if their credit were as good there as it is in this country.

"I think, if the Jesuits have so little desire to assume the duties of missionaries at this post, it is because they do not like the proximity of the French establishment. They give many false reasons for neglecting this duty; but, at least, if they do not wish to come to Detroit, why do they oppose other missionaries who desire to come and take possession? They delay making any decision, in the vain hope that the savages will return to their old haunts, panic-struck by the terrors which the Jesuits endeavor to instill into their minds. I am willing to stake my life that this will never happen; they have not sufficient control over the minds of the savages to produce this result.

"Permit me, in closing this letter, to beg of you to impart to me the knowledge by which I may gain the friendship of the Rev. Father Jesuits. For myself, it would be better to walk in the way which dazzles the eyes of all the earth, and yield to the current toward which all men suffer themselves to be drawn. This would be easy for me, if I considered only my individual interest; but when the object is to have the king's interest advanced, they will oppose every movement, saying they know better than I. In that case, what shall I do to remain in the path of their friendship? This is what I have not yet been able to do, but perhaps you may make some suggestions that will enable me to do better in future.

"I beg of you to grant me the honor of your recommendation to M. Pontchartrain, concerning the kindnesses that I ask of him. You have been pleased to do me good in the past, for which you have my deepest gratitude; I hope you will continue the same favor. I am, with very great respect, sir,

"Your very humble,

"Very obedient servant,

"LA MOTTE CADILLAC.

"FORT PONTCHARTRAIN, Aug. 31, 1703."

The "Company of the Colony," becoming dissatisfied with the first contract which gave them the exclusive commerce of Detroit, subsequently entered into a new agreement with M. Cadillac. The substance of that contract is thus given by him to Count Pontchartrain:

"I agreed with the directors, by the advice and consent of the governor-general and intendant, that I would take one-third of the commerce of this post, and the company should be released from all pecuniary responsibility toward the other officers.

"Some envious persons obtaining knowledge of this agreement, reported to the directors that it was burdensome to the company. Accordingly another contract was made, by which the company agreed to pay me the sum of two thousand francs a year, and furnish the necessary supplies for myself and family. It was also agreed that they should pay M. de Tonti the sum of one thousand three hundred and thirty-three francs per year.

"In consideration of the payment of these sums, I pledged myself not to traffic with the savages, directly nor indirectly, and to hinder, as much as should be in my power, any other person from trading at that post; also to prevent any frauds or embezzlements on the part of the employees of the company. The surplus funds of the company the directors left to my care and management for their interest."

This last agreement was made in 1702, and was continued, to the entire satisfaction of all parties, until the close of 1703.

In the early part of the year 1703, M. la Motte Cadillac discovered that M. Tonti and two of the commissioners had traded with the Indians, contrary to contract. He also detected these two commissioners, Arnaud and Nolan, in embezzling the furs of the company. Having proved these embezzlements against them, M. de Cadillac reported the occurrence to the directors by the next convoy which went to Montreal, also informing the governor-general and intendant of the circumstances.

The accused commissioners were near relatives of Messrs. Lotbinieres and Delino, the principal directors of the company. In order to shield them, the directors sent M. Vincelot, another relative, to Detroit, to investigate the subject. It is very easy to infer what report would be made on his return.

M. de la Motte Cadillac having gone to Montreal early in the autumn of 1704, was arrested, by the orders of the governor-general and intendant, on various charges preferred against him by the directors of the company. The principal charge was, that he had transcended his duty as military commandant, and played the petty tyrant. The suit against him was not decided until June 15th, 1705. He was acquitted by the intendant, and immediately asked permission of the governor-general to return to Detroit, which, during his absence, had been under the command of M. de Tonti; but, on some plausible pretext, his request was not granted.

Impatient at the delay, and aware of the powerful combination against him, M. la Motte appealed to the colonial minister. By the next vessels he received orders to appear before Count Pontchartrain at Quebec.

In consequence of this new delay, M. la Motte asked the governor-general to send M. Bourmont to command at Detroit. The request was granted, and M. Bourmont immediately proceeded to Detroit.

On the 25th of September, 1705, M. la Forest was appointed second in command at Detroit, and the long-delayed permission was also given to M. de la Motte to return to his post; but, preferring to have a full investigation of his affairs before the highest tribunal, he obeyed the orders of Count Pontchartrain, and remained at Quebec.

# CHAPTER VII.

Examination of M. Cadillac before Count Pontchartrain—Cadillac received with reproaches—His defense—Gives a minute account of the settlement of Detroit—Journey thither—Conduct of Father Vaillant—Danger of mutiny—Harmony restored—Arrival at Detroit—Population of the Indian villages in the vicinity in 1704—Great number of beaver—Complains of the duplicity of the Jesuits in seeking the destruction of Detroit—All arises from personal enmity—Account of the embezzlements of the two commissioners—Nineteen packs of furs found—Other proofs of their guilt—Cause of Cadillac's arrest.

Highly indignant at the supposed failure of all his plans in regard to the establishment of Detroit, Count Pontchartrain met Cadillac with bitter reproaches. He was, however, permitted to make his defense, and the conversation which ensued between them, was soon afterward committed to writing by M. la Motte, accepted by the minister as correct, and is still preserved among the colonial archives in Paris. The reader will find the following translation more satisfactory than any more modern statement of facts.

"Whence comes it," exclaimed the Count, when M. Cadillac was brought into his presence, "whence comes it that you have failed to establish Detroit? I am informed that it is through your neglect that the project has not succeeded. You have sufficient genius to accomplish it, if you had wished. I will punish you for your indolence, and will teach you to give me a detail of plans which you have no desire to execute.

To this, M. Cadillac indignantly replied:

"Monseigneur, unjust reproaches do not seem to satisfy you; you even add threats: these things do not intimidate me, they only show that my enemies have belied me to your highness. I can assure you that I have done my utmost to make the enterprise successful, and have prosecuted my plans with all imaginable activity, but I have been obliged to yield to the torrent. If I may have the honor of repeating to you what I have already said in the assembly, I think you will justify my conduct."

The complaints of M. Cadillac's accusers had indeed influenced the mind of the colonial minister; but he was a just man, and, aware that M. Cadillac had a right to a patient hearing in his own defense, he acceded to the request, and question and answer elicited a statement of facts which, to the present generation, is so much history that otherwise would have been irrecoverably lost.

"Was it not in 1699," asked Count Pontchartrain, "that you first proposed to establish a trading-post on the strait, which forms the connection between Lakes Erie and Lake Huron?"

*La Motte.* "It was, my lord.

*Count.* "How were you received on your arrival in Canada?

*La Motte.* "Perfectly well. The Jesuits, having been advised by the first vessel, that you had resolved to establish Detroit, came down to the quay to welcome me with many civilities, which I took good care to reciprocate. As soon as they were assured of the confirmation of the report concerning the proposed establishment, they devoted themselves to the work of petitioning the governor-general to send Jesuits to Detroit to establish themselves as missionaries among the savages, to the exclusion of all other religious orders. Their request was immediately granted, and they appointed Father Vaillant.

*Count.* "At what time did you leave Quebec to go to Detroit?

*La Motte.* "I left on the 8th of March, 1701, and arrived at Montreal on the 12th, where some changes were made in our arrangements, the Recollets having obtained permission to have one of their priests accompany me, and remain at Detroit in the capacity of chaplain to the troops, while the Jesuit went as missionary. This transgression against the Jesuits set them in commotion, and they sought to persuade themselves that I had caused the change; and this circumstance was the commencement of their opposition to the establishment, which still continues.

"On the 5th of June I left La Chine with fifty soldiers and fifty Canadians, with M. de Tonti as captain, and Messrs. Dugué and Chacornacle as lieutenants. I had orders to go by the Grand river of the Outawas, notwithstanding the entreaties which I made against it. We arrived at Detroit on the 24th of July, and I immediately commenced fortifying myself there; causing the necessary buildings to be erected, and the soil to be broken up and prepared for sowing in autumn.

*Count.* "I have heard that Father Vaillant, by his exhortations, contributed much to the advancement of this work.

*La Motte.* "He employed himself so well, that if the soldiers and Canadians had been willing to believe him, they would have departed, two days after their arrival, to return to Montreal, upon the strength of the promise which this Father made them, that he would cause the intendant to pay their wages for a year, though they had only been employed six weeks.

*Count.* "How did you discover his ill-will, and unravel this intrigue?

*La Motte.* "I perceived it by the discouragement which everybody manifested in regard to the establishment, which caused me to sound one of the most honest men privately, and he revealed to me, in good faith, the arguments which the Jesuit had employed to induce them to quit the post, and return with him.

*Count.* "Did you not make known to this Father that you had discovered his perfidy?

*La Motte.* "With your permission, I will relate the circumstances. We were still encamped at the mouth of the Sable, when I called together the soldiers and Canadians: Father Vaillant was present; he did not know my design, and was ignorant that I had discovered his. I asked the Canadians why they wished to return to Montreal; begging them to tell me who could have inspired them with sentiments so adverse to the king's interests. Then addressing myself to an officer, I requested him to tell me what he knew of it. Father Vaillant saw plainly by this proceeding that his plot was known, and that the moment was approaching when he would be overwhelmed with shame and confusion. He rose from his seat, placed himself in the shadow of my tent, from whence he took a bee-line for the woods, running with all his might, while the soldiers and Canadians who saw him go, were almost convulsed with laughter. My tent prevented me from seeing him, and when I asked them the cause of their excessive laughter, one of them said, 'he did not know what dreadful punishment I had threatened to inflict on Father Vaillant, that he should escape to the woods in such haste; but, judging from the speed with which he went, we should not probably see him again very soon.' I contented myself with explaining to these people the intentions of the king, and the advantages of his service; after which they confessed, without hesitation, that their discouragement had arisen from the instigations of this Father. Afterward, I had reason to be better satisfied with them.

*Count.* "But did you not afterward make known to him his error by reprimand, or in some other way which might be disagreeable to him?

*La Motte.* "No. I believed it expedient to keep silence. I paid him as many civilities as I would an archbishop, being satisfied with informing the governor-general of the affair, and rendering an account of it to you.

*Count.* "I remember that you wrote me of it; I was also otherwise informed, and his Superior had orders to send him to France, and give you another man, who would better enter into your plans.

*La Motte.* "Your orders would have produced the desired result, if they had been fully executed. How strangely that religious order dares to set aside its service to the king! This Jesuit has been permitted still to remain in Canada, more than ever opposed to me, and using every means in his power to instill his own hatred into the minds of the society. Although your order was not fully carried out, the Jesuits were greatly offended by it; and it is not difficult to perceive that they have sworn to effect my ruin in some way or other.

*Count.* "It appears, however, that M. de Callieres wrote an agreement, containing many articles, which would enable you to live in perfect harmony with the Jesuits; and I have been informed that all the difficulties which might at any time occur, would speedily be removed, if the contract were fulfilled on both sides.

*La Motte.* "It is true that this agreement might have put an end to all disputes between us, but the fox eats the hen sooner or later. The bad conduct of Father Vaillant having caused the king to order him to return to France, and I, on my part, having discovered a conspiracy against me, entered into by the governor-general, the intendant, and the Superior of the Jesuits—my plans having been betrayed to them by M. de Tonti, captain of the troops, who was given to aid me—the Superior was under the necessity of subscribing to the agreement with a view of continuing the peace until the departure of the vessels. He then intended to carry out his plans for the immediate destruction of the post at Detroit.

*Count.* "I see plainly that the orders of the king lose their force as soon as they have passed the Grand Bank;

and the governor-general and intendant make others according to their own ideas.

*La Motte.* "Yet even they do not give such orders as they wish; they are obliged to yield to the authority of the Jesuits. It is true that in conforming to the will of the Jesuits, by a blind acquiescence in all they require, both parties fish in the same fishery, while the people suffer. Yet the sufferers are forced to applaud what in their hearts they condemn.

*Count.* "It was not possible to avoid giving the commerce of Detroit to the Company of the Colony; they promised to use every effort to make the establishment succeed.

*La Motte.* "If you had known them as I do, you would have hoped nothing from them. That company is more knavish and chimerical than any ever organized. I would as soon see Harlequin emperor in the moon. It is they who have entirely upset my plans, by unitedly and secretly opposing your intentions; being slily aided by the Jesuits in the country.

*Count.* "At what time did you learn that the king had granted to this company the commerce of that place?

*La Motte.* "I received the first notice of it on the 18th day of July, 1702. I was desired by a letter, which I received with some relics from Montreal and Quebec, to come to an understanding with the company concerning the interests of the establishment.

*Count.* "I wrote to the company that the king desired them to make a handsome addition to your salary, it being unreasonable that you should sustain that establishment at your own expense, after being deprived of its commerce, which had hitherto been your only means of indemnification. Are there many savages at Detroit?

*La Motte.* "The villages in the immediate vicinity of the fort contain more than two thousand souls. We number four hundred good men, bearing arms.

*Count.* "How have you induced these people to leave their former villages, their fields, and their grain? It must have been at great cost to the king. I judge so by the immense expense incurred for the savages who settle at Montreal and Quebec. They are allowed soldiers' rations, even to the little children; besides the frequent presents they receive.

*La Motte.* "I hardly know how I have managed, but I have not expended a sous. The governor-general and intendant have not been willing to allow me the value of a pistole to use for presents; on the contrary, they and the Jesuits have exhausted all their skill in vain attempts to prevent the savages from coming to settle there.

*Count.* "If these hinderances were removed, it appears that the better part of the savages would be united at that place?

*La Motte.* "Without doubt, they all know that the climate is good, and the soil productive.

*Count.* "You say the country is good, and produces abundantly; but I have been informed, repeatedly, that the land is good for nothing, producing very little grain; that there is scarcely any game or fish, consequently, but a small settlement could ever be sustained there. Such accounts have induced me to make efforts to obtain all possible information before urging forward this establishment.

*La Motte.* "When a man wishes to kill his dog, he says he is mad. This report of the country is merely an artifice of the Jesuits, who have succeeded in attaching the governor-general and intendant to their party. The rest of the inhabitants are of no account with them; indeed, the people always say Amen, to all, and for all, that the society propose in regard to the country.

"Sir, you might have learned the real state of the establishment, and the truth in regard to the country, by secretly sending an honest man to investigate. If he were known as being sent out by you to report concerning the state of affairs, it would be necessary that he be well supplied with good preservatives to prevent his being affected by the pestilential air of the country. On his return, he would have assured you, as I do now, that in all New France there is no better land; finer grain cannot be found, nor in greater quantity. In regard to the number of the inhabitants, there are enough to the right and left of the fort, and extending into the depth of the land, to settle all Persia.

"They must have been very bold and rash to dare tell you such falsehoods, but it all shows how the plow is held in that country.

"As for game, there are no beaver that equal those obtained there, and it cannot be denied that in three years, there have been more than thirty thousand of them killed. There is no habitable land that furnishes more game than Detroit.

*Count.* "I am convinced of the truth of your statement. Enlighten me also concerning the offense which this establishment gives to the Iroquois.

*La Motte.* "That is merely a *ruse* of the enemies of the post. Being informed that the Count wishes peace to exist between the French and the Iroquois, in order to produce a vascillation concerning the augmentation of the forces at Detroit, they have industriously circulated a report that the Iroquois are dissatisfied with it. So far from this being true, there are now at Detroit thirty families of that nation, who have settled there. So long as Detroit is fortified by the French and their allies, the Iroquois will never make war against it. The Jesuits know this well, though they intimate otherwise, and to accomplish their designs they would not hesitate to instigate our savages to attack the Iroquois, who themselves desire peace.

*Count.* "Nevertheless, at the council which was held at Quebec by order of the king, that all doubtful points in regard to this establishment might be discussed and settled, all were of the opinion, that the disaffection of the Iroquois was the greatest obstacle to sustaining the post at Detroit. Why did you not then make known your opinion, and set aside the difficulty?

*La Motte.* "I had no knowledge of such a council being held, therefore I was not able to refute what was said. The letter which you did me the honor to write under date of June 20th, 1703, was not delivered to me till July, 1704. I then called together all the people in Detroit who were present at the council at Quebec, and they signed a statement that the governor-general guarded the place of meeting, and allowed no one to depart till he had signed against this post.

"All the French who are settled at Detroit, asked permission of me to settle there, from their own personal knowledge of the goodness of the soil, as you saw by the affidavits which I took the liberty to send you under date of June 14th, of this year.

*Count.* "I can no longer doubt that every thing in that country is managed by intrigue and faction. Had you been called to that council, as I wished and ordered, this affair might have terminated differently. The orders of the king seem to become greatly weakened beyond the Grand Bank—I will provide against it. It surprises me that the governor-general and intendant have not decidedly declared themselves either for the preservation or the destruction of Detroit. Have they not some private reason for acting thus?

*La Motte.* "The governor-general and intendant have wisely held themselves in a state of apparent neutrality. They have satisfied themselves with making the people speak, who were so managed as to sign the death-warrant of this establishment, while the chief officers did nothing directly, the better to gild the pill for you.

*Count.* "What you say may be true, but you should have warned me sooner. Perhaps they may also have other reasons for not loudly declaring themselves against that post.

*La Motte.* "No doubt they have displayed so much discretion only from fear that, in causing this establishment to fail by authority, the colony might also be overthrown. Then, if it should happen that our savages should go to the English, or rather, if the latter should come to establish themselves at Detroit, the Court would have just reason to reproach them for it. Therefore, they have kept silent, and apparently neutral, that in case of any untoward event, they might throw the blame upon the council, which was convened at Quebec by order of the king and colonial minister. My own opinion is, that the savages will not leave Detroit, and I have thought that the Jesuits, in despair of success, perhaps in concert with the governor-general and intendant, may attempt to instigate our allies to revive the war against the Iroquois, to induce you to decide upon the final abandonment of Detroit. This is merely a conjecture of my own; I may be mistaken.

*Count.* "It is shameful that you were not present at that council, which I had ordered for the sole purpose of informing myself fully concerning that post. I am no better satisfied that my letter to you was so long delayed.

*La Motte.* "Apropos to the letter, they have intercepted and opened that which I had the honor to write you last year, and taken copies of it, which have become public. This shows how little respect they have in that country for His Majesty's minister; it is also a violation of the rights of men, never tolerated except by enemies in time of war.

*Count.* "What do you say!—is it really true that there are persons bold enough to open letters addressed to me? Do they not know that letters are sacred, and that such curiosity is a crime, and an outrageous insult to a minister of the State? No person is permitted to open a letter sent me by a commanding officer, without first being requested to do so.

*La Motte.* "No one could be ignorant of this; but it is entirely beyond doubt that my letters have been opened, and that copies of them have been taken. I do not even know whether the originals have ever been sent you. The copies are exactly the tenor of my letters; by this means, all my business plans have become well known.

*Count.* "It is not difficult to understand, that this would enable your personal enemies, and those opposed to the establishment, to use all their influence against you. I recollect that in your letters, you informed me of their real character, and their reasons, public and private, for opposing your plans. Their opposition seems to arise from motives of individual interest, and the hatred they bear you; and this hatred seems to have increased in proportion to your success. I fear that, although the Iroquois hold in respect the fortifications at Detroit, these designing men will induce other tribes than those settled at Fort Pontchartrain, to make war upon the Iroquois, and thus bring about the destruction of that post, which, according to the best of my knowledge, is not well garrisoned.

*La Motte.* "No doubt there is danger to be apprehended in that direction; and I thank you for the justice you are disposed to do me, in thus penetrating the designs of my enemies.

*Count.* "I wish you to tell me, without any disguise, whether the complaints of the directors are true. Have you contravened the orders of the king, and engaged in trade at Detroit; or have you been guilty of those embezzlements from the company, of which you are accused? If you are guilty, acknowledge it; if innocent, justify yourself, and you shall suffer no injury for having done your duty and executed my plans.

*La Motte.* "If I were guilty of any of these offenses you have mentioned, I should deserve condign punishment; but I can assure you, sir, I am as innocent of all these accusations as the angels are of sin. The origin of all my difficulties with the company is, that I have convicted M. de Tonti and two commissioners of the company, of having traded with the savages at Detroit, for their own benefit, although they had bound themselves by contract to abstain from all such traffic.

*Count.* "Is there proof of the existence of such a contract?

*La Motte.* "Proof incontestable has been obtained to that effect, which they have not been able to deny.

*Count.* "You have doubtless seized the furs which these commissioners have attempted to smuggle.

*La Motte.* "That has indeed been done; but what makes the crime more enormous, is, that the furs have been taken from the very storehouse of the company, or rather the commissioners have sold the goods of the company to the savages, and appropriated the product to themselves.

*Count.* "Where did you find the packs of furs which you speak of having seized?

*La Motte.* "I found nineteen packs of a prime article, which had been concealed by two of the commissioners in a hut in a Huron village.

*Count.* "Have these commissioners confessed that these nineteen packs belong to them, and resulted from their trade?

*La Motte.* "They have not only confessed the fact to me, but they signed a deposition to that effect, which is their own condemnation.

*Count.* "Does it appear that these furs are the profits of their own goods fraudulently conveyed, or of the goods of the company?

*La Motte.* "Their statements differ very much; but

it appears evident that the goods were stolen from the storehouse of the company.

*Count.* "Is that the only seizure you have made?

*La Motte.* "There are also four packs of beaver and other furs, which I seized even in the storehouse of the company, bearing the mark of M. Arnaud, principal commissioner.

*Count.* "How did you discover the theft of these four packs in the storehouse?

*La Motte.* "There were two beaver-skins found with the mark of the company, and the number 229 upon them. They had served as an envelope for forty prepared roebuck-skins. The two beavers were not yet spoiled, although they had been thrown into a cellar, full of water, belonging to an unoccupied house. Finding them in such a place made me suppose that the storehouse had been robbed; accordingly, I went to make an examination, and found these four packs, which M. Arnaud had concealed. No doubt he had also stolen No. 229, and many others.

*Count.* "Do you not suppose that these commissioners have been guilty of other embezzlements, though these are enough to cause them to be hung?

*La Motte.* "I know they have stolen from the company, or defrauded them of about one hundred and eighteen packs of furs.

*Count.* "What! one hundred and eighteen packs—that is a great number. What would be the probable value of that quantity of furs?

*La Motte.* "According to my estimate, at the current price, the average value of each pack would be at least forty crowns. Hence the loss to the company is about fourteen thousand francs.

*Count.* "No doubt you have given information of this fraud to the proper authorities, that the evil might be remedied, and the two commissioners, Arnaud and Nolan, severely punished.

*La Motte.* "I have only too faithfully performed that duty; it would have been better for me if I had remembered the proverb, 'Every one must live, thieves as well as others.'

"I wrote a statement of the affair to M. Callieres, but he died before my letter reached Montreal; consequently it was delivered to M. Vaudreuil, commander-in-chief. At the same time I also sent a detailed account to M. Lotbinieres, one of the directors. In my letter, I begged him to send me his orders concerning the affair, before the departure of the convoy from Fort Pontchartrain for Montreal; informing him that if he and the commissioners could settle the matter between them, I was satisfied, provided they shielded me from all blame.

*Count.* "But why is it that you did not inform all the

directors instead of writing only to the governor-general and M. Lotbinieres?

*La Motte.* "I thought best to do so for two reasons. An officer being engaged in this bad business, it seemed proper to notify the governor-general only, as a mark of deference to him; and I wrote to M. Lotbinieres, because M. Arnaud, who was the author of all this mischief, is his son-in-law.

*Count.* "I have seen no reason to blame your conduct until now; but, as M. de Callieres was dead, and M. de Vaudreuil, the commander-general, received your letter, doubtless he sent his orders informing you what course to pursue.

*La Motte.* "He wrote me not to precipitate matters, as he wished first to see the intendant, who was at Quebec.

*Count.* "M. Vaudreuil was wrong, for I noticed that you particularly requested an answer before the departure of the convoy from Fort Pontchartrain; but by this reply you had no guarantee that you would be exculpated by the directors. What course did you pursue in this dilemma?

*La Motte.* "I was indeed very much embarrassed by the reception of such an order. I wished to obey it, yet there were many considerations against it. First, if I deferred notifying the directors of the nefarious conduct of their commissioners, by the convoy which was to be conducted by Nolan himself, they could not be informed of it, and obviate the difficulty, till ten months thereafter, which would have been so long a delay that it might have proved a serious injury to the company. Secondly, the wages of the commissioners being once paid to them, the company would not be able to obtain any compensation for their losses, as both of the commissioners were insolvent merchants. This would have given the directors just cause of complaint against me, because the contract declares that the commissioners shall lose their wages if they are detected in any premeditated fault. And, thirdly, M. de Vaudreuil being then only commandant, his order was not sufficient to release me from my obligations to the directors, who might have sued me for a breach of contract. I accordingly sent an accusation against the commissioners to all the directors, accompanied with vouchers. It would have been better for my own interests, if I had allowed them to pillage the storehouse of the company, without saying a word; for, doubtless, the directors kept their relatives there for this very purpose.

"M. de Lotbinieres replied to my letter, regretting the fault of his son-in-law, Arnaud, but desired me to pardon him, and he would agree to settle all things with M. Delino, in regard to Nolan, his brother-in-law, without any one knowing it. M. de Monseignat, also a brother-in-law of Arnaud, wrote me in the same style, but I did not receive their letters until some time after the convoy, by which I had sent an account of the seizure, had left Detroit."

## CHAPTER VIII.

M. Cadillac's defense continued—Count Pontchartrain investigates the conduct of Cadillac's accusers—Questions Cadillac concerning the price and sale of goods—Requires a minute account of all the circumstances which caused the difficulty between him and the "Company of the Colony"—Cadillac details facts, and gives explanations and arguments—Conduct of M. Denoyer—His imprisonment by Cadillac—M. Vincelot sent to Detroit—His character.

*Count.* "Explain to me who are the two commissioners, Arnaud and Nolan.

*La Motte.* "They are two merchants, who conducted their business so badly, that they became overwhelmed with debts. M. Nolan is brother-in-law of Messrs. Delino and Lotbinieres. M. Lotbinieres is the father-in-law of M. Arnaud, and uncle of M. Vaudreuil, the governor-general. M. Monseignat is also brother-in-law of M. Arnaud. Messrs. Lotbinieres and Delino are directors, and bosom friends. The first has the full protection of his nephew, the governor-general, and the second is equally the favorite of the intendant, though not related to him. This, at least, is public opinion.

*Count.* "I see that you have been unfortunately situated, especially in your official station; but I am much deceived if these persons do not pay dearly for their rashness. Let us investigate farther. Who are your accusers; and of what do they complain?

*La Motte.* "The directors of the company preferred the complaint; and the very commissioners whom I have convicted of fraud and embezzlement, are their principal witnesses.

*Count.* "Did the commissioners accuse you to the governor-general and directors of any wrong-doing before you detected them in their embezzlements?

*La Motte.* "None at all. It was ten months after I sent the directors an account of that procedure, signed by themselves, before a complaint was preferred against me.

*Count.* "That being the case, their testimony is not admissible, and ought at once to be rejected; but I would like to know of what the directors accuse you.

*La Motte.* "The first accusation is, that I have compelled their commissioners to sell goods to the savages under price, consequently at a loss, and to the injury of the company.

*Count.* "Have you ever done this intentionally?

*La Motte.* "The accusation is the greatest falsehood in the world, for, in 1702, the directors, far from complaining of me concerning the interests of the company, were perfectly satisfied. I can prove this by their own writings; such proof it is impossible for them to deny. It is also true, that they have paid me my salary to the end of the year 1703, which shows that they were satisfied. The whole affair is a trick of Messrs. L'otbinieres and Delino, who govern the other three directors. I have convicted their near relatives of fraud, and now they seek to screen these friends, by destroying my reputation for uprightness.

*Count.* "That, I call sport unto the death; but it is bringing their friends out of difficulty in a most shameful way. Their injustice shall be punished as it deserves, if you succeed in proving what you have asserted. You say that the directors appeared satisfied with your course until the close of 1703; did you not use coercion toward the commissioners in 1704, and cause them to sell goods at low prices? If so, confess it frankly, and give your reasons; no doubt they were sufficient to justify you.

*La Motte.* "If I had done so, I could easily confess it without running any risk, having for a guarantee the order of the governor-general, signed also by the intendant, and even the directors. These are the very words: 'The commandant will leave to the commissioners of the company the liberty to traffic for furs, observing only that this is done according to the orders of M. de Callieres. He will also prevent the sale of goods at higher prices than those decided upon by the principal commissioners of the company.' This order was in reply to a paragraph in a long memorial presented to Messrs. Vaudreuil and Beauharnais. The following is the substance of the orders returned: 'The directors consider it advisable that the commissioners confer with the commandant on all business of importance to the interests of the company; but they think the principal commissioner ought to decide in regard to whatever concerns the commerce of the company, according to the orders which he may receive from the directors, or which he may find most advantageous; always excepting those specific cases in which the commandant has a right to require obedience to his orders.'

*Count.* "These orders of the governor-general and intendant were judicious; otherwise, no doubt the commissioners would have sold goods to the savages at an exorbitant price, without troubling themselves about the removal of the savages from our interests to the English. Have you caused the sale of goods to be continued at the same prices as those directed by M. de Callieres, when you commenced the settlement at Detroit?

*La Motte.* "No. The orders of M. de Callieres were, to sell to the savages at Fort Frontenac at twenty-five per cent., and to those at Detroit at fifty per cent. He did this with a design. On the ratification of a general peace between the French and their allies, and the Iroquois, our savages would, at once, think of the commerce, and to retain them still in our interest, it would be policy to give them goods at reasonable prices. Messrs. Vaudreuil and Beauharnais, from the orders they have given, seem to be of the same opinion. Even the company, in writing to their commissioners, acknowledge that they cannot disapprove of the course which I have sought to have them pursue.

"The last letter of M. de Vaudreuil, dated April 24th, 1704, contains these words: 'Although I directed you, sir, to allow M. Denoyer to execute the orders which he had recently received from the directors, I always supposed that, in consequence of the contract, the service of the king would not be affected by them, I will now say to you, sir, that in some circumstances it would not be bad policy to sell goods even at the old rates. Endeavor to manage as well as possible for the interests of the company.'

*Count.* "With the orders that you have received, together with the letters of the directors, you certainly cannot be accused of using violence, even if you have caused these orders to be obeyed to the letter.

*La Motte.* "Perhaps you will rather think me reprehensible for allowing the commissioners to add so much to the wealth of the company. Instead of selling their goods according to the orders of M. de Callieres, confirmed by those of M. de Vaudreuil, at the rate of fifty per cent., the powder of the company has been sold at four hundred per cent.; balls, at six hundred per cent.; tobacco, at three hundred; vermilion, glass beads, cutlery, iron-ware, and old iron, at two hundred; no kind of goods has been sold at less than one hundred per cent., the whole tariff of prices being regulated by the price of furs at Quebec, which the directors send to me as well as to the commissioners.

*Count.* "You surprise me! I cannot help blaming you for allowing the commissioners to sell their goods to our savages at such exorbitant prices; especially at a time when we need to conciliate them, on account of our war with the English. I fear this conduct of the company will lead the savages to commit some act of revenge against the colony.

*La Motte.* "You ought rather to blame the governor-general and intendant, who, forgetful of their own orders, have done much more for the company than they could expect me to do in such a troublesome juncture, having allowed the commissioners to continue to vex me by such prices, even when they knew that the English had sent necklaces to the savages at Fort Pontchartrain, with a tariff of their prices, in which they offered to sell goods to our savages two-thirds less than our commissioners sell them.

*Count.* "The company having sold their goods at such

exorbitant prices, have, no doubt, derived great profits from the commerce of that post.

*La Motte.* "On the contrary, they have lost. The directors have conducted the business of the company very badly, not knowing how to manage the commerce of that country. They have also incurred incredible expenses in order to favor their relatives and friends, and gain credit to themselves. Then, the price of certain furs has diminished every year, though this is an event attendant on all trade, and one that cannot be foreseen and avoided. And, finally, the commissioners, relatives of the directors, and protected by them, have levied largely on the supplies of the storehouse. Who knows how much has been plundered?

"Messrs. Lotbinieres and Delino have instituted proceedings against me, to enable them to impeach my testimony against them and their relatives. They are pretending to investigate the affair concerning their commissioners, and have chosen a deputy to go to Detroit, and collect testimony against them, or, rather, against me; their design being to extricate themselves and their relatives from this difficulty, by imposing on me atrocious calumnies which they cannot prove.

*Count.* "Whom have they sent to Detroit to make this investigation?

*La Motte.* "His name is Vincelot. He was proposed by the directors, and deputed by the intendant. He sprang from a degraded race, and is a man of no ability. He is cousin-german to M. Pinard, one of the directors, and, consequently, my adversary. This fact nullifies the procedure, making it illegal.

*Count.* "No doubt your detection of those embezzlements is indeed the true cause of the procedure, and M. de Vaudreuil, finding himself involved in the affair, is quite willing it should turn thus; but, if you have done your duty as a good officer and an honest man, you must not suffer for your faithfulness. Have you any writing to show that you have not used violence toward the commissioners? I have thoughts of prosecuting both the directors and commissioners.

*La Motte.* "I have an agreement, made with the commissioners, signed by them, by the chaplain of the fort, by M. de Tonti, and myself, which proves conclusively that I have used no violence.

*Count.* "What other accusations do they bring?

*La Motte.* "They accuse me of a capital crime. They say I have used abusive words toward their commissioners, because they did not render me certain acts of respect, which I pretended were my due.

*Count.* "I do not understand that; could the directors doubt that their commissioners owed you the highest respect in a place where you are commandant, by the authority of the king?

*La Motte.* "They doubt it so much, that they have preferred this charge. It is true that I have sometimes reproved their commissioners, but it has been when I have surprised them in flagrant offenses; as when I convicted them of embezzlement.

"The third charge is, that, M. Denoyer having been sent to fill the place of their principal commissioner, on his arrival at Fort Pontchartrain, I detained him more than two hours in my room, while I read and declaimed against the letters which he had brought from the directors, in order that M. Radisson, the former principal commissioner, might have time to conceal the papers which he and I did not wish to have seen. 'By this means,' they say, 'the directors have not been able to obtain the necessary information concerning the state of their affairs.'

"The facts are simply these: M. Denoyer, having delivered to me the letters which the governor-general, intendant, directors, and private individuals had written, I invited him to take breakfast, while I was occupied in their perusal, and he accepted the invitation. The letters were long—that of the directors covering fourteen pages—and I was engaged more than half an hour in reading them. As soon as I had finished, I assured this new commissioner of all the protection he might need in the discharge of his duties. I also informed him, that it would be proper for him to execute the orders with which he was charged, as quietly as possible, on account of the savages. I told him they had never yet seen seals set upon coffers, closets, and caskets, nor even upon the doors of the storehouse, nor had they ever seen a guard placed there. They would consider such things an infringement of the liberty which is so precious among these nations. I then dismissed M. Denoyer to execute his orders. He hastened to the house of M. Radisson, whom he found conversing with Messrs. Châtellerault and Demeule, two other commissioners who had come in the same boat with M. Denoyer, and who were relatives of Messrs. Delino and Lotbinieres.

*Count.* "Then it is not true that M. Radisson had concealed any papers?

*La Motte.* "I have no knowledge of his doing so. M. Radisson maintains that it is all an imposition of M. Denoyer. It is true that neither he nor the directors have been able to prove it. But even if M. Radisson had concealed any papers, what right have the directors to accuse me of connivance with this commissioner?

"The fourth accusation is, that, the directors having accused M. Radisson of misconduct in regard to the interests of the company, I have become his protector, causing the savages to demand the dismissal of M. Denoyer, and the reinstatement of M. Radisson. They also say that I have instructed the savages to ask that my wife, and the wife of M. Radisson, be permitted to remain at Detroit, hoping, by this means, to secure my own and M. Radisson's return to that post. What semblance of truth can they present for the assertion that I have influenced the savages to demand the dismissal of M. Denoyer in favor of M. Radisson, when the directors acknowledge that I am not satisfied with the latter? It is certain that M. Denoyer, whom I had only known three days, during which he had enjoyed my hospitality, could not in that time have done or said any thing to seriously displease me. It is an absurd subterfuge to say that the savages demanded his dismissal so soon after his arrival. Equally ridiculous is the assertion of the directors, that I influenced the savages to ask that my wife, and the wife of M. Radisson, might remain at the fort, to secure our return. There might be some degree of probability in such an assertion, if I had received any orders from the governor-general, or the Count, to leave the post; or even if I had been ordered to descend to Quebec or Montreal, to render an account of my conduct. On the contrary, when I asked permission to go to Montreal, on my own business, M. Vaudreuil granted my request, at the same time expressing his approbation of my conduct. My arrest, soon after my arrival, was entirely unexpected to me.

*Count.* "I should judge, from your account of the affair, that the directors, failing to find other proof sufficient to condemn you, now seek it among the pagan savages. I believe such testimony has never been received in a court of justice.

*La Motte.* "How could a judge allow the testimony of a people who have neither faith nor law; who will testify to any thing, provided they are paid for it; and will unsay the same thing in half an hour, if, for the service, they can be baptized in a drink of brandy?

*Count.* "Is that all the directors have to say in reference to the savages?

*La Motte.* "No. They assert that I have influenced the savages to object to the removal of the furs from the fort, until the storehouse was filled with merchandise, and all the French had the liberty to traffic with them. The directors say my object was to compel the company to make large imports of merchandise to that post, of which I intended to make myself master, as usual.

*Count.* "Did the savages really make any such demand, and for what reason?

*La Motte.* "Soon after the arrival of M. Denoyer, and the two commissioners who came with him, they maliciously made the savages understand that they came to send away the furs, and did not intend to bring any more merchandise. This offended the savages, who had always been promised the rights of an extensive commerce, by the establishment of Detroit. In this course of conduct, no doubt the commissioners obeyed the secret orders they had received from those under whose authority they were sent out.

*Count.* "But what do the directors mean when they assert that your object has been to cause them to make large importations to that post, in order that you might become master of them, as usual?

*La Motte.* "Who can divine what they mean? If I had appropriated their goods to myself, or wasted them, these charges would be well founded; but even they do not accuse me of this. What difference would it make to me whether the company made large or small importations, since I had no interest in them? On the contrary, if I were trading on my own responsibility, as they have dared to assert, it would have been better for me that they should send only a few goods, as it would enable me to sell mine (if I had any) more advantageously and easily.

*Count.* "Is there any really substantial article in the accusations of the directors?

*La Motte.* "They exclaim loudly against my presumption in imprisoning M. Denoyer, their principal commissioner, who was sent to succeed M. Radisson. They recalled M. Radisson because I accused him of misconduct. Yet the directors say this accusation was made by me with his consent, to cover our mutual embezzlements. Would M. Radisson consent that I should prefer an accusation against him, that would revoke his office, which was worth to him eighteen hundred francs a year besides his expenses; thus involving him in the loss of his wages, a sullied reputation, and the difficulties and expenses of a lawsuit? I leave it to the judgment of infants.

*Count.* " It appears as you say; but let me understand about the imprisonment of M. Denoyer. First, let me inquire if you were forbidden to imprison, or if you had the power to inflict this punishment upon the officers and others at your post?

*La Motte.* "My powers were very ample. They gave me authority to punish, according to the circumstances, by reprimand, arrest, imprisonment, suspension, or, in case of a clear, positive disobedience to orders, to run my sword through the body of the offender. This extent of power has been given me on account of the great distance of that post from the seat of government, and it has enabled me to immediately suppress all seditions and factions.

12

*Count.* "Now tell me why you were obliged to imprison M. Denoyer, the principal commissioner?

*La Motte.* "A soldier of the garrison having been killed by some of our enemies, our savages reported that they had found the stake to which he was tied. A party of one hundred savages of the different nations living around the fort, was immediately formed to pursue the enemy, and avenge the death of the soldier. They came to me, and demanded seven or eight Frenchmen to go with them. I ordered M. de Tonti to assemble the temporary servants of the company, and call for volunteers. From them he was to select eight good men, and give them food and ammunition from the storehouse of the company, as had been customary. M. Denoyer pretended that I could not take any detachment from the servants of the company, even for the service of the king, without his permission. He forbade their leaving the fort, without first asking him. 'This should be so, or he would burn his books.' The Canadians, who had been drafted, were pledged to the service of the company; they, therefore, informed M. de Tonti of the orders of the commissioner, and he brought the complaint to me. I immediately sent for the Canadians, and, having taken their several depositions in the presence of witnesses, I sent for M. Denoyer. I asked him if he pretended that I could not draft the servants of the company for the service of the king, without his permission. He had the impertinence to maintain to my face, M. de Tonti being present, that he did so pretend; and asserted that he did not now believe I had the power. This reply, made with all possible arrogance, obliged me to send him to prison. Therefore, I said to him: 'I will teach you, little commissioner, to neglect your own duty and act the seditious, by attempting to alienate other minds from obedience.'

*Count.* "Is it possible that this commissioner dared show such insolence; and that a seditious person is so far protected by the company, that they even wish to accuse you of a crime for inflicting so slight a punishment? If you had done otherwise, you would have deserved to suffer the penalty of military law. There is nothing so injurious, as to allow a revolt to go unchecked at its commencement; and it is of great importance that a commandant be very watchful, and that he do not permit the authority of the king to be in any degree diminished. Has the governor-general received full information of all this? It seems incredible that he should allow it. How long did you keep this commissioner in confinement?

*La Motte.* "Soon after my arrival at Montreal, I rendered to the governor-general a very exact account of the whole transaction. Some time afterward, he knew that the directors had preferred this charge, among others, against me. He manifested no opposition to it, which proves that, on account of M. Lotbinieres, his uncle, the whole plan has his connivance and protection. At least, it shows the little skill he possesses in maintaining the authority of the government, and protecting those officers in its service who understand their duty. As for the prison, it is nothing more than the sergeant's room, in which this illustrious commissioner Denoyer remained only about three hours!

*Count.* "Really, that was a great punishment! Be assured, I will not pass by in silence the small degree of attention paid by the governor-general to this affair. Did the imprisonment take place before, or after the savages demanded the dismissal of M. Denoyer?

*La Motte.* "These are the facts: M. Denoyer arrived at Fort Pontchartrain, on the 5th of June. On the 8th, the savages demanded his removal, by a necklace, which he accepted against my entreaties, and, if I may use the term, remonstrances. I told him I would settle the affair with the savages, not doubting that I understood their reasons for making the request, and thinking I could remove the bad impressions of him which they had received. He would not yield to my persuasions; but gave up his instructions, all his papers, and the effects of the company, into the hands of a man named Châtellerault, second commissioner. So true is this, that he has stated these facts himself, which makes me believe that he had instructions to conduct in such a manner as to cause the savages to demand his dismissal, and then charge the blame upon me, in my contemplated absence. The directors and their commissioners had in view my removal, and the consequent failure of the establishment. M. Denoyer was imprisoned on the 22d of June, fourteen days after the savages demanded his dismissal. Some days later, I imprisoned him a second time, for having disobeyed a standing order, that no officer or other person should leave the post without my permission. M. Denoyer, as if to continue his former disobedience, caused his canoe to be put into the water and loaded for Montreal. He had not mentioned the subject to me, as he always pretended not to be subordinate to me. I found this canoe, belonging to M. Denoyer and the other two commissioners, ready loaded and manned with eight men, while its owners were yet under arms, according to the custom of distant posts. M. Denoyer and the other two commissioners were immediately arrested and sent to prison.

*Count.* "You did right to punish such an infringement of the universal rule in distant posts. Was M. de Châtellerault the second commissioner in fault?

*La Motte.* "Yes, since he had received the instructions, papers, and effects of the company, it was really his duty to ask permission for this boat to descend to Montreal. This contempt of my orders, together with the fact that they had not, since their arrival, paid me the customary visit of respect always considered due the commandant of a fortified town, especially so at these remote posts, caused me to perceive the intrigue between these commissioners. The order that no one shall leave the post without permission, is necessary to prevent the embezzlements that might otherwise be made.

*Count.* "Are factions and revolts frequent in that country? Have you a good garrison? You ought, at least, to have a hundred tried soldiers at your fort.

*La Motte.* "The preceding year, the commissioners and temporary servants of the company revolted against M. de Tonti, who commanded during my absence, and he permitted the sedition to go unpunished; and probably these new ones thought I would not dare to punish them. There is not another commandant in that country who has not experienced very strong rebellions. During the twelve years that I have commanded in that region, no open rebellion has occurred. The beginning of a revolt has been checked by the immediate punishment of the instigator, for which I have always, till now, been commended. As for the garrison, the governor-general, intendant, and directors, have done so well by their treatment of the soldiers, that they have reduced the number to fourteen. They are treated like galley-slaves. For three years past they have received neither clothes nor pay.

*Count.* "At the time of the meeting at Quebec, were not the temporary servants of the company more numerous than your garrison?

*La Motte.* "Yes; there were at that time thirty servants of the company, who might have raised a sedition that would have been serious in its consequences, if they had been disposed to second the movements of the commissioners. The directors say that these acts of violence —for so they designate the punishment which I inflicted upon their commissioners—prove that I have interests separate from those of the company, and for this reason they are opposed to my return to Fort Pontchartrain. They even objected to my remaining at Montreal, at the time of the departure of the convoy for that post, lest I might have some communication with those going thither, and inspire them with opinions contrary to the interests of the company.

*Count.* "Have they demanded any thing more?

*La Motte.* "Yes; they ask that I be ordered to remain at Quebec, to reply to any accusations which they may hereafter bring against me. Finally, they have concluded to hold me responsible for all the harm that has befallen the company. They have obtained the consent of the intendant to grant them a hearing, and he has commanded me to remain in Quebec till farther orders.

*Count.* "Strange that they should inform against you upon points which can be vindicated immediately. I see, by your account, that you have vouchers for your conduct in every thing that affects the interests of the company. Indeed, I know they were satisfied with your conduct until the close of 1703. This is also fully evident from the fact that they have paid you four thousand francs for your services. Doubtless, the directors have preferred these charges against you to retaliate for the information you gave against the two commissioners, Arnaud and Nolan, their relatives. But it is absurd that they should inform against a commandant for an act of imprisonment, when he holds the full power to inflict that punishment, especially when the offense tends to rebellion. It cannot be that the intendant has consented to grant their request?

*La Motte.* "On the contrary, he has permitted the directors to institute a complaint against me, on every head contained in their memorial, and ordered a copy to be transmitted to me, that I might prepare myself to answer. He has also requested M. Ramesay, commandant at Quebec, to require me to remain in that city till I had given satisfaction to the directors.

*Count.* "It appears, from this, that the intendant has issued orders for your arrest, on a mere complaint, without any legal process. Has M. Ramesay really caused you to be arrested on this requisition of the intendant?

*La Motte.* "He has; though not without first repeatedly informing the intendant that he could see nothing in the memorial of the directors, but a mere complaint without any proof; therefore, he did not believe he ought to arrest an officer holding his commission from the king himself, and especially the commandant at Fort Pontchartrain, a distant post established at the head of the colony. He also wrote to the governor-general concerning the affair. In reply, the governor-general informed him that he had done right in executing the order of the intendant and ordering my arrest.

*Count.* "I no longer doubt that the governor-general, intendant, and directors, have connived together, their object being to save the two commissioners, at the expense of your reputation, and to overthrow the establishment at Detroit, by depriving you of the command. All things at that post would then be under the undisputed management of the Jesuits, who, it is reported, really possess all the authority in the government, and in the administration of justice. Do not be discouraged; if your statements are true, which I do not doubt, you shall not suffer for having obeyed my instructions and maintained strict integrity. Have you any thing to say against the proceedings of M. Vincelot, who was delegated by the intendant to investigate your affairs at Detroit?

*La Motte.* "M. Vincelot is cousin-german to M. Pinaud, one of the directors, who is my enemy; this is sufficient to make the whole proceeding absolutely null and void. Then the governor-general sent M. Louvigny, an officer of Quebec, and brother-in-law of M. Nolan, under the specious pretext of commanding the convoy to Detroit; though the real object was to aid M. Vincelot in his efforts against me, hoping that their united influence might effect the abandonment of the post. It is also necessary for me to say that, when Messrs. Arnaud and Nolan were recalled, their places were filled by two other relatives, Messrs. Châtellerault and Demeulle.

*Count.* "Pray, stop; I shall soon believe that all who are in the employ of the company at Detroit, and wish to retain you at Quebec, are the relatives of the three directors, and also allied to the governor-general."

# CHAPTER IX.

Cadillac's defense continued—He gives his reasons for appealing to a higher court—Narrates the measures taken to secure the destruction of Detroit—Offer of a pension to M. Tonti—Government sends M. Decouverte to the Ottawas and Miamis with goods—M. Mantet sent with presents and necklaces—M. Vincennes sent to the Miamis with three canoes loaded with goods—Ruin of Detroit determined at Quebec—Fort at Detroit set on fire—Church, house of the Recollets, and dwelling of M. la Motte Cadillac burned—All the provisions of the fort consumed—Generosity of the savages—Miamis attack the Detroit savages—M. Cadillac negotiates a peace between the several nations—War-party of the Illinois made prisoners by the French—Brought to the fort—Whipped with rods—Ottawas of Michilimackinac remove to Detroit—Sixty Ottawas make a descent upon the Iroquois at Fort Frontenac—Paganism of the savages.

*Count.* "What were your reasons for bringing your cause before a higher court?

*La Motte.* "I have taken exceptions to the intendant, because, upon the complaint of the directors, without proof, he caused me to be arrested at Quebec, thus preventing my return to Fort Pontchartrain; a proceeding contrary to law, and a manifest act of violence, which proves him my adversary. He cannot pass sentence where he has no legal power to judge. Holding my authority directly from the king, and having always had the power to imprison or otherwise punish offenders, during the twelve years that I have commanded the posts in that distant region, for which I was never before informed against, I consider myself amenable only to the governor-general and the court.

"The intendant having lent the directors considerable sums by orders on the Exchequer, the furs at Detroit are mortgaged to him, he being surety to the office of the Exchequer for the sums lent. Therefore, the surety is no less interested than the creditor in preserving the property of the debtor. The testimony of the intendant is quite necessary to me, as he possesses private knowledge which would be unfavorable to the directors.

"I have also objected to M. Vaudreuil, because M. Lotbinieres, first director of the company, is his uncle, and father-in-law of M. Arnaud, one of the commissioners convicted of embezzlement. Also, because Messrs. Vaudreuil and Lotbinieres, especially the first, have letters concerning those embezzlements, which they will surrender only by the orders of a superior. I have protested against the procedure of M. Vincelot, because he is a man of no character or ability. His parents were people of bad reputation. Besides, the testimony of M. Vincelot is objectionable, as he is cousin-german to M. Pinaud, one of the directors.

"Finally, I have appealed to a higher power on account of the plot between the governor-general, intendant, directors of the company, and the Jesuits. They were unable to overthrow the establishment while I remained there, and no doubt they believed that, by causing me to be detained here as prisoner, under these diabolical pretexts, they would succeed in shielding their guilty relatives, by preferring against me the same accusation of which I convicted them.

"Having been unable, with all their authority, to prove any thing against me, and thus consummate their plans, they have sent M. Louvigny, major of Quebec, to Detroit, to corrupt the savages, and cause them to take part against me. M. Louvigny himself has been convicted, by the sovereign council, of commercial transactions, and of contravening the orders of the king.

"The commissioners, Arnaud and Nolan, having accused me to the directors, left Quebec as soon as they heard of my arrival at Montreal. The directors sent them to Michilimackinac in a boat, belonging to the Jesuit Fathers, heavily loaded with goods. By this means, an opportunity was afforded to M. Arnaud to bring his beaver and other furs from Michilimackinac, whither he had transported them, after having stolen them from the storehouse of the company at Detroit. These peltries were in the house of one of the Jesuit Fathers at Michilimackinac, which proves the protection extended by the governor-general, the Jesuits, and directors, to these commissioners. I spoke of it one day to the governor-general, who replied that 'the commissioners had gone to Michilimackinac without his knowledge, the Jesuits having said nothing to him about it.'

"Nearly all the witnesses who deposed at Detroit concerning the dishonesty of the commissioners, having arrived at Montreal, were immediately sent to the country of the Outawas, charged with goods, to prevent the confrontations and proofs. The depositions of all those who have accused me, having been taken, they also have been sent to the Outawas. In the mean time I am persecuted, imprisoned, and deprived of the little property I possessed. All this is done to gain time, in which to effect the overthrow of Detroit. They also wish to annoy me, and make me ask their pardon, and beg for mercy. But I will do no such thing. I await your judgment and that of the king. I wish to have this affair fully investigated. They have attacked my reputation, and I demand satisfaction. I have served the king with industry, zeal, and assiduity, in proof of which I have many certificates. All the letters of my superiors are full of expressions of satisfaction in regard to my conduct and services.

*Count.* "Will you now inform me, minutely, concerning the measures that have been taken for the destruction of Detroit? Speak plainly, and be assured of my protection, provided you accuse justly, and alter the truth in nothing.

*La Motte.* "I will not depart from this principle. My patroness is Truth, and I believe myself invincible while I fight under her banner. I will simply give you the facts, and you may draw your own inferences; the public have drawn theirs.

"Last year M. de Tonti, having descended from Detroit to Montreal and Quebec, found himself denounced, with the commissioners of the company, for trade and embezzlement. Far from punishing him, the directors have sent him back again to Detroit, finding him a good instrument to use secretly against me, and against that post. As an additional encouragement, they gave him a pension of six hundred francs a year, by contract, under private seal. The understanding was, that he should send his wife back to Montreal, as a means of making the savages believe that they intended to abandon Detroit. As soon as I heard of it, I proposed to send my family to Quebec or Montreal, for the same sum; but they would not listen to it. I did this to try them.

"At the time of M. Tonti's return, they sent M. Mantet to Michilimackinac, with two canoes loaded with goods and brandy, under the pretext of conveying thither the amnesty. Yet he departed for the Outawas six or seven weeks before the arrival of the vessels that brought the news of the said amnesty. They also sent M. Decouverte to the Outawas and Miamis, with two canoes loaded with goods and brandy, under pretext of settling some differences between our allies.

"According to the confession of M. Vaudreuil, M. Mantet was charged with presents and necklaces to settle these difficulties. It is therefore evident that the mission of M. Decouverte to the Miamis has only been to prevent that nation from coming to settle at Detroit, and, in case of ill success, to create disturbance.

"M. Vincennes was also sent to the Miamis, with orders to go by the way of Detroit, being really sent to M. Tonti. He had three canoes loaded with goods, and more than four hundred quarts of brandy. His pretext was, that he was going to terminate the war commenced by the Miamis at Ouyatanon, against the nations settled at Detroit, and against the Iroquois. This war was already ended, and the governor-general and intendant were so informed. Besides, it would be strange to send an ensign *ad honores* to settle difficulties between nations at a distant post, where there was already a commandant appointed by the court.

"When I questioned M. Vincennes concerning his errand, he told me that the governor-general had an interest in the goods which he carried. I mentioned this to M. Vaudreuil, who replied that he would *discharge M. Vincennes*, as he had only given him permission to take two canoes.

"Father Marest, Superior of Michilimackinac, and of all the missions to the Outawas, M. Tonti, captain at Detroit, and M. Mantet, met at Quebec; and it was there and then that the ruin of Detroit was determined upon by the Superior of the Jesuits at Quebec, the governor-general, intendant, and directors. To effect this, they decided to issue permits, and re-establish the mission at Michilimackinac. That their plans might not fail, Father Marest returned with a boat-load of goods. M. Mantet accompanied him with two other boats, and M. Tonti went with them as far as Detroit.

"M. Callieres had made an arrangement, to which the Superior of Quebec had subscribed, fixing the destination of Father Marest at Detroit; yet the governor-general and intendant wrote me that they could not prevent his return to Michilimackinac, 'for several strong reasons.' Thus you perceive that Father Marest has had permission to take one boat-load of goods to Michilimackinac, thus preventing the savages from coming to Detroit to trade.

"M. Mantet has taken two boats, M. Decouverte two, M. Vincennes three, and M. Boudor one. M. Boudor has the savages quite at his disposal, and has carried into the country of the Outawas more than twenty thousand francs' worth of goods and brandies.

"M. Tonti has also been well paid. He has sent three boat-loads of goods to the Outawas, where they have been sold for his benefit. Twelve boat-loads of goods have been sent to the Outawas, beside large quantities carried thither by the savages. It is true that permission has been given, under pretense of their going to the Illinois, who are too far distant to come to us; but it was only a pretense.

"Orders were, some time since, issued by government, forbidding any one in all the colonies to sell brandy to the savages, under any circumstances whatever; and the penalties attached to the law were inflicted with all possible severity. While they punish with rigor all violations of this ordinance at any of the posts, they allow great quantities of brandy to be carried into the depths of the forests—and the Jesuits do not complain of it. They now maintain a strict silence on the subject, after having made so much noise about it in the days of Count Frontenac and M. de Callieres. They did not then so rule the country.

"The fort at Detroit has been partially burned. The fire was the work of an incendiary. It was set in a barn, which was filled with Indian corn and other grains. This barn was flanked by two of the bastions.

"The flames being increased by a high wind, the church, the house of the Recollets, M. Tonti's house, and my own, were all consumed. My loss was about four hundred pistoles. I might have saved my house, if I would have allowed the storehouse of the company and the property of the king to burn. I had one hand severely burned, and lost most of my papers.

"The fort was repaired in two or three days, all the savages assisting me with the best possible grace. They also manifested their generous feelings toward me on this occasion. Having lost all my own provisions, and the supplies of the garrison and of the servants of the company, the savages made to me, personally, a present of a hundred bushels of corn. They also furnished all the grain necessary for the subsistence of the garrison, at the usual prices, taking no advantage of our necessities. The garrison of one hundred men that was given me in 1701, had become reduced, at that time, to fourteen, so that it was impossible for me to guard all the fort; indeed, I could fully protect only two of the bastions, and that with much fatigue to the soldiers. Having received neither clothing nor pay for three years, they were also much discouraged. One of the soldiers fired upon the savage who set fire to the barn; but we could not learn who he was, nor have we since been able to obtain any definite information concerning him. All the nations settled around Detroit aver that it must have been a foreign savage, or some Frenchmen who will be well paid for committing the deed.

"Soon after the attempt to burn the fort, the Miamis of Ouyatanon came to Detroit, and made an attack on the savages there. They killed an Outawa, two Hurons, and a Pottawatomie. This act of hostility exasperated all the nations at Fort Pontchartrain, and warlike preparations were immediately made. I succeeded in persuading them to wait a few days, and then dispatched a messenger to the camp of the Ouyatanons, who were four hundred strong, telling them if they did not come promptly and make reparation for this insult, I would go myself and exterminate them; but, if they would come, I would send them a white flag for their protection. They immediately sent their chiefs to Detroit, replaced the dead with the living, according to their custom, and made large presents to the relatives of those who were killed. Thus a bloody war was prevented. Father Mermet, Jesuit, is missionary to the Ouyatanon Miamis. This attack was made after the Miamis of the river St. Joseph had left their villages to come and settle at Detroit.

"About the same time that the Ouyatanons attacked Detroit, the Illinois also sent thither a war-party of fifteen persons. They were discovered and made prisoners.

"When they were brought to the fort, the French contented themselves with whipping the prisoners with small rods, giving them to understand that I treated them as a father, preserving to them the lives which they deserved to lose. I then sent four of them back to their tribe, with the demand that some of the principal chiefs should come and give their reasons for presuming to make war against the nations of Detroit. They were so much intimidated by this, that a treaty of peace was easily concluded, which still continues.

"The Illinois stated that Elouaoussé, one of the chiefs of the Outawas, had been sent to their country, to persuade them to engage in a war against his own nation at Detroit. He had induced these fifteen young men to join him, and they departed on the expedition without the knowledge of the old men of the nation, who would have nothing to do with the affair.

"Father Gravier is missionary to the Illinois, and M. Delieta, a relative of M. Tonti, also resides there. Probably their design in instigating the destruction of the nation of Detroit, by the Illinois and Miamis, was to cause the savages to retire to Michilimackinac to avoid the war. The Illinois who are not boatmen, would not be able to cross the straits which unite Lake Huron with the Lake of the Illinois. Elouaoussé, of whom I spoke, did not leave Michilimackinac for the Illinois till some time after the arrival of Father Marest and M. Mantet. The few Hurons who remained at Michilimackinac, have left that place, and joined those at Detroit. All that nation are now established there. I had the honor to assure you, by letter, last year, that this would be so in spite of the declarations to the contrary, made by the famous Father Carheil, their missionary.

"The Outawas of Michilimackinac, with the exception of seventy or eighty, have also come to Detroit. This *transmigration* has surprised the whole body of the Jesuits in that country. They did not expect it. The governor-general and intendant were quite unprepared for such intelligence, as they had placed full confidence in Messrs. Mantet and Decouverte; and especially in the representations of Rev. Fathers Marest and Carheil.

"Last year I had the honor to send you a copy of a memorial of the Jesuit Fathers, particularly of those of Michilimackinac, in which they intimated to me that if the savages came to Detroit, they would follow. The savages have come, but the Fathers remain immovable in their parishes.

"Sixty warriors of the Outawas, who still remained at Michilimackinac, made a descent upon the Iroquois, and surprised and captured nearly forty of them, under the very walls of Fort Frontenac. Having killed one of the Iroquois, they placed a Huron tomahawk upon his body, to signify that he must have been killed by some of the Hurons of Detroit. The Outawas could not reach the villages of the Iroquois by the usual route, without passing Detroit, where they would be opposed by the nations dwelling there; so they crossed over to the other side of the river, and descended to Fort Frontenac.

"It is not at all probable that sixty men would have had the boldness to declare war against the five nations of the Iroquois, unless instigated to such an act by those whom they considered wiser than themselves. Probably the motive presented, was the hope of the re-establishment of Michilimackinac, by depopulating Detroit. The instigators knew very well that Detroit could not sustain itself against the hordes of the Iroquois, without a strong French garrison, and that the savages would very naturally return to their old hunting-grounds, to escape the dreaded Iroquois. This event occurred after my descent to Quebec, and while I was detained there a prisoner. Soon after the attack, M. Mantet arrived at Montreal; and fifteen days after, M. Decouverte came also. Both brought a number of boats loaded with beaver and other furs—the recompense for such a fine errand.

"M. Vincennes is now actually at Detroit, with four

hundred quarts of brandy, and is keeping a public house. He was the precursor of M. Louvigny, major of Quebec, and of M. Vincelot, sent by the intendant to obtain evidence against me. In corrupting the savages, brandy has not been spared.

"The directors have paid M. Louvigny two thousand francs for making this journey, which occupied him only fifty-five days. An officer was never before known to receive pay for escorting an envoy. M. Vincelot has also received the sum of one thousand francs for the voyage. He returned with M. Louvigny. See the generosity of the directors, at a time when the company is overwhelmed with debt, and the colony in the greatest distress, and without resources!

"The interpreter sent by M. Callieres to Detroit, was M. Champigny. He has been withdrawn, because he was an honest, able man. They have put in his place a man named Rivan, who does not understand the Outawa language, of which he is the interpreter—but he is a brother-in-law of M. Vaudreuil.

"The Outawas accused Quarante Sous, a chief of the Hurons, of having told them that it was I who had instigated the demand for the dismissal of M. Denoyer. Quarante Sous denied it, and asserted, in the presence of M. Louvigny, M. Vincelot, and all the French, that the accusation was false—that I had never spoken to him of

M. Denoyer. 'I do not understand the language of M. la Motte,' said he, 'neither does M. la Motte understand mine, and where is the interpreter?' The Outawas hung their heads, and confessed that they knew nothing about it. All of my witnesses from Detroit, said boldly that every thing had been done to intimidate them, yet they all testified decidedly in favor of my acquittal.

"In taking the testimony of the Outawas, M. Vincelot made them raise the hand and take an oath that, by their hopes of Paradise, they would speak the truth. Such a thing was never before known among the Outawas. I would be willing to stake my life against the production of one previous example. They would as soon raise the foot as the hand; and would be baptized a hundred times a day for a hundred drinks of brandy. We may infer the value of their oath. It is an indisputable fact, that there is no wigwam without its divinity—as the eagle, the serpent, the bear, and many other animals—to whom they sacrifice in their necessities, especially in times of war and sickness. The only good that the missionaries do, consists in the baptism of children who die after having received it, and perchance administering the same rite to some old man at the hour of death.

"What officer would command in that country, if the

testimony of the savages was received in the courts of law? It would have been more prudent for M. Vaudreuil to recall me at once, if he wished to destroy this post and protect his relatives in their dishonesty, than to proceed in this manner; because, hereafter, the savages will have neither respect nor fear for the commanding officers.

"M. Vaudreuil has not been sufficiently cautious; he has not foreseen the consequences of this affair, nor the severe blow which his conduct gives to the authority of the king. Messrs. Frontenac and Callieres would not have made such a mistake.

"M. Lacorne, lieutenant of the troops, whom the governor-general has appointed to the command at Fort Frontenac, made a martial feast to the Iroquois; put the hatchet into their hands, and directed them to go and make war against the nations at Detroit. He is a good officer and understands the colonial service, and would never have declared war against the savages at Detroit, without orders from the governor-general, either verbal or written.

"This last attempt to destroy that post is outrageous, and proves, too well, that the war which the Illinois and Ouyatanons had commenced against our savages, and the attack of the sixty Outawas from Michilimackinac upon the Iroquois, and M. Lacorne's declaration of war, all emanated from the same source. The only evidence we had of the instigation of the Jesuits in the other difficulties, was the word of the savages; but M. Lacorne's proceedings unravel the mystery.

"M. Vaudreuil himself, has sent an Outawa named Sans Souci, formerly a soldier under his command, to Michilimackinac, with two canoes, loaded with seven or eight thousand francs worth of goods and brandy, under pretense of bringing Ouendigo, a savage belonging at Michilimackinac. If this sort of pretext is good to cover an illegal traffic, there was no need of suppressing the permits. Can any one doubt that Sans Souci is interested with the governor-general in this commerce?

"M. St. Germain has leased M. Vaudreuil's grant of land, and gives him for it three thousand francs a year, besides having built a house, which is to become the property of M. Vaudreuil when the lease expires. There is not more than a quarter of an acre of the land broken up; therefore, the tenant must of necessity traffic with the Indians, otherwise he could not pay so large a rent, or build so good a house, for the benefit of M. Vaudreuil. Indeed, it is notorious that M. St. Germain has carried his beaver to the English, and it is a greater vexation to the neighboring inhabitants, who are forbidden to make any trade with the savages.

"M. Decouverte, on his return from the country of the Outawas, brought with him beaver to the amount of six thousand francs, as any one may see at the office of Receipt. Of this, M. Vaudreuil has received a thousand crowns."

REV. GABRIEL RICHARD.

Vicar General Sulpitian

# CHAPTER X.

Disaffection of the Iroquois toward Detroit—Detroit Indians invited by the English to Albany, in 1703—Return disaffected toward the French —Firing of the fort—The consequences—Letter from Father Marest, at Michilimackinac—Additional account of the difficulties with the Indians—Fears for the safety of the French—M. Chartier resolves to leave the mission-house at St. Ignace, and go alone to Fort Michilimackinac—Prevented by the offer of Merasilla, an Outawa-Sinago—He assures the missionary of his own safety—Asks a flag and letters to the French at Michilimackinac—Three Frenchmen return with him—Michilimackinac more securely fortified—M. Arnaud makes presents to the savages—The old men in council disapprove of the conduct of their tribe in going to Detroit—Great anxiety about the missionaries at St. Joseph—Friendship of Koutaouiliboe—Onaské sends an apology to the governor-general for his seeming remissness in duty to the French—Savages returned from Detroit report two Frenchmen killed, one a Recollet priest.

The settlement of Detroit in 1701, called forth the remonstrances of the Iroquois, which were entirely unheeded by the French. Disaffection on the part of that powerful confederacy of nations was the consequence, though they still continued to observe the conditions of the treaty made at Montreal the previous year.

In 1702, war was declared against France by England, Germany, and Holland. This renewal of hostilities had no perceptible effect upon the colonies in America, until the following year, 1703. In the summer of that year, the Indian nations in the vicinity of Detroit were invited by the English to Albany, and a number of the chiefs of the Outawas accepted the invitation. They returned disaffected toward the French, having been induced to believe that the post at Detroit was established for the purpose of effecting their subjugation.

The firing of the fort, soon after their return, and before M. la Motte's departure for Montreal, was, no doubt, an outburst of their aroused indignation; and the subsequent attacks upon Fort Pontchartrain, during his prolonged absence, by the Miamis of Ouyatanon, and the Outawas of Michilimackinac, are no doubt traceable to English as well as Jesuitical influence.

In addition to the account of these difficulties, given by M. la Motte to Count Pontchartrain, is the following letter, written by Rev. Father Marest, missionary at Michilimackinac, to the governor-general:

"MICHILIMACKINAC, August 14, 1706.

"J. M. J.:—

"MONSIEUR:—I did myself the honor to write you, by Toupikanich, concerning the bad news we had heard from Detroit, that a war had broken out between the Hurons, Miamis, and Outawas. At the time I wrote, we were ignorant of the fate of the French at Detroit, and also at Michilimackinac.

"The savages whom we sent to Michilimackinac, returned after going almost to the very gates of the fort, without bringing us any assurance of the safety of the French.

"M. Chartier, though he had cause to fear the savages at Michilimackinac, on account of some captives who were there, was the first to offer to go on this hazardous mission, saying 'he was ashamed to remain, and rely solely on the reports of the savages, for every one knew that they always mix the false with the true in any news they undertook to report.'

"But an opportunity was providentially afforded us of learning all we wished to know, without incurring any risk. Merasilla, an Outawa-Sinago, who was going to Detroit with the people of Toupikanich to avenge the death of his brother, who was killed the day after he was made chief, and by this means restore the name of Kischkouch, when he heard that we intended to go to Michilimackinac, begged of us to ask the savages to release him, that he might accompany us thither. The savages granted our request, but reproached him with having no love for his brother. But, nothing daunted, he requested an interview with M. Menard and myself.

"The parley took place the next morning, which happened to be St. Ignace' day, after mass had been said for that saint. All the French who wished, were permitted to be present.

" No one could have spoken in a more engaging, sensible manner, than did Merasilla. He said there really was cause to fear for us, and for the French at Michilimackinac; but he hoped to be able to relieve all the French from any trouble they might be in. He requested us to give him a flag, and a letter to the French; these would be sufficient evidence to them that he had not come to imbrue his hands in their blood. He said, if he found the French at Michilimackinac still alive, and desirous to revenge themselves upon their enemies, if all things were favorable to such an attempt, he would return immediately with the letter which the French would undoubtedly send in answer to ours. If he found that the French had already been massacred, without allowing the savages there to suspect that he had seen us, he would come with the utmost dispatch and warn us, that we might retire to a place of safety; and if there were any immediate danger of an attack upon us, he would aid us in defending ourselves.

" You may judge how gladly his proposition was received, though it is always said that a man risks his life, if he trusts to the fidelity of a savage. But we made him such promises, in our own name and in yours, that the hope of reward was to him a very strong inducement to keep his word. We told him that as soon as he returned, we would recompense him abundantly, whether the condition of things were good or bad, and that we would inform you of the essential service he had rendered us, and you would never forget it.

"To give us every possible assurance of his fidelity, Merasilla left his whole family with us as hostages, and with only three savages, departed in a canoe for Michilimackinac. He executed his commission with the utmost secrecy. He said nothing to the savages, nor to the French, except to the one to whom he gave the letter, until after he was fully informed of the state of affairs. All the French at Michilimackinac greatly admired his judicious conduct. On his return to the mission, each of the Frenchmen there made him a present to the value of four beavers; for which it is but just that the king should remunerate us, as it is in his service that we are exposed to so many dangers. You will greatly oblige all of us, myself in particular, if you will also recompense him liberally. He will then feel, that to render good service to the French who are under your orders, and especially to a missionary, is a matter of some importance.

"Three Frenchmen returned with Merasilla from Michilimackinac, who informed us it was not without reason that we had been told that we risked much in attempting to go to Michilimackinac. For eight days the occupants of that post had been as if the tomahawk were suspended over their heads. Two of the principal women in the village, who had always until then appeared very friendly to the French, went weeping from hut to hut, demanding the death of the French who had killed their brother. Three or four times the French had been obliged to make presents to the Indians, who considered these gifts as a kind of contribution, or honest plunder. They had also been obliged to sell goods to the savages at their own price. But, since the last news from Detroit, by which it appeared that the French there had not shared in the second attack made on the Outawas, affairs at Michilimackinac had been more quiet.

"The day before the Frenchmen left Michilimackinac to come to us, all the Outawas in the village, about one hundred and sixty in number, including those who came to invite them, started for Detroit. If the French there should take any part in the difficulties between the different tribes, there would be more reason than ever to fear for the safety of the French at Michilimackinac.

"Notwithstanding this news, we all resolved to proceed together to Michilimackinac. For my own part, I considered it quite as safe to risk being detained as a hostage by the savages, as to incur their displeasure, which I should most certainly do if I attempted to go to Montreal. Besides, I believed that my presence would serve as a restraint upon the savages, and thus be some security to the French.

"On our arrival at Michilimackinac, on the 9th of August, every one seemed rejoiced. The savages declared that they were now convinced that their father Onontio would not abandon them; that whatever might happen at Detroit, the French would always be secure here. Indeed, they said they did not believe Onontio had any thing to do with the affair at Detroit, since, though he had knowledge of it, he had sent them good promises, and the missionary had returned to them, in spite of all the dangers of the way.

"The French have been actively engaged in fortifying this establishment for the safety of themselves and their effects, as no one can depend on the word of the savages, since the chiefs, however good their intentions, are not masters. For our better security, M. Arnaud has found it necessary to make presents to all the savages. In this he has acted for the public good, and deserves to be repaid. He will present his bill to yourself and the intendant. You are not ignorant how zealous M. Arnaud is for the public good, especially when he knows that his services will meet your approval. His generosity ought not to go unrewarded. M. Menard, who came up with me from Montreal, will also present you with his bill of expenditures in the service of the king.

"It is not just that these two men should be obliged to defray the expense of presents to the savages; especially as the king in these troublous times has provided no presents with which to settle difficulties. I have myself paid the value of a score of beavers, for services. You will permit me to say that, as I came here by your orders, in the midst of so many dangers, it seems only right that some provision should have been made for my journey, and I hope hereafter this subject may receive your attention. Still, I am very glad to be here, and hope my presence will be of service to the French.

"I believe, if M. Menard and myself had arrived here before the departure of the Indians for Detroit, we might have prevented their going, by informing them of some things we heard by the way; but this was not permitted. The old men in council have condemned the departure of their tribe, but say they could not restrain the young men, after they had learned the treason of the Hurons. Besides, they went to aid their relatives, by their tomahawks and with provisions.

"Before we left St. Ignace, Toupikanich informed us that a party of a hundred men would soon arrive, on their way to Detroit; but they did not appear while we remained there. Therefore M. la Motte ought not to find fault because we did not stop them.

"About that time, a party of warriors were to leave

Michilimackinac, and, having engaged the Sacs and Foxes to join them, intended to attack the Miamis on the river St. Joseph. M. Arnaud induced them to wait until our arrival; and we were enabled entirely to divert them from their object. To effect this, we gave them the necklace you had sent to settle their difficulty with Detroit, and prevent their going thither. This necklace, with tobacco, had the effect to stop Onaské and Koutaouiliboe, who were living beyond the precincts of the village—and through their influence the whole project was easily overthrown. Several canoes have indeed departed since, but there was not a sufficiently large number of savages to make a successful attack.

"I asked the savages if I could send a canoe manned with Frenchmen to the river St. Joseph, with any degree of safety? They replied that I could, and urged me to do so, seeming to take an interest in the Fathers who are there. The truth is, they do not feel at liberty to make war upon the Miamis while the missionaries remain there, and for that reason would prefer that they should come to us. I had previously engaged some Frenchmen to carry the news to the river St. Joseph, and to relieve our Fathers if they were in any difficulty; but one of them has been so much intimidated by the representations of his friends, that he dare not trust himself among the savages.

"As affairs are at present, I do not think the removal of the Fathers is advisable, for that is the most important post in all this region except Michilimackinac; and if the Outawas were relieved from the restraint imposed upon them by the existence of the mission, they would unite so many tribes against the Miamis, that in a short time they would drive them from this fine country.

"All the old men of this village who are friendly to the French, among whom is Koutaouiliboe, have behaved so well during all the trouble at Detroit, that they deserve to be rewarded for their zeal. Koutaouiliboe has long been our friend. He possesses sound sense and a good reputation, and has affection enough for us to deserve our consideration. He desires me to say, to you in particular, that he cannot settle all these bad affairs alone, and he wishes you, next autumn, to send the French chief you intend for them, and they will pay the amount in beaver. They no longer know where to find martens and wild-cats. He says, they all wish to have no more difficulties here.

"Onaské wishes me to inform you that 'the reason he has appeared to grow remiss, was from the fear that some trouble might occur in his absence, and there would be no one to settle it.' He says, that while he was at the Isle en Huronne, the small-pox desolated his village, and he invited the Kickapoos of Detroit to return here; but they did not obey him, and now they have been killed by the Hurons. He took the French in his arms, when the people who came from Detroit had a bitter heart toward them; for that reason I found them in good condition. He was very glad to see me, and hoped I would remain. He was glad that the French had made a fort for me, and for themselves. It would strike fear into the hearts of their enemies, and cause jealousy among the tribes at Detroit. He had done all he could to prevent the young men from descending to Detroit; and since I was here, he had nothing to fear from those who should come from there, and he would not allow any trouble to originate here. If Le Pesant left Detroit, he did not believe he would come here, but would probably go to Manitoulin.' Onaské begs you 'always to love his village, and not to believe the representations of Le Pesant, who gave six packs of beaver to the Iroquois to induce them to come with him and destroy Michilimackinac. He hopes you will continue to hinder the Iroquois from coming here, and instruct them not to receive the Huron, if he wishes to return to his wigwam.' You will, of course, manage these things as you think proper.

"I have, at last, found another Frenchman who is willing to go to the river St. Joseph, and I hope the four will now depart immediately. We have reason to feel anxious concerning the safety of the Fathers, on account of so many war-parties going down on that side. At least, we shall have news from St. Joseph, unless our men find too many dangers in the way."

"MICHILIMACKINAC, August 27, 1706.

"A few canoes of the savages of this place, who went to Detroit, having returned, I am permitted to give you their report; they arrived here on Monday, August 23d. The chiefs of Michilimackinac, who remained at home, have always maintained that their men had not gone to fight, but to withdraw their brothers, the young men, from Detroit. Those who went last, report that they met these young men on their way home. Five or six days had already elapsed since they left Detroit, and they were nearly exhausted with hunger. Ten canoes have gone to Saginaw for provisions. Le Pesant and Jean la Blanc, with many others, are still delayed by the wind. Those who have arrived, say that a great battle was fought at Detroit, and that the French were going out with the Miamis and Hurons to attack the Outawas in their fort. Two Frenchmen had been killed in the combat, by a Miami. The Outawas feared that they had killed some of the Iroquois of the Saut, if any were with the Hurons.

"The savages all say that the Miamis were masters in

the fort of the French, stealing their corn and other provisions, and committing all manner of depredations. It was also reported that they had burnt an Outawa. The Hurons burned a young Outawa woman in their fort. They sent four Outawas captive to the Miamis of St. Joseph; two of them escaped; but they said the Miamis had not ill-treated them, and the blame of the whole affair must rest on Quarante Sous. The same Hurons had two other Outawa prisoners, whom they wished to give either to the Miamis, who were soon to return from Detroit, or to M. la Motte.

"The greater part of the fields at Detroit had been ravaged. Only a few of the Miamis remained at Detroit, and the Loups had withdrawn. No news had yet been received from M. la Motte. M. Menard will give all the circumstances at length; you may depend upon his report.

"We are impatiently awaiting the return of M. Boudor and the Outawa chiefs. I have not yet sent to the river St. Joseph, but hope to very soon.

"I hasten to close this long letter, by assuring you that I am with respect, sir,

"Your very humble, and
"Very obedient servant,
"JOS. T. MAREST."

## CHAPTER XI.

La Motte's reply to two letters of the governor-general—Gives an account of the attacks of the savages mentioned by Father Marest—Jean la Blanc demands peace by a branch of porcelain—M. Bourmont receives the branch, and refers the affair to the decision of M. la Motte—M. la Motte thinks this outbreak no sudden freak—Savages probably instigated by others—Desertion of the French soldiers on their way to Detroit—Expresses thanks that powder is no longer allowed to be sold to the hostile savages by the traders—Arrival of one hundred warriors, Sauteurs and Amikouecs—Numerous councils held between them and the French—M. la Motte demands of them the death of Le Pesant and three or four others—Hurons and Miamis determined to plunder the traders at Michilimackinac.

On the reception of the first letter from Father Marest, containing an account of the trouble at Detroit, the governor-general wrote two letters to M. la Motte, who was returning to his post at that place. To these communications M. la Motte wrote the following reply:

"Fort Pontchartrain, August 27, 1706.

"Monsieur:—I received, on my way hither, the two letters with which you were pleased to honor me, dated 27th of June and 3d of July. By the first, you inform me that you are not surprised at the attack which the Outawas have made upon us, and upon the Miamis. Not so with me, for I confess frankly that I was extremely surprised at this undertaking of a nation which never before manifested a warlike disposition toward us.

"The affair of the Mississaques of which you speak was a quarrel between this nation and the Miamis, who had nothing in common with the Outawas. The commandant of this post had pacified the parties, and settled the difficulty. In fact, as soon as the Outawas had commenced the attack, the Mississaques drew outside of Detroit, that they might not be suspected of having given any aid to the Outawas. They have even come here, since my arrival, to 'lament our dead,' according to their custom.

"It appears that the Outawas premeditated what they have done; and according to the letter of M. Bourmont, of which he has shown me a copy, it appears equally certain that they intended to destroy the French, for they killed the Rev. Father Constantine, who was in his garden outside the fort, and La Rivière, a soldier who had gone to give warning to the missionary. This soldier received a wound from the knife of a savage; and while attempting to save himself, he was pierced by three or four gun-shots before he could reach the gate of the fort.

"Who does not know that the savages are cunning and perfidious? 'The old men,' say the Outawas, 'did not meddle in this affair—it was the young men.' Fine excuse, if we can make up our minds to receive it.

How is it then, sir, after committing this black deed, Jean la Blanc, who is the second chief, and the old man of the village, comes to demand peace by a branch of porcelain?* M. de Bourmont received it, referring him to what you and I would do about it on my arrival. Only four hours after, Jean la Blanc, who is the second chief, and the old man of the village, came to attack the fort with a great number of warriors. They kept up a brisk fire upon it from five o'clock in the afternoon until midnight. In short, they continued the siege forty or fifty days, even to the day of their departure.

* "The porcelains in this country are shells; these are found on the coasts of New England and Virginia. They are channeled, drawn out lengthwise, a little pointed, without ears, and pretty thick. The fish contained in these shells are not good to eat; but the inside is of so beautiful a varnish, with such lively colors, that it is impossible to imitate it by art. . . . .

"There are two sorts of these shells, or, to speak more properly, two colors, one white and the other violet. The first is most common, and perhaps on that account less esteemed. The second seems to have a finer grain when it is wrought; the deeper its color is, the more it is valued. Small cylindrical grains are made of both, which are bored through and strung upon a thread, and of these, branches and collars of porcelain, or wampum, are made. The branches are no more than four or five threads or small straps of leather, about a foot in length, on which the grains or beads of wampum are strung. The collars are in the manner of fillets or diadems, formed of these branches sewed together with thread, making four, five, six, or seven rows of beads, and of proportionable length; all of which depends on the importance of the affair in agitation, and the dignity of the person to whom the collar is presented."—CHARLEVOIX.

"What did this same Jean la Blanc mean, when he returned to the fort with a flag-staff in his hand, and having approached the bastion, said to M. Bourmont, 'With what I hold in my hand I fear nothing, for it comes from M. Vaudreuil. It is not you who will settle this affair, it is he; I listen to his word, and do what he bids me.' After which he entered the fort, having demanded admission of M. Bourmont, where he repeated the same thing.

"What language is that? who can understand it? Is it the young men, or the old, who have been concerned in this action?

"The whole course which the old men, or rather this nation, have pursued, proves only too well that this resolution has not been taken suddenly. I think this design would never have been executed, if M. Tonti had not previously laid out two large forts, one for this nation and the other for the Hurons, on which he made the French work in spite of themselves. I learned his design before my departure from Detroit, and advised him to do nothing about it, because it was not prudent, on the right and left of ourselves, to fortify nations upon whom we could not rely. On the contrary, *our fort* should have kept them in dependence. It was a great mistake, but there was a remedy, and I had proposed to myself a means of causing these forts to be abandoned.

"But M. Tonti committed a much greater mistake by selling to the Outawas, for the benefit of the company, so much powder that at the time of the attack there remained only thirty-one pounds, as appears by the inventory with his signature. Fortunately M. Bourmont had fifty pounds which he brought from Quebec the preceding autumn. Great strength! mighty means of defense! A royal fort established by order of the king in a wilderness teeming with savages, yet destitute of gunpowder!

"The Outawas were well informed of this fact; they also knew that the garrison consisted of only fifteen men! But, sir, even with a knowledge of these facts, why should the savages make an attack on the fort, and kill the French? Why fight the Miamis, who have lived there peaceably for five years, eating and drinking together every day; and who had never for twenty or thirty years quarreled among themselves?

"It was said that the attack was made on the Missisaques; but that could not have been, as the Mississaques have not only shown no disposition to avenge themselves, but have gone away, not wishing to be in any way concerned in the bad conduct of the Outawas.

"You were right in supposing that I would find no Outawas here on my arrival. I was of the same opinion as soon as I learned, at the distance of two days' journey from Montreal, that they had made an attack on the fort, and had killed the poor Father, the soldier, and the Miamis. The report that some of the Outawas had been left at the fort as hostages, until my arrival, was false. They were not so well disposed toward the French as that would signify.

"There is no doubt, sir, as you have said, that if M. la Forest or myself had been on the spot, these difficulties would not have occurred. Perhaps we might have been able to detect those secret plans, by means that escaped the observation of M. Bourmont.

"But this outbreak is no sudden freak; and if the savages have become so seriously disaffected as present appearances indicate, no doubt the cause may be imputed to my unjust detention at Quebec by your order, in consequence of a well-concerted series of charges preferred against me by the company of the colony. I am aware that at first you might have believed me guilty; but after I was acquitted by the intendant, I had the honor to request, with all possible earnestness, your permission to return to the post to which I was appointed by the king—not having been the choice of any governor—but you refused to grant my request. I must believe you had good reasons for so doing, though I have not the honor of knowing them.

"Your orders to go to Fort Pontchartrain were not

given to M. la Forest until the 25th of September, just after I had received an order from Count Pontchartrain to come to Quebec, if I were at Detroit; consequently it was my duty to remain, and M. Bourmont was sent to command until I could return.

"You are already aware that M. Bourmont, who left Quebec on the 29th of September, did not arrive here until the 29th of January. If he, young and vigorous, had so much difficulty in accomplishing the journey, would M. la Forest, who is between fifty and sixty years of age, have been able to succeed, especially as he was then in ill health? I am more vigorous than he, because I am younger, but my duty to the colonial minister compelled me to remain at Quebec.

"On my way hither I passed Sonnontouan, the village of that dangerous spirit Pimabanso. I had some disposition to give him trouble; but he is an evil spirit, and always gets himself out of difficulty. I have just learned that he is near here, coming from Orange laden with brandy, as is his custom.

"I have no doubt that you will cause some of the deserters from this post to be punished, and that you will send the rest back, or replace them, in order to complete the number that you granted me. May I not also hope for an increase of fifty men? I trust you will either grant me that number, or else release me from the responsibility of any troubles that may arise at this fort.

"I hope you will be able to arrest, and return to me, two men of my company named St. Jean and Parisien, who ran away from me on our way to Detroit. After we had crossed the Grand Traverse, I left four or five canoes which did not go as well as the others, ordering M. Dufiguier to tell them that I would go on to the Fort du Sable, and await them there, as they could come thus far with perfect safety. The other boats soon arrived. But St. Jean and Parisien entered the Goyagouin bay, and proceeded to the great village of Sonnontouan to carry letters to the Jesuit who resides there, and who, it appears, had charged them with his letters to Montreal. I awaited them at the Sable eight entire days, because I heard by the Iroquois that there were Outawas at the Portage. I have written evidence of all this. They did indeed come to the Fort du Sable after they were sure I had left, though I first obtained a promise from the Iroquois that if the deserters should come, they would escort them to the portage of Niagara. Seven or eight Hurons went to the Fort du Sable and offered themselves as an escort, but St. Jean and his party would have nothing to do with them. Do not these rascals deserve to pass the winter in a dungeon, and to be sent back here in the spring?

15

"I am very much obliged to you for having forbidden the four canoes which have gone to Michilimackinac, to carry powder there. I do not know whether your orders have been executed, for a hundred well-armed Mississaques came here with a letter to me from Father Marest, who furnished them with powder for their journey. They say the French were not willing to receive their beaver, but traded with them for all their martens. I have forbidden them to trade for powder here, fearing they might be but the messengers of the Outawas, or, at least, would share the powder with them.

"A hundred other warriors have also arrived, Sauteurs and Amikouecs, whom Father Marest and Maurice Menard had collected around Toupikanich. It is believed that they come to assist the Outawas, as they had with them two Outawa men and one squaw. When they saw the Outawa fort on fire, they conferred together, and seemed to decide that it was necessary to hold a parley with us. For that purpose they raised three good white flags of such cloth as they would not be apt to purchase, and I granted them permission to land near the fort. As they had not appeared to be concerned in the affair with the Outawas, we felt obliged to receive them; but the result was the holding of many councils, and sometimes I was under the necessity of using very large words.

"The Hurons and Miamis, who are no fools, from the

first opposed these councils, for they were confident this movement had only been made by the Mississaques and Sauteurs to favor the Outawas. Their reasoning was very good. They said, if these tribes had come on a peaceful errand, they would not have come as soldiers, nor in such large numbers; neither would they have brought with them two Outawas, whom we at once recognized as among those who had fought against us. I made great efforts to destroy this idea. I knew our allies had good reasons for thinking as they did, but considered it best, under the circumstances, to tell them I would not permit them to kill people whom I knew to be innocent—I would rather die with them.

"Upon hearing my decision, the Miamis armed themselves and left the fort, and went to the village of the Hurons. I immediately caused the gates to be shut, and doubly guarded. Finally, the Miamis met us in council, and I settled the affair peaceably; all now appear satisfied.

"I learned accidentally at Sonnontouan, on my way here, that five Outawas, two Miamis, and two or three Hurons had gone to Orange to get brandy. I do not know what has become of the Outawas; the Miamis have returned, and report that the English detained them there, on account of the difficulties at this post.

"The Hurons, Ouyatanons, and some of the Miamis

are here, and have, in all the councils, expressed the following sentiments: 'We will never listen to a treaty of reconciliation with the Outawas. We will hear, on this subject, neither the governor nor you. Onontio might give us all the goods in Quebec and Montreal, and we would reject them' (I very much doubt it, however). 'We beg you to join us. We are killed for wishing to give life to your fort, and to avenge you. M. Bourmont had no powder; we gave him ours to defend you. We do not wish for peace—it must not be spoken of. If you make peace with the Outawas, we shall have bad thoughts.'

"This last sentence means, in good French, that if I make peace with the one, I may expect war with the other. But I do not trouble myself about that. I shall succeed in my designs—not, however, without some difficulty. I replied to them as follows:

"'We have been struck by the same hand; but I do not wish to make war in your mode, I wish to do it in mine. You go in small parties, and often put over the fire little kettles. As for me, I declare to you all, Hurons, Miamis, Ouyatanons, Chavouanons, and Iroquois, to all who hear me speak, I wish to boil only one great kettle, and to put all the Outawas into it at once. Now, listen to me: if they discover us on our march and flee, they cannot sow; if they have sown, we will destroy their corn. The governor will give them no powder, and these people cannot live by the bow and arrow. They are dead men, without costing you the loss of a single man. If they shut themselves up in their villages and fortify themselves there, I promise to fire the palisade, and give you admittance. I will do it myself, at the head of the French soldiers and of your warriors, and I promise you not to leave a single Outawa on the earth.'

"Since that time, it has been necessary to pass day and night in council, and I am quite exhausted. I scarcely know how I have found time to write so long a letter; I cannot take a copy of it.

"These nations wished to proceed immediately to Michilimackinac with a hundred warriors, and desired me to go with one hundred French soldiers. I have persuaded them to defer the expedition until next spring, when they have concluded to go with an army of eight hundred warriors.

"It is for you, sir, it is for you to decide what is best to be done. You still have time to send your orders this autumn, by a light canoe, which would probably reach here before winter sets in; but if they should be overtaken by cold weather, the men could come by land. My own opinion is, that this attack of the Outawas ought not to go unpunished. In order to completely quiet these troubles, it will be necessary to put Le Pesant and three or four others to death, and to pardon the rest. This punishment would render the chiefs of each nation more wise and circumspect, since the chiefs are always the authors of such mischief. Le Pesant is old, and his missionary will pray God for him after his death, and give him absolution at death, if he demand it.

"I should have immediately sent a canoe-load of men to inform you of all the events transpiring here, that you might take such measures as you should think necessary, if the soldiers, who were sent by M. Bourmont, and also my correspondents at Montreal, had not assured me that no one troubled himself to send them back, or even to assist in defraying the expenses of their voyage. Therefore, sir, unless you think proper to give me some certain assurance that the envoys whom I send to inform you of what is passing here in your own government, shall have their expenses defrayed by the king, consent, if you please, to receive reports from me only by such opportunities as may present themselves. I am not rich enough to do otherwise.

"Why is it that since last January each soldier has only been allowed three sous a day for food? This has not been the case before in ten years. Why does not the intendant feed these troops as well as he does those at Quebec? Will you have the kindness to give attention to this matter?

"Allow me to inform you that the Hurons and Miamis are going to Michilimackinac, determined to plunder all the French traders who are on their way thither, and thus prevent them from carrying powder and ball to the Outawas.

"Finally, sir, it appears to me that your action in regard to the Outawas is of great importance. Of this you are already well aware, knowing, as you do, our interests, and the manners and customs of this people.

"Your very humble, and

"Very obedient servant,

"LA MOTTE CADILLAC."

# CHAPTER XII.

The governor-general orders the principal chiefs of the tribes engaged in the attack on Detroit, to descend to Montreal—They arrive June 17, 1707—Governor-general refuses to see them—Council called the next day—Jean le Blanc's speech—Second council, June 20th, speech of the governor-general—Third council, Jean le Blanc's reply—Fourth council, governor-general again addresses the savages—Demands the death of Le Pesant—Finally refers the affair to M. la Motte Cadillac at Detroit—Last council: Jean le Blanc consents to the demands of the governor-general.

In accordance with the advice of M. la Motte, the governor-general ordered the principal chiefs of the Outawas to come to Montreal, that he might examine into the affair. Obedient to the command, Jean le Blanc, and a number of other chiefs, made the journey in the spring of 1707. They arrived on the 17th of June, and proceeded immediately to pay their respects to the governor-general. To their great dismay, he refused to see them. The next day, however, a council was called, and Jean la Blanc, the second chief of that powerful nation, the Outawas, made the following speech:

"My father, my father—I am so embarrassed that I know not if I shall have strength to speak to you. Our custom is, as soon as we have debarked, to come and salute you. We were surprised, yesterday, to learn that you did not wish to receive us.

"My father—You see your children, the Outawas; behold in what state we are to come here below! We have no more of the old people; and of all our chiefs, whom you have seen here at other times, there now remains to us only Le Brochet, who is on his way hither.

"My father, my father, M. de Vaudreuil—I wish you to hear me, and listen to me tranquilly. I have committed one fault, which is very great. I cannot say that I was intoxicated, for I had not the water of life of the English to induce me to do this bad action. But I will tell you, with all truth, what was the cause of my misfortune.

"We had departed, as you already know, our father, to make war upon the Sioux, to avenge the Sacs, our allies. After having passed the fort of the French, as we were near that of the Hurons, a savage came to tell us that our children were dead; that after three days' march of our warriors, the Ouyatanons would come to eat our women and children. Then, my father, we said, 'We will strike the Miamis before they strike us, or we are indeed dead.'

"You have known, my father, from Mishonaky, and you ought to have known by your letters, all that has passed in this affair; and especially our great misfortunes, as the 'gray coat' and the soldier have been killed, though without design.

"When they had finished fighting, that is to say, several days after we had attacked the Miamis, I went alone to the fort, to speak to M. Bourmont. I carried a branch of porcelain, and entreated him to be willing to listen well to me. I told him it was to be wished that Onontio M. Vaudreuil, and even the great Onontio, the king, could hear me, as they would listen to my reasons. I demanded of him the coat which you gave me when I came here below, and which I had left in the care of the best of my friends. I demanded of him this coat, my father, in order to make use of it to find the nations clothed in the coats of my father, and to settle all the bad affairs. He would not listen to me. The day following, I returned six times, and each time I took with me a man of the different nations, and presents of necklaces and beavers, in order to be able to speak to him; but he refused to listen to us, as on the preceding day.

"My father, my father—You have known all that has happened, and how all has occurred. I have nothing to fear, because I have a good father; therefore, I conceal nothing from you: I show you all that is in my heart. Here is my body; do with it what you will: put me in the big kettle, if you think proper. But I am not the most guilty; for what I have done, was done as by a man without his senses. It is Le Pesant, that bear, who is above upon his bed, who has not been willing to listen to all the reasons which we brought, to prevent him from obliging us to commit this bad act.

"My father—Since I have commenced speaking, I am gaining courage. I beg you to remember that it was my father Talon, my own father, who first came from the upper regions to find the French. He came across the woods to Three Rivers, where he was well received by him who commanded there. The next year he returned, and found there M de Courcelle, who gave him the name of Talon, saying it was necessary to bind the commerce together; and, since the door was open, they must continue to see each other, as it gave him a key to this door, in order to open it when he should think proper, whatever difficulties might occur.

"My father—I keep this key, being one of his children. I make use of it to-day to open your door. It is true that I have almost closed the door against myself, by my bad conduct; but of what use is this key, if it may not serve me in an affair of consequence; and who is permitted to use it, if not I, to whom my father has left it?

"My father—I have left Michilimackinac, to come to see you. I have come by the old way, so much traveled by our ancestors. I found it all filled with impediments. I have cleared it; I have taken away the trees that obstructed it. I have removed the rocks in the rapids; I have rooted out all the bad plants, in order to make it, in future, a fine passage for my brothers, the French, and for ourselves. I give you this necklace, my father, that this gate may remain open to you. We have lost every thing, in losing our old men; we have no wisdom to conduct us. How can we have, being without a leader? At Michilimackinac we have seen M. Louvigny, M. la Motte, M. Tonti, M. Mantet, and M. la Forest, with the Illinois. While they remained there, we always lived peaceably, and were always obedient to the will of our father. What has happened to us at Detroit is very painful; I am vexed with myself when I think of it. I killed myself when I killed the soldier, and the 'gray coat,' the child of the father who gives us life! Have pity on us, our father, for I am in despair at the bad conduct which I have committed. Behold all your children here present; they say the same thing. We have killed the 'gray coat,' it is true, but we hope to bring him to life again. When I say that we will bring the 'gray coat' again to life, it is not with necklaces and furs; for I know well that, though we might have a house full of them, they would not be a sufficient recompense for the blood of our father. What then can I do? I can only satisfy you, my father, by giving you these two captives, who are our own blood, since we have adopted them. Receive them, my father, to cover that of Father Recollet; else take my body. I can offer you nothing more; have pity upon me! Restore tranquillity to the lakes and rivers, that all your children may be in peace; and that they may cook their meat, and drink of the wave, with all safety.

"There are those, my father, who call themselves your children, who have wished to astonish me, by taking me by the end of the finger; but you, my father, have always held me by the hand. It is true that I have thought to escape you. I beg you now to take my hand more strongly than ever. What can I fear, if you do not abandon me?

"My father—You must have seen, by your letters, and by what Mishonaky has told you, how many nations Quarante Sous has invited to eat us. I confess to you that the Hurons, after having been so long our friends, have villainously betrayed us. I am cut to the heart, and I can only be healed by telling you all my thoughts. The Hurons have not only killed us in battle, but what touches me the most, they have killed our men who, for the love of them, went with them to war against the Flat Heads. The Hurons would, long since, have been no more, if I had left their interests. Many nations have asked of me this roebuck, to eat it; but I have not been willing to give it up. Yet it is he who has betrayed me to-day.

"My father—The Hurons have committed four treasons in succession, in what has passed at Detroit. I know not the number of people I may have killed for them; but they have killed for me thirty men.

"My father—It is I, it is the Outawas, who have killed the 'gray coat;' by mistake, indeed, but we have killed him and the soldier, and we have caused all the misfortunes which have occurred at Detroit. As for Techenet, it is M. Bourmont who has killed him, seeing him fight against us; for the father and the soldier were both killed in the first fire; and all that happened afterward was done coolly, as M. Bourmont caused it to be done.

"My father—All my bad feeling toward the Miamis and Hurons arises from their having often reproached me with being without a father. They said you had forsaken me; and a proof of that was, that I had no longer any powder, while they were treated to it in abundance. 'What!' said I to myself, 'am I not the oldest of my father's children? Why should he abandon me?'

"M. la Motte has invited me, by Beauvais, to come to see his village. M. d'Argenteuil has also sent me word that he could not come to see me now, but he hoped he might do so soon. I have replied to M. la Motte, that if I had two bodies, I would willingly divide into two parts, to go to see him; but that, having only one, and being called by my father, I was going to learn his wishes."

In accordance with the Indian custom, the governor-general deferred his answer until a future time. Two days after, on the 20th of June, the council again met, and M. Vaudreuil made the following reply to the speech of Jean le Blanc, addressing himself alike to Le Blanc, and to all the other chiefs who had accompanied him to Montreal:

"I am not surprised, Jean le Blanc, after what has happened at Detroit, to see you embarrassed in speaking to me; you should have foreseen at that time what would be the consequences of such conduct. If I did not wish to receive you immediately on your arrival, as I received Le Brochet, Meyaouka, and two others, it is because I regarded them as obedient children, who, in these bad affairs, always maintained good principles. But as for you, I can yet regard you only as a rebellious child—one who has displeased me with his bad conduct. I know all that has passed at Detroit; every thing has been told me by M. la Motte, M. Bourmont, and Father Marest, as well as by yourself.

"Did you say the truth yesterday when you told me that you would give me your body to do with it whatever I might wish, even to put you in the big kettle, if

I thought proper? In this, you betray your despair of my forgiveness for those things that you have done; that is something, but it is not enough. I am a good father, it is true; but for that very reason, when one offends me, the offense is very great.

"In coming here, you have given me a proof of your obedience, and also of your confidence in my kindness. But I have not yet received any evidence of your true and sincere repentance, and perseverance in well-doing. Therefore, what have I to depend upon when you have returned to Michilimackinac? What pledge will you give that you will not, on the very first day, insult my children?

"When you came here two years ago, you, Jean le Blanc, with Le Pesant, did you not tell me that the Outawas of Michilimackinac were not like those of Detroit, who had attacked the Iroquois without cause; that, although the Miamis had struck you twice, your broken head was quite closed up since the peace, and wherever you might find the Miamis you would not attack them, unless they first attacked you, but then you would avenge yourselves. Did I not then tell you, that in case of any farther trouble it would be necessary for me to refer you to the commandant of Detroit, who, knowing all the circumstances of the case, and having my orders, could always tell you my wishes?

"Have you kept your word? Did you inform M. Bourmont before you attacked the Miamis? Is it true that the Miamis made the first attack upon you, and you tried to prevent it?

"No! All this is only a pretext, of which Le Pesant, the bear, who is now at Michilimackinac, high up in his bed, was glad to make use, in order to give trouble. Since you failed then to keep your word, what ground have I to believe you now? I ought rather to think that only the danger in which you are now makes you promise so fairly.

"The more I examine into the events that have transpired at Michilimackinac, the more I see of your disobedience. Sometimes I behold my children, the Iroquois, bound and ready to be burned; sometimes I see the French, whole families, taken prisoners and held as hostages. These are every-day occurrences; and if I forbid you to go to war, it is to restrain those among you who are constantly seeking occasions for war.

"It is not that among the large tribe of the Outawas there are none who listen to my voice; I know that Meyaouka, who is here, loves peace, and Le Brochet also. I know that Sakima has a good mind, and since he has come here he shows a disposition to satisfy me. I know that there are still some others above who have good sentiments.

"But who will satisfy me that, when you have returned, Le Pesant, that bear, who dreams upon his mat only of making war, will not spoil the present peaceful spirit you possess, and prevail upon you to commit a greater fault than that which you have already committed?

"Your present offense is much greater, since you have not only without cause attacked the Miamis, my allies, and armed in my service, but you have also attacked myself by killing a missionary, whose loss can hardly be repaired. He was of so much value among us that if Le Pesant, who is the sole cause of all this mischief, had come here, I do not know what I might have done. But I leave to you the care of avenging me, and rendering suitable satisfaction. You should have brought me his head. My blood still flows. I see it continually before my eyes; and though you have come here, I cannot yet staunch it. The two captives whom you present to me, though adopted by you, are foreign blood. Father Recollet and the soldier were my blood—my own blood.

"The blood of the French is usually repaid among us only by blood. Thus, you see, I ought not to be satisfied with what you have done; indeed, it is almost impossible to satisfy me at all for the loss which I have sustained, unless it be by sacrificing the head of him who caused it.

"You have told me yourself that he caused all your

misfortunes, and so long as he lives will only make quarrels for you with all the nations, and will finally be the cause of your ruin. Reflect on what I have said to you, and give me your reply."

The next day, June 21st, 1707, the council having again convened, Jean le Blanc made the following rejoinder to the speech of the governor-general:

"My father, my father—I come again before you. Count Frontenac always told our old men, that we would still be his children, although they were dead. I speak to you as if they were present.

"We are your children, my father; we come to you by a necklace. I am in despair, my father, about being able to repair the evil I have done. I speak for my people, I lend them my voice.

"I have nothing to offer you but my body. I am in despair, being unable to make amends for my faults. I follow in the footsteps of our old men—I follow in the footsteps of my own father; they have always been obedient, I will be so too. I have committed a great fault; but can it be repaired? My father—I am desperate about what has happened. You have demanded the head of that bear who is above. True, it is he who is guilty—it is he himself; but I cannot promise you satisfaction.

"If I were to say to my father, 'I will give you

the head of that great bear,' it would be impossible for me to keep my word, and I should be sorry to lie to you.

"I dare not promise you, my father, to do what you demand, because that great bear is allied to all the upper nations. Not that I would fear him if he were there alone, for none of us love him, as he is the guilty one. But, as he is allied to all the lakes, my father, I am troubled about the consequences. As all his allies prevented me from making efforts to bring him here, I cannot do with him what I would desire.

"My father—My consolation is that he is old, and cannot go far, and when he is dead we shall have no more trouble. But while waiting, we promise you to listen to him no more. And, if we can appease your anger, we will give you our word that he shall not cause us to commit any fault.

"My father, my father—We are your children, we are all French; it is terrible that we must perish for the love of our brothers. This is the first fault that we have committed—the first fault with which any one can reproach the Outawas.

"My father—We have always been friendly to the French; shall we now perish by their hand?

"All of us who are here, my father, are chiefs and principal men; we are resolved to do your will. Pardon us, our father! We promise you that you shall never have sorrow on our account, and that we will have no other will than yours."

Another council was held, June 22, 1707, when the governor-general addressed the savages of Michilimackinac, as follows:

"I have thought upon what you replied to me yesterday. I am very willing to believe that you cannot deliver to me the head of Le Pesant, as I requested you.

"Yet his blood is necessary to satisfy me: the death of a missionary can be expiated only with blood.

"I pity you; for all the nations have seen your fault, and are waiting in suspense to hear what satisfaction I may require of you. All the nations, therefore, must know how penitent you are for your fault, and how submissive you are to my will.

"It was at Detroit that you offended me; it was there that you killed Father Recollet and my soldier; and it is there that I wish you to make satisfaction. For that purpose, I wish you to carry to M. la Motte the two captives, whom you brought here to present to me.

"That I may be certain of your obedience, and that all the nations may also witness it, you must not return by the great river of the Outawas; at least, not all of you. It is necessary that you, Jean le Blanc, and some others, with the captives, should go by the way of the lakes. I will give you letters to M. la Motte and the French, for your security.

"But, by whatever means M. la Motte may settle the difficulties which you have made, and also satisfy the nations whom, as well as myself, you have offended, I will order him not to include Le Pesant in the pardon, which, perhaps, he may grant you on my account.

"I will agree to any settlement that M. la Motte may be able to make between you and the other nations, if Le Pesant be not included. I am very willing to grant you a general amnesty of all the past. Jean le Blanc, behold the open door! see that you make use of it!

"The necklace which you gave me yesterday, I return to you. When you have done what I have commanded you, and when La Motte has found means by which to grant you the pardon of your fault, and to settle the affair with those nations whom you have attacked, bring back the necklace to me by the way of the lakes or the great river. Both these ways will be open to you, in case I shall myself confirm the pardon which may have been granted you in my name. When the necklace is returned, I will willingly forget your fault. But if you all, Outawas of Michilimackinac, do not give me this proof of obedience, you have every thing to fear from my just resentment.

"Father Marest has informed me that he intends to

bring me some captives to satisfy his brothers, the Iroquois, and that he would come down now, but for that. I charge thee, only thee, Brochet, to tell him that I depend upon his word.

"As to the complaint that you make against the Hurons, it is not they who have killed you, it is yourselves. If the Outawas had not attacked the Miamis, as you did, without cause, the Huron nation would still be our ally, Father Recollet would be living, and you would be at Detroit enjoying an abundance, and not in misery, as you now are.

"Jean le Blanc, M. la Motte knowing what you have told me, has invited you to go and see him; profit by the good opinion which he has of you.

"Although you have offended me in the most tender point, having plunged the poniard into my bosom, you see that I yet have pity for you, by furnishing you the means of settling the difficulty which you have made. Outawas, profit by my pity!

"I have given my orders to M. la Motte, to remember all who are here present—Outawas, Kiskakons, Sinagos, you of the Nations du Sable, and of the Fourche.

"Remember, all of you, the word which I gave you yesterday, no longer to recognize Le Pesant in any thing, and to regard him in future as a decayed, rotten member, and separated from your body.

"Remember that you have promised me to make no more trouble, and never to give me cause of sorrow.

"Outawas! the blood of the French is of value; remember well all my words!"

The last council of this long session was held on the 23d of June, and to the clear statement of the terms and conditions of peace made by the governor-general, Jean la Blanc replied:

"My father—I am sorry that M. Bourmont is not here to give you his statement, as I do mine. I believe he is ashamed, since he has not come, like me, to tell you his story.

"My father, my father—I beg you to listen to me; and you, interpreters, take good care that you forget nothing, and that you correctly interpret what I shall say unto you.

"Last year, when I arrived at Michilimackinac, I said to Father Marest, that I should die for the loss of my father. But when I saw the little Fox arrive, I said to him that I no longer feared any thing; for my father had called me, and I was going to offer him my body.

"My father—I see plainly that my complexion is not to your liking. I go to obey your will. I go to find M. la Motte, and to die with my brother, Father Recollet.

"My father—I am a child of obedience; I go to Detroit. I have already said to you that I will deliver to you my body. I am going to Detroit, and from there I will go to Michilimackinac, in order to make smooth the old way. I will do your will, my father; and, since I do what you require of me, I beg you to grant me what I ask of you.

"My father—We have not yet determined who are to go to Detroit with me; I have brought them here, that you may decide. My father, I obey your will.

"My father—Our people will be in trouble about me. When I departed they came to see me, in great distress lest I should never return. I beg you, since I obey you, to send one of your chief men to assure them that I have only gone to do your will.

"I ask this, my father, because the boat that goes by the great river will reach Michilimackinac sooner than I shall; and when he shall say to the people that I have gone to see La Motte, the old men will send a boat to inform the other nations, and to explain to them the object of my journey.

"The Sacs, the Malominies, the Mascoutins, the Kickapoos, the Outagamies, and the Pottawatomies, are people who will like to hear the good news. They are our allies, and are those to whom our old men will give notice, that the land may be united.

"I came to bring you my body. I have always believed that I should not return by the same route that I came. My design has always been, after having seen you, to go to see M. la Motte.

"My father, my father—M. la Motte has acted like the porcupine; he would not go to see his little ones. He called us—the four Outawa nations—to Detroit; but, after having made an opening in the tree, as does the porcupine to give food to her children, he left us. If he, or M. Tonti, or M. la Forest, had been at Detroit, all this trouble would not have happened.

"My father—I beg you to send by the great river, a man who will be attentive to our interests; and to give me an interpreter who understands me well, that I may not be wearied by the way. Give me also men strong and swift, that we may go the quicker."

This request for an envoy was well understood by the governor-general, as a mere subterfuge of the savages to enable them to get possession of a French hostage for their own security. Aware that a discussion of the subject and a continuation of the councils, could not be productive of any good, he merely replied to the chiefs that he had no envoy to give them, and that they were now perfectly aware of his wishes.

With assurances of protection on his part, and fidelity and submission on theirs, the council was dismissed.

## CHAPTER XIII.

The chiefs proceed to Detroit—First council held by M. la Motte, August 6th, 1707—M. la Motte addresses the savages—Second council: Otontagon replies—Third council: M. la Motte addresses the Hurons and Miamis—Sastarexy replies—Fourth council: a general council of the Outawas, Hurons, and Miamis—M. la Motte's speech—Otontagon, Sastarexy, and Onaské address the council—M. la Motte demands the delivery of Le Pesant into the hands of the French—The chiefs finally accede to the demand.

Obedient to the orders of the governor-general, Jean le Blanc, Kinongé, Meaninan, and Menekoumak, four chiefs of the Outawas, proceeded to Detroit, to meet M. la Motte. The remainder of their party returned to Michilimackinac by way of the Ottawa river.

On the arrival of the chiefs at Fort Pontchartrain, a great council was convened, August 6th, 1707, and continued from day to day until August 10th.

M. la Motte Cadillac, who had been fully acquitted by Count Pontchartrain of all the charges preferred against him, and restored to his official station as commandant, was now convinced, by the course pursued by M. Vaudreuil, that it was deemed expedient by the colonial government to wear, at least, the appearance of friendship.

Gratified at the favorable change, whatever might be

the motives, he brought all the energy of his mind and the fruit of his long experience to bear upon the adjustment of this difficult and important affair.

Adapting his mode of expression to the customs of the savages, he opened the first council with the following characteristic speech:

"Otontagon, Kinongé, and others, hear me patiently. I will not repeat the words you have said to Onontio, nor his replies; you know as well as I what they were.

"M. Vaudreuil writes me that he sends you here with the two captives you offered him. He makes me master of peace, and leaves the whole matter with me, telling me to use whatever means I think best to restore tranquillity to the nations.

"Otontagon, hear me! I have lighted a great fire. I have planted four great trees near this beautiful fire, two on my right hand and two on my left.

"Outawas! you are the largest tree: I have said to myself, 'It is well: now I will often repose under the shadow of this tree: I will refresh myself there: under its shadow I shall have only good thoughts!'

"Could I believe that any one had attached to the top of this great tree a sharp and heavy hatchet, which I did not see, because it was covered with foliage?

"While I slept peacefully, and dreamed only of peace, a wicked bear climbed to the top of this tree. He shook it with all his might, and the hatchet which hung there fell upon my cabin, and crushed it.

"When I saw my cabin in ruins, my heart was displeased; it darted to the right and to the left; it ascended even to my throat. I then said, 'I will cut down this tree, I will root it out, I will reduce it to ashes.' But when my heart had nearly regained its place, I said, 'Why destroy this tree, its leaves, and its fruits? I pity the women and children. This drunken bear has done all the mischief; he has intoxicated all the children; he has deprived them of their senses. He must die, and I must give the others life.'

"Outawas! listen well to my final resolution. I demand that you deliver to me Le Pesant, he whom you call the wicked bear; that you place him at my disposal here in this place where he has offended me. I wish you to give me full power over him, to give him life or to put him to death.

"If he refuses to embark, I command you to cut off his head in your own village. This is the only means by which I can give you peace. I do not kill him, but he kills himself.

"Outawas! avoid the perils which threaten you! Save your own lives! Have pity on your women and children! Nothing can make me change my determination. It is your business; attend to it! Deliberate among yourselves; decide on the course you will pursue, and give me a reply in a few words, before the going down of the sun.

"Onontio and I have one heart, and the same thoughts. Those that say differently of us are liars; he will confirm all I do, whether for peace or war."

A second council was held in the afternoon of the same day. Otontagon's speech:

"My father—We are surprised at your requirements. The bear whom you demand of us is very powerful in our village. He has strong alliances with all the nations of the lakes. He is a great tree! Who is strong enough to root it up?

"We have thought on this subject; it is difficult; but as nothing can move you, and as your heart is hard as a rock, we must obey you. We only beg of you to spare us the pain of bringing him to you ourselves. Send a boat with us to Michilimackinac, and we will put Le Pesant into it, as you demand; and you will be master of his life or of his death. If he refuse to embark, we will cut off his head. He is my brother, my own brother; but what can I do? You must be obeyed, and this is what you have demanded, and what we have decided among ourselves."

M. la Motte immediately replied:

"By this means you will have peace; your women

and children will rejoice, and I will forget the mischief you have done me."

The third council was held August 7th. M. la Motte addressed the Hurons and Miamis:

"Sastarexy! Miamis, listen to me! I have promised you that I would never make peace with the Outawas, except by the death of Le Pesant, because I have always regarded him as the author of all the mischief which has been done here. You have said that you would be content with this satisfaction.

"I have demanded Le Pesant of the Outawas, and they have given me a favorable reply."

La Motte then repeated to the Hurons and Miamis the proceedings in the councils held with the Outawas.

Reply of Sastarexy, chief of the Hurons:

"My father—Let us say to you that we cannot believe that the Outawas will do what they have promised; for who is he that can overturn so great a tree, whose roots, they themselves say, are so deep in the earth, and whose branches extend over all the lakes? There is meat here, why go farther to seek it? One is certain, the other uncertain."

M. la Motte's rejoinder:

"You have always told me that you would be satisfied if Le Pesant were destroyed. I have promised you that it shall be done. The more difficult the thing appears, the more it will convince you of the great power of Onontio and myself, and that nothing can resist the might of the French."

The fourth council was held August 7th—a general council of the Outawas, Hurons, and Miamis. M. la Motte's speech:

"Otontagon, and all the Outawas, listen to me:

"Here are the Hurons and Miamis who listen to the French, and who regard us. I have related to them the proposition I have made to you, and your replies, and the promise you have given to do me a favor.

"Otontagon, you who bear the words of your people, relate to the Hurons and Miamis what you have decided in regard to Le Pesant."

Otontagon replied:

"If I were not in the presence of my father, I should be angry, because our brothers, the Hurons, take us for liars; and you also, Miamis, our allies.

"We are a people strong and resolute; it were to be wished that Le Pesant were here present; I would myself immediately cut off his head, and he should not again see the light! It is enough that La Motte requires a thing; he never changes his mind, and can we change?"

Reply of Sastarexy, the Huron:

"My father—For a long time the Outawas have continued to kill us. They have always said to us, wait, wait! I beg you to render us justice. Our chiefs have been killed; they are yet extended, bleeding, on the ground."

La Motte then brought forward a captive, whom he offered to the Hurons, saying:

"Sastarexy, my son, here is a little meat, which I give you to resuscitate the dead. I do not say it will entirely restore them. As soon as the Outawas have made the satisfaction which I have demanded of them, I will throw water upon the earth, and that will wash it. I will so entirely cover the blood, that it shall appear no longer."

He also presented a captive to the Miamis, addressing them in like manner. The Miamis made the following answer:

"My father—I have already said that Pakoumakoua was to come to hear and answer you. He has fallen sick; but he said to us, 'My children, go and see what your father wishes, and return and bring us the news.'

"I will say to the old men, that it is well; that peace is made. I beg of you that I may leave this meat here till the old men shall come; they may take it themselves, if they think proper. For me, I can decide on nothing; I came here only to hear."

The news brought to Michilimackinac, by the Outawas who returned from Quebec by way of the Outawa river, created the utmost consternation among the tribes concerned in the difficulty. After consulting together, and asking the advice of Father Marest, their missionary, Onaské and Koutaouiliboe, two chiefs of the Kiskakons, resolved to descend to Detroit, under the protection of a flag of truce, and add their influence to conciliate M. la Motte, whose resolute character was well known. They arrived on the 8th of August, in the midst of the councils, very much to the surprise of all parties. Their white flag was respected, and they were admitted into the council. The manner of their reception may be inferred from the colloquy which took place between M. la Motte and Onaské:

"What brings you here, Onaské? Did Onontio tell you to come? Is peace made? Are we friends? Am I avenged?"

Onaské replied: "My father, you have long known me; I go everywhere with my head lifted up, because I never have any bad affairs. I said within myself, M. la Motte, my father, knows me; I believe I risk nothing in going to see him. I have confidence in him."

*M. la Motte.* "How dare you say that you never have bad affairs; that you never make war? Your people, your nation, did they not come to Detroit to aid the Outawas, who have killed me? I think you are very bold to come here, while my land is still smoking with my blood and that of my children. When people grow old, they usually grow wise; but you have grown foolish. Tell me, then, your real design in coming here; you must have other reasons than those you have given. Speak!"

Onaské immediately responded: "It is the misery in which I am, that has caused me to throw myself into your arms. We are wretched. Our children have eaten grass all summer; they are compelled to boil it and drink the soup! Misery is a strange thing!

"I have risked every thing, even death! Death, did I say? I will die by the hand of my father; perhaps he will have pity on me. We shall have no Indian corn this year, and our children will all die! But for me, the whole nation would have come to Detroit; but I said to them, be patient and await my return."

La Motte, assuming an appearance of great displeasure, exclaimed: "If you die of famine, so much the better! You have killed my children—you have struck me—and Heaven punishes you for it. I will soon otherwise avenge myself. Go away; you are very bold!"

The next day, August 9th, La Motte held a council with the Hurons, and related to them the proceedings of the previous day, in the council with the Kiskakons. He then addressed Sastarexy, the Huron orator, as follows:

"Sastarexy, my son, I have never had any thing concealed from you; my heart has always been yours, even to the palm of my hand. I beg you now to tell me your thoughts; not entirely—I am satisfied if you only show me what are your designs; whether for peace or for war. Open your heart to me to-day."

After some deliberation, Sastarexy replied:

"My father—We have always told you that we would follow your footsteps; you shall always be our guide. We are your obedient children; we are under your protection. You have given us a good land, and you were under many obligations to do so. Nothing can induce us to leave this land, and we will never disobey your wishes. Make peace or make war, we will approve of whatever you do; it is not for a good child to find fault with what his father does. We have all confidence in you."

*M. la Motte.* "I thank you, Sastarexy. It is true that formerly the Outawa was my eldest son; but since then he has removed his fire from here, and committed an enormous disobedience. If he returns to his duty, he shall be my younger son.

"And you, Hurons, congratulate yourselves that to-day, by your obedience, you have taken the place of your elder brother in my heart and in my favor. Congratulate yourselves in having profited by a goodly heritage."

The last council was held by M. la Motte Cadillac, with the four Outawa chiefs from Montreal, and the two chiefs of the Kiskakons from Michilimackinac. M. la Motte first addressed the Outawa chief, Otontagon:

"You, Kinongé, and the other chiefs, are well informed of my resolution, and you know the promise you have made me. Upon the fulfillment of that promise depends the peace which you desire. Onaské! Koutaouiliboe! listen while Otontagon tells you the result of the councils, and decide what you will do.

"Have pity on your children, who have eaten grass all summer, and for whom you have felt such tenderness that you were willing to risk your life by coming here."

Otontagon then tremblingly related, in a few words, the demand of M. la Motte, and the engagement into which they had entered for its accomplishment.

Onaské immediately replied: "I thank you, my brothers, Otontagon, and all the Outawa chiefs. It is very true that this affair is of great importance; but our father, M. la Motte, demands Le Pesant's life; if he wishes, it must be so. I know my father, and he knows me; when he wishes a thing, it must be done; he does not change his mind. In this I agree with him.

"Otontagon, my nephew, Le Pesant is your flesh; Kinongé is also your flesh. Be firm; it is just that this dog, who has bitten both of us to the bone, should be destroyed.

"Who can effect any thing in my nation but me? I speak in the hearing of Manitouabe, of Koutaouiliboe, of Sakima, and of Nanakouena. I am strong! I thank my father for having declared to me his thought. I thank you, my brothers, for the promise you have made him. We must either keep it, and live in peace, or die!"

La Motte then remarked: "I had resolved to cause your furs to be taken away; I would not have given you even a bone to gnaw, and you should have had nothing to support your children. But, on account of your words, I allow you to trade, and to take away with you what will be necessary for your subsistence; but do not abuse my kindness.

"If you fail to fulfill your promise, you will fall into greater misery than before. I shall have dull ears forever, and will never again entertain thoughts of peace. Tell your people that peace will be concluded only when the satisfaction which I demand shall be rendered; and until then, they must come here no more.

"After the surrender of Le Pesant, you may all come with a high head; I will smooth the way."

# CHAPTER XIV.

Outawas and Kiskakons return to Michilimackinac—M. St. Pierre and soldiers from Detroit accompany them—Grand council convened—Difficulties settled—Le Pesant delivered up—Sent under guard to Detroit—M. St. Pierre returns to Quebec with Koutaouiliboe and Sakima—They arrive at Quebec, October 7th, 1707—Council convened—Speech of Koutaouiliboe, giving a minute statement of affairs at Detroit and Michilimackinac—Second council, governor-general's reply—Dismisses the chiefs with presents—Letter from the governor-general to Father Marest, missionary at Michilimackinac.

FINDING themselves compelled to accept the terms of M. la Motte, the chiefs of the Outawas and Kiskakons returned to Michilimackinac, accompanied by M. St. Pierre. On their arrival a grand council was held by the French envoy and the surrounding nations, which had been gathered by the instrumentality of Koutaouiliboe. All difficulties were satisfactorily adjusted, and Le Pesant was delivered into the custody of the soldiers sent from Detroit for that purpose.

M. St. Pierre, whose mission was accomplished, immediately set out on his return to Quebec, accompanied by Koutaouiliboe, chief of the Kiskakons, and Sakima, chief of the Sinagos. These chiefs were charged with a letter to the governor-general from Father Marest, missionary at Michilimackinac. They arrived at Quebec,

October 7th, 1707. In a council held soon after their arrival, Koutaouiliboe gave the following minute account of the proceedings at Detroit and Michilimackinac:

"My father—Sakima and I have finally arrived before you, to show you how obedient we are to your orders, and to inform you of all that has occurred at Michilimackinac and Detroit during the past summer.

"My father—When we sent Jean le Blanc and the other chiefs from Michilimackinac to appease your anger, they promised to use the utmost diligence to return, as we were waiting very impatiently to know your will. But you thought proper to send Jean le Blanc and the principal chiefs to Detroit. As soon as the rest of the party, who came by the great river, arrived at Michilimackinac, they gave us an account of their voyage, and told us that M. St. Pierre, whom you had sent with Jean le Blanc to Detroit, was to return by the way of Michilimackinac and speak to the nations.

"I rose up then, my father—for you know I have always had a French heart—and demanded of the young men, as well as the old, whether they were all asleep, and if they did not understand the news which was brought to them from Montreal. 'What,' said I, 'M. St. Pierre in Detroit, and coming this way to speak to the nations, and you pay not the least attention to the word of your father! Go, young men, bear this news to the

Sauteurs, the Noquens, the Folle-Avoines, the Pottawatomies, the Sacs, the Puans, and the Outagamies—that on the arrival of M. St. Pierre he may find them all here, that nothing may retard the will of Onontio.' We waited long, and St. Pierre did not come; then I said to the old men, 'What does this mean? Can it be that some accident has befallen M. St. Pierre, and thus the message of our father is delayed? I will go to Detroit to meet M. St. Pierre, and if he has not arrived I will wait for him.'

"My father—When I arrived at Detroit I found M. St. Pierre acting as interpreter for M. la Motte. He demanded of me, in an angry tone, where I was going. My heart was frozen by the manner in which M. St. Pierre spoke to me, when I had come to Detroit only on good business, and had left Michilimackinac only to be sooner informed of the will of my father. The next day M. la Motte sent me word by M. St. Pierre, that I might return with Onaské, if I wished, but the women and children, and all my peltries, must remain till affairs should be settled. I replied to M. la Motte, that the business on which Onontio had sent M. St. Pierre was important, but my peltries were of no consequence; that as I had come to Detroit in good faith, if he would not let me barter them there, I could easily carry them back again.

"My father—When I saw that M. la Motte would not receive my furs, I was convinced that something had been concealed from me; for our people had told us, on their return from Michilimackinac, that you, my father, had demanded the head of Le Pesant. I then asked Jean le Blanc why the Kiskakons, being French, were not permitted to trade at Detroit, while the Outawas, who had caused all the trouble, had entire freedom. He told me he was very glad to see me, and would hide nothing from me. He said that you, Onontio, had demanded the head of Le Pesant to atone for the blood of Father Recollet. Not being quite able to promise you full satisfaction—because this wicked bear was like a great tree, having such strong roots that it was difficult to tear it up—Onontio had sent him to Detroit to meet M. la Motte in council, that they might find means to give satisfaction to Onontio, and make peace with the other nations. But La Motte, who, in Detroit, was another Onontio, sternly demanded Le Pesant as the only satisfaction, and he had finally concluded to surrender him.

"The next day Otontagon and Kinongé, or, as you call them, Jean le Blanc and Brochet, Onaské and I, met M. la Motte in council, and we all promised to deliver up Le Pesant to M. la Motte; and I told them if Le Pesant would not come to Detroit, I would cut off his head in our own village. M. la Motte then told me that I might trade with my furs. What, then, was his thought? Did M. la Motte suppose that, by retaining my furs, he would cause me the sooner to execute his will? Does he not know that interest is nothing to me, but that I am always obedient to my father? I told M. la Motte that Le Pesant was not our relative, therefore it was for Jean le Blanc and Kinongé to deliver him up. As for us, we should always be ready to give them all the help they might need. It was enough for us that we were doing the will of Onontio.

"In the evening M. la Motte told us that M. St. Pierre would depart for Michilimackinac on the morrow, and it would be best for us to embark and follow his flag, as there were three bands of Miamis who might easily attack us on the way. When M. St. Pierre drew near Michilimackinac, he said that he would not land—he would only draw his boat upon the sand, and Le Pesant must be delivered to him immediately, or have his head broken. I replied: 'My brother—What you say is of value; but all men have not the heart placed alike, hence business is not always as quickly done as one might wish. Although we have given our word to Onontio and M. la Motte, this affair is of the utmost importance, and we cannot be too cautious in our movements in regard to it. When M. Louvigny came to take away the Iroquois, he found it necessary that he should know all hearts, and listen patiently to all the reasons.'

"I need not tell you all that took place; but on landing, M. St. Pierre found that the young men whom I sent out before going to Detroit had notified the nations, and there were assembled the Kiskakons, the Sinagos, the nations of the Sable and Fourche, the Sauteurs, the Noquets, the Folle-Avoines, the Pottawatomies, the Sacs, the Puans, and the Outagamies. They had come to meet M. St. Pierre in council, having forgotten all their old quarrels between themselves, and meeting together as real brothers.

"Three days after our arrival, when the distant nations had departed for their homes, we brought this affair of Le Pesant into the council. We had not dared to speak of it while the nations were assembled, as he is allied to almost all of them. I will boldly say to you, my father, that it was Onaské, Sakima, Meyagila, and I, the chiefs of the Kiskakons and Sinagos, who obliged Le Pesant to embark for Detroit to meet M. la Motte, according to your wish. If there had been only Jean le Blanc, he would never have dared attack this great tree. But your children of Michilimackinac were all resolved to break his head if he would not embark, rather than to see ourselves, for the love of him, exposed to your anger.

"My father—Our fear is that M. la Motte will not put Le Pesant to death; and that, remembering that we delivered him up, he will seek to avenge himself.

"My father—Sakima begs that you will pardon him for not having brought with him captives to offer to his brothers the Iroquois. He would not have come down now, if the desire of testifying to you his obedience had not overcome his fear that you would reproach him for having failed to fulfill his promise. He renews that promise to you, my father, and you will not have cause to complain of him."

The next day the council was again convened, and the governor-general replied as follows:

"Koutaouiliboe—I have learned from the account you gave me yesterday, also from M. St. Pierre, and from the letters of M. la Motte, all that has occurred at Michilimackinac and Detroit in regard to Le Pesant, that bear who has made trouble for so long a time. I am glad that my children at Michilimackinac have at last opened their eyes to their own interest; and that according to my will they have sent to M. la Motte the only obstacle that prevented my making a solid peace with them.

"At Detroit, M. la Motte is another myself, as he has my orders, and I am persuaded that he will follow them in every point, and that, having Le Pesant in his hands, he will dispose of him as shall be necessary to promote a lasting peace.

"I am glad to see you here. I always knew that Koutaouiliboe had a good mind and a French heart, and I have for him a real esteem. I have not the less for Sakima, although he has not brought me by this voyage the captives he promised, to give to his brothers the Iroquois. I will not speak of it, however, on condition that he will send them to me as soon as possible next year, that the Iroquois may not reproach me with telling a lie, and seeking to deceive them.

"I will not detain you, my children; the season is far advanced, depart when you please. Carry to your brothers the good news that peace is made; that by their obedience in sending Le Pesant to M. la Motte, they have entirely disarmed my anger.

"You can now go to Detroit and come to Montreal; these two doors are open to you; only remember all your life, and tell it to all your nation, that the blood of the French is valuable, and the people who in future shall shed it shall not have my pardon, unless they bring me the head of him who has committed the deed. I am very glad that all the nations were assembled to meet M. St. Pierre, and that you were united, as real brothers ought to be. Continue in sentiments that are so advantageous to you; and since the country is once more united, take care to do nothing in future that might disturb its quiet. Always listen to my words, and to what M. la Motte shall say in my name, when you are at Detroit, and listen also to Father Marest, when he shall carry you my message. As you all have the French heart, I recommend Father Marest to your protection, that you prevent any insult being offered him. On your arrival at Montreal, I will cause two blankets to be given each of you; also powder and balls, tobacco, and provisions sufficient for your journey. They will also give you ten pounds of tobacco to carry to Father Marest. Be careful always to remember what I have said to you."

On the return of Koutaouiliboe and Sakima to Michilimackinac, M. Vaudreuil sent the subjoined letter to Father Marest. It shows the perfect understanding which existed between them, and in some respects confirms the statements of M. la Motte:

"Rev. Father:—I received your letter of the 8th of September by M. St. Pierre, who arrived here the 7th of this month with Koutaouiliboe, Sakima, and another young man. I have showed many attentions to Koutaouiliboe; and you will see by my reply to them in council, of which I send you a copy, that I expressed myself well pleased with the conduct of the Outawas in sending Le Pesant to M. la Motte.

"What you say of Jean le Blanc gives me much pleasure, though M. St. Pierre endeavored to make me suspicious of him. I hardly believe, after what I have said to him, and what he has promised, that he will, in future, make any trouble. I believe he will do his best to settle this difficulty with M. la Motte.

"As the court wishes the establishment of Detroit, that, of course, is also my pleasure; and it is for M. la Motte to decide whether it will be more advantageous to his post to have the Outawas return there, or to allow them to remain at Michilimackinac.

"Although M. Pontchartrain found fault with you for being absent two years from your mission at Michilimackinac, he, at the same time, signified to me that his majesty wished the permanent settlement of Detroit by the French, and that the savages should also be established there. It is therefore necessary to allow them very great liberty on this point, that they may not complain that they have been retained; and that M. la Motte also, may not report to the court that the savages have been in any way prevented from coming to establish themselves at his post.

"I was interested in your account of the assembling of the different nations at Michilimackinac, awaiting the arrival of M. St. Pierre. He also spoke of it. I am very glad affairs have so terminated that they, at least in appearance, have separated good friends. If they come to Montreal next year, as you inform me they propose to do, I will use every means in my power to establish a permanent peace. I shall also inform Ounkimavendellé, that he must keep himself quiet if he wishes to gain my favor and to render himself respectable. I am glad you gave two pounds of powder to the chief of the Sacs; if he comes here, I will assure him that a man who enjoys your approbation is certain of my favor. You know, Reverend Father, that hitherto I have paid attention to all those whom you have recommended to me.

"I agree with you, Reverend Father, that the affair of Le Pesant is one of the most important that has ever occurred in the upper country. I have always regarded it as such. Whether M. la Motte causes him to be put to death, or not, I am persuaded that there is nothing to fear for you, since it is by their own act that the Outawas delivered him to M. St. Pierre, in order that M. d'Argenteuil might take him to Detroit. They have thereby submitted to whatever might occur.

"I have noticed, Reverend Father, what you spoke of in regard to M. la Motte's accusing you of being the cause of the quarrel that occurred at Detroit; and that you returned to your mission, well aware that you would find, on your arrival, not only the Outawas of Michilimackinac, but also those of Detroit.

"M. Raudot and myself will render to you, at court, the justice you deserve; and if M. la Motte has no other affront or grievance against you, it will not be very difficult to destroy what he may advance in regard to this matter. I exhort you to live on good terms with him as far as possible: the service of the king, and even the advancement of your mission, depending very much on the good understanding between the officers of the upper country and the missionaries.

"I cannot give you any definite orders in regard to the course you are to pursue, if your savages leave the mission; I think, however, that while awaiting the orders of the court, if they go to Detroit or elsewhere, you cannot do better than to go with them. I cannot see, Reverend Father, what inconvenience you will experience by writing to me your sentiments upon what passes above; I need the information, and it seems to me, if any one ought to be well informed concerning what is passing at Michilimackinac, it is you.

"Say to Rev. Father Chardon that I am very glad he has resolved to continue at his mission.

"Our vessels have not yet arrived, therefore I can send you by this opportunity only ten pounds of powder, which I beg you to share with Onaské, and such others as you think fit. I will also send you ten pounds of black tobacco, if it is to be found in Montreal, in part payment of the twenty pounds that M. St. Pierre was to remit to you.

"I have given to Koutaouiliboe, Sakima, and the young man who came with them, each a coat, a calico shirt, some provisions, and powder and balls, for their return journey; and to each of the first two, a blanket. The season being so far advanced, I apprehend that they may not be able to reach you, therefore this prevents me from sending you any thing more by them. I am, with all possible consideration,

"Rev. Father,

"Yours, &c."

## CHAPTER XV.

M. la Motte pardons Le Pesant—Dissatisfaction of the Miamis—They demand vengeance upon Le Pesant—Kill three Frenchmen and commit other depredations—Hurons and Iroquois raise war-parties to attack the French—M. la Motte complains that it is Jesuitical influence which occasions these disturbances—Asks for a re-enforcement of troops and a better fort—Advises the destruction of Fort Frontenac—Thinks a new fort below Fort Frontenac would afford better protection to the passage to Detroit and Montreal—Complains of the *Coureurs des Bois*—Inspection of the several posts by M. d'Aigrement—He remains nineteen days at Detroit—Accuses M. la Motte of tyranny—Measures the valuable lands at Fort Pontchartrain—Only twenty-nine of the inhabitants landholders—Taxes—Asserts that the maintenance of Detroit must be prejudicial to all Canada—Trouble at Detroit with the Miamis—Detailed account—Proceeds to Michilimackinac—Considers it an important post—Describes its location and advantages—Urges the necessity of sending a commandant with a good garrison—Approves of the "permits."

UNFORTUNATELY for the settlement at Detroit, M. la Motte was induced to pardon Le Pesant. This injudicious leniency provoked the Miamis, who accused M. la Motte of a breach of contract. They demanded vengeance upon Le Pesant. Finding that their wishes were entirely disregarded, they killed three Frenchmen, and committed other depredations in the vicinity of Detroit.

M. la Motte was making preparations to avenge himself, when he received intelligence that the Hurons and

Iroquois had raised war-parties to come and massacre all the French. This new danger, from an unexpected source, induced M. la Motte to effect a treaty of peace with the Miamis. The treaty was soon violated by the savages. M. la Motte then marched against them with a large force, and compelled them to offer terms of submission.

These frequent outbreaks on the part of the savages, were not the only difficulties in the way of the commandant of Fort Pontchartrain. The old feud between the Jesuits and Franciscans, though smothered by the stern command of government, was not forgotten.

Jesuitical intrigue was often apparent, not only in the violation of treaties on the part of the savages, but also in the disaffection of the French; and to counter-plot successfully, required the utmost exercise of M. La Motte's ingenuity. Of this he complains, in a letter to Count Pontchartrain. A summary of the letter is preserved in the Colonial Archives at Paris, from which the following extract is taken. It is dated Detroit, Sept. 15, 1708.

"La Motte still complains that the Jesuits are so much opposed to the establishment of Detroit, that they must either leave, or he will abandon the fort; demanding, however, that the government indemnify him, if he should leave.

"He asserts that the Jesuit Fathers have prevented the Outawas from coming to Detroit to settle, and offers to prove it by a letter written to him by Father Mantet, missionary of Michilimackinac, dated October 23, 1677, but not received by La Motte until 1707. He says that the letter has been written thirty years, yet no one has dared to contradict its contents.

"He also thinks it necessary for the firm establishment of Detroit, that there should be five or six hundred inhabitants, and troops in proportion; that a good fort of earth be made on the site of the present insecure fortification, and a smaller one on the other side of the river, directly opposite, as these defenses would certainly make the French masters of this passage of the nations. He advises to destroy Fort Frontenac, and build another twenty-five leagues farther down, at a place named La Galette, which would be in every respect a good depot between Montreal and Detroit.

"He says he knows a passage by which a canal could easily be constructed to form a connection between Lake Erie and Lake Ontario. But he complains that it is impossible for him to accomplish any of his purposes, because the great project of the people of Canada is the establishment of Michilimackinac, with the permits and *coureurs des bois*. This proposed re-establishment has great allurements for the governor-general, because it makes him master of the commerce. If Michilimackinac were abandoned, the savages would no longer resort to Montreal, and, consequently, the governor-general would not receive his annual presents from them. All Canada regards Detroit as an obstacle to the re-establishment of the permits; hence their opposition to it.

"He says Michilimackinac could not sustain itself in case of a war with the Iroquois, because it could have no communication with Montreal. But Detroit does not labor under that embarrassment; he can go to Montreal whenever he wishes, and he can put so many armed enemies on the war-path of the Iroquois, whenever it pleases him, that they will be glad to leave him in repose.

"After a recapitulation of the plans which he proposed in 1703, La Motte complains of the many expenses which he has been obliged to defray, individually, and asks that some provision may be made by government for such contingencies. He says he is under no obligation to bear the expense of the new fort, which he is building at Detroit, nor to erect the church. He offers, however, to build the choir of the church, and to give the land on which it stands, provided he may have the advowson of it.

"He says if His Majesty is not willing himself to give any thing for the nave, he might order the inhabitants and merchants to contribute a given sum for that purpose, and offers to donate five hundred francs as his part."

A few days prior to the date of M. la Motte's letter to Count Pontchartrain, M. d'Aigrement, who had been sent by M. Vaudreuil to inspect the several posts on the frontier, having spent nineteen days at Detroit, passed on to Michilimackinac. On his return, the result of his investigations was sent to France. The following transcript gives the other side of the picture:

"*Summary of an inspection of the Posts of Detroit and Michilimackinac, by M. d'Aigrement, dated Quebec, Nov.* 14, 1708.

"M. d'Aigrement left Niagara, June 29, 1708. He sailed along the north coast of Lake Erie, a distance of ninety leagues, and arrived at Detroit on the 15th of July. He remained at Fort Pontchartrain of Detroit nineteen days,* and became convinced during his stay that M. la Motte Cadillac, who commands there, is generally disliked by the French and savages, with the exception of three or four of the former, whom he employs in his secret trade, and whom he influences more than

* "La Motte contends that this sojourn was not sufficient to gain any correct knowledge of the country. He says that during his stay, they did not have two hours conversation together, and that M. d'Aigrement made secret inquiries in regard to him, a course well calculated to call forth discreditable remarks from the French and savages."

the others. This hatred is in consequence of the tyranny which he exercises over the entire settlement. Among the many instances which came under his notice, are the following:

"La Motte requires of a blacksmith, named Parent, for permission to work at his trade, the sum of six hundred francs and two hogsheads of ale, and the obligation to shoe all the horses of M. la Motte, whatever number he may have, though at present he keeps but one.

"Of a gunsmith named Pinet, he requires three hundred francs a year, and the repairing of twelve guns per month, which makes one hundred and forty-four a year. Estimating this work at one pistole per gun, M. la Motte draws from the work of these men, seventeen hundred and forty francs.* Evidently this state of things cannot last long, for they will be obliged to leave Detroit.

"M. la Motte has caused a windmill to be erected, in which he takes the eighth minot as toll, while others take only the fourteenth. He gives for his reason, the great cost of the mill.†

* "M. la Motte says that he made agreements with these workmen at Montreal, when they were in no wise under his control; that some time after their arrival at Detroit, they themselves desired a different commission—the very one of which they now complain. Besides, the taxes that he requires of them are not new, the Company of the Colony having used the same prerogative."

† "This reason of M. la Motte's deserves attention; yet one does not feel quite satisfied with it; he appears too covetous."

"M. d'Aigrement caused the valuable lands at Fort Pontchartrain to be measured, and found three hundred and fifty-three roods of it in all. La Motte has one hundred and fifty-seven; the French inhabitants, all together, have forty-six; and the Hurons one hundred and fifty. The one hundred and fifty roods of La Motte have been broken up by the soldiers and savages, nineteen roods of which belonged to the company—so the cultivation of it has cost La Motte nothing.

"There are but twenty-nine of the inhabitants of Detroit who have taken ground-plots within the fort, where they have built small log-houses, thatched with grass. The whole number of the French settlers is sixty-three, thirty-four being traders. It is certain that if M. la Motte had not introduced the trade in brandy, but very few of the traders would remain, and no more would go there. Brandy and ammunition are the only profitable articles of commerce to the French, the English furnishing all others.

"The savages make great complaints against M. la Motte; they say plainly, that if he remains there they will not settle at Detroit. They demand the lieutenant, M. d'Argenteuil, as commandant. This man has much influence among them, but has little management. The savages promise great faithfulness to the king.

"In order to prevent the disturbances which would arise from the excessive use of brandy, M. la Motte causes it all to be put into the storehouse, and to be sold to each in his turn at the rate of twenty francs per quart. Those who will have it, French as well as Indians, are obliged to go to the storehouse to drink, and each can obtain, at one time, only the twenty-fourth part of a quart. It is certain that the savages cannot become intoxicated on that quantity. The price is high, and as they can only get the brandy each in his turn, it sometimes happens that the savages are obliged to return home without a taste of this beverage, and they seem ready to kill themselves in their disappointment.

"M. la Motte has bought of four individuals one hundred and four quarts, at four francs a quart, and sold it at twenty francs—thus making a profit of four-fifths. The inhabitants of Detroit pay M. la Motte two francs ten sous a year for each lot of land measuring one rood, fronting on the river, by twenty in depth; and for the ground in the fort, they pay two sous for each foot of front, and double that amount when this plot borders on two streets. All the inhabitants also pay to M. la Motte a tax of ten francs a year, which he claims for himself. This tax is levied for the privilege of free trade with the Indians. M. d'Aigrement also recounted many acts of petty tyranny on the part of M. la Motte, especially exercised toward the poor soldiers that were under his immediate control.

"This inspector asserted that there can be no doubt that maintaining the establishment at Detroit must be highly prejudicial to Canada; for, said he, 'our allies, the Hurons, even now carry their peltries through the country to the English; and they have also introduced to the English the Miamis, of whom they formerly made such good use in the war which we had against them.'

"In the month of April, 1707, the Miamis having killed three Frenchmen, M. la Motte sent orders to the Outawas to come to his aid, having heard that the Iroquois, Hurons, and Miamis were determined on the destruction of the French. Three hundred good men of the Outawas immediately set out, under the command of the two officers sent by M. la Motte; but they were surprised to learn, before they reached Detroit, that M. la Motte had already made peace with the Miamis.

"The conditions of the peace were, first, to deliver up the murderers within forty days; second, to return, within fifteen days, a little Outawa whom they had taken captive; third, to pay for the cattle which they had killed; fourth, to restore the goods which they had stolen from the French.

"The fifteen days having elapsed and the little Outawa not having been sent back, M. la Motte resolved to make war upon the Miamis, although the forty days that he had given them for the delivery of the murderers had not yet expired. He called together the French and savages, and after having lifted the tomahawk in council, he departed with four hundred men to attack the fort of the Miamis. But he conducted the march without that order and precaution which were necessary, despising all the advice given him by the chiefs and his own officers. When he arrived near the fort of the Miamis, which he expected to take without opposition—there being but sixty warriors of the Miamis, and his force amounting to four hundred men—he found the Miamis ready to defend themselves. They fired on the advancing army, wounding many persons, and obliging La Motte to retreat to some distance from the intrenchment. At this juncture the Miamis raised a white flag, that M. la Motte had given them the previous year, which rendered it necessary for him to hold a council with them.

"The principal chief of the Miamis who came to the council reproached La Motte for having broken his word, the forty days which he had given them not having expired. La Motte replied that he had a right to attack them, as they had failed to bring back the little Outawa who was among them within fifteen days, as they had promised. He demanded that this little Outawa should now be restored, and that they should also give him three captives to replace the dead. They not only complied with these requisitions, but they also promised him that they would deliver up the murderers within six weeks, if possible, but if not, they would come after their harvest and settle at Detroit. As a pledge of their truthfulness, they gave three of their chiefs into the custody of the French as hostages. They also presented to M. la Motte fifty packs of different kinds of furs, for himself and for the troops and allies. In this affray there were seven Frenchmen wounded, and four savages killed and two wounded.

"After his return to Detroit, M. la Motte, not having heard from the Miamis, sent a canoe with four Frenchmen to their camp. The Miamis kept two of the Frenchmen, and sent back two of their own men instead, to signify to M. la Motte that they would do as they had promised; but this is improbable, as they have abandoned their fort. If they come to Detroit, it will be very difficult for them to agree with the Outawas, as no one can bring about a good understanding between all the different nations which La Motte has intended to assemble here. There are ancient enmities that will always prevail over all he can say to them. If it were possible to succeed in causing them to live together in peace, there would arise another difficulty. The Iroquois would gain all these nations over to the English, on account of their greater facilities for commerce. An example of this is already seen. Detroit has not sent to the office at Montreal more than seven hundred weight of beaver this year, while Michilimackinac has sent forty thousand pounds. It is certain, however, that the Detroit tribes have traded as much as usual, therefore the rest must have passed to the English.

"If Michilimackinac is abandoned and the Outawas go to Detroit, as M. la Motte intends, it is certain that the low price of the English goods will cause the trade in beaver to pass into their colony, without our being able to prevent it. We should also lose the beaver from north of Lake Superior, which is the best there is: it will pass to the English at Hudson's Bay.

"M. d'Aigrement disputes the account given of the soil about Detroit, by M. la Motte and others. He describes it as consisting of a sandy surface, nine or ten inches deep, beneath which is a clay so stiff that water cannot penetrate it. The timber, he says, is small, stunted oaks, and hardy walnuts; he acknowledges that the land produces good Indian-corn, but says that is because the soil is new. He does not believe that the fruits of Europe can be brought to perfection there, because the roots of the trees stand in water. Considerable cider*

* Doubtless made of crab-apples—a spontaneous production of the country.

is made there, but it is bitter as gall. It is true that the country is warm, being only forty-three degrees north latitude; but the difficulty arises from the fact that the ground is new and full of water. There are some small chestnuts which are pretty good to the taste, but they are the only kind of fruit that is good. The grass-hoppers eat all the garden-plants, so that it is necessary to plant and sow the same thing even to the fourth time.

"Even if the land were ever so productive, there would be no market, and the trade of this post would never be useful to France—the result of which would be that the establishment would always prove a burden to the colony, and of no use to the kingdom. It may be said that, if we abandon it, the English will take possession; but that is not to be feared—it being more advantageous to them that we should incur the expenses and let them reap the benefit, as they now do. The Indians are very willing to make use of the goods of the English, but they would not suffer the English to take possession of their lands, even for the purposes of trade.

"The former interpreter at Detroit, brother of the secretary of M. Vaudreuil, has been discharged. His successor is much better—he is an upright man.

"After having remained nineteen days at Detroit, M. d'Aigrement started for Michilimackinac, August 3d, and arrived there on the 19th of the same month.

Michilimackinac is one hundred and thirty leagues from Detroit. Here he remained four days, during which time he observed that this is the advance post of all Canada; the most important, as well for its advantageous position, as for the commerce that might be made there. It is the rendezvous and highway of all the nations of Lake Superior, and the entire upper country. If the nations wish to make war upon each other, the Outawas who inhabit Michilimackinac would be capable of preventing them, and might be the mediators in their differences, as has been the case in the past.

"This post is inaccessible to the most powerful enemies of the Outawas, who are to the south, and are not boatmen. The fish are very good, and very abundant. The land is not very good, but the savages raise from it enough Indian corn for their own use and that of the traders. The beaver found there is the best in North America; but to insure its passage into France, it is necessary to establish a French commandant there, with at least thirty soldiers. The savages desire this. It would also be necessary to induce the Hurons to return, whom M. la Motte decoyed away, as they are much better qualified to cultivate the land than the Outawas.

"These Hurons would never have abandoned this country, if there had been a French commandant; they left solely on account of their hatred of the Outawas, who held them in a kind of slavery. Those whom M. d'Aigrement saw at Detroit, say they like much better to be at Michilimackinac, and would attach themselves to a French commandant there. They hate the Outawas, but appear to have a real affection for the French.

"If we do not send a commandant with a garrison to Michilimackinac, it is to be feared that the Hurons who are at Detroit will settle with the Iroquois, in consequence of their feeling of dissatisfaction toward M. la Motte. They would have done so before this, if the Iroquois would have permitted them to make a distinct village among them. Thus far the Iroquois have not been willing to allow the Hurons to come among them, except on condition of combining with them, and the name of Huron becoming extinct. Since there are now at Michilimackinac only a few wanderers, the greater part of the furs of the savages of the north go to the English trading-posts on Hudson's Bay. The Outawas are unable to make this trade by themselves, because the northern savages are timid, and will not come near them, as they have often been plundered by them. It is therefore necessary that the French be allowed to seek these northern tribes at the mouth of their own river, which empties into Lake Superior. It would be advisable to re-establish the permits, to give only twelve the first year; and after that to increase them even to twenty, but not to exceed that number. This would suffice for the quantity of beaver we should need. These permits would be sold at a fixed price, and the amount given to indigent families, as heretofore. It would be necessary to forbid the governor-general granting private permits, on any pretext whatever.

"To be still more certain of obtaining the beaver, it would be expedient for the contractor to give more than thirty sous a pound; it might be necessary to increase the price even to forty sous, in which case he would be able to purchase as much as he would desire. All this trade would come to Michilimackinac; and it would be necessary, in order to prevent any of the furs being subsequently carried to the English, that the commandant of that post should keep an exact account of the quantity of furs, more or less, which should be loaded into each canoe to be sent to the intendant. By this means, each canoe would be obliged to deliver, at the office at Montreal, the same quantity which had been charged at Michilimackinac. The contractor should remunerate the commandant for this service.

"There still remain at Michilimackinac fourteen or fifteen Frenchmen, who could not possibly subsist there, if the merchants and others in Montreal did not send them goods. These are not the only ones who trade there; many canoes go up under pretext of government service, which are really loaded with goods. As those who conduct the canoes are usually the favorites of M. Vaudreuil, there is reason to believe that he has an interest in this trade. It is certain that if there were no French at Michilimackinac, most of the beaver now bartered there would go to the English.

"Previous to the departure of M. d'Aigrement from Michilimackinac, a band of the Outawas, who had been to Montreal, arrived there. They had with them five casks of brandy, and were all so much intoxicated the next night, that they set fire to their own wigwams, which would all have been burned, but for the timely aid of the French, and who for this service were much abused by the savages.

"The government at Montreal should prevent the savages from carrying away such large quantities of brandy, as it is the cause of most of the quarrels arising among them. They also squander the greater part of their beaver in presents and in brandy, and have not enough remaining to purchase half the articles that are indispensable to their comfort. The Outawas informed M. d'Aigrement that they obtained permission to bring away their brandy, by means of large presents which they made to M. Vaudreuil. He does not know certainly that this is true, but he is certain that the other presents received by M. Vaudreuil this year will amount to more than five hundred pistoles.

"A chief of the Outawas, who has been at Detroit, and is now at Michilimackinac, complained that M. la Motte refused to deliver to him a necklace of porcelain, and a feast-kettle which the chief had given to one of La Motte's agents, in security for five beaver-skins which he had borrowed. The chief wished to return the loan two-fold, and receive back his property, but was refused. He thinks the refusal arises from the fact that he did not wish to return to Detroit. M. la Motte told this chief, and many of his nation, that if they would not return to Detroit, they would all die. The savages are so superstitious that they now believe, when any of their people die, that M. la Motte has caused their death. Some have even gone to reside at Detroit, to avoid this death which M. la Motte pretends to have power to inflict.

"M. d'Aigrement begs to be believed that the account he has given of the conduct of many individuals, has been quite against his own inclination, not having any reason to complain of them on his own account, but because he must obey the orders of His Majesty. He infers, from all he has seen, that Fort Frontenac, on Lake Ontario, ought to be maintained, unless it is thought advisable, hereafter, to establish a post at La Galette, twenty-five or thirty leagues lower down. He considers the post at Detroit very injurious to the colony, and to the commerce of the kingdom; but thinks it very important to preserve the trade at Michilimackinac, where the Outawas are established."

## CHAPTER XVI.

War between France and England—English attempt the reduction of New France—Port Royal taken—Fifty thousand crowns raised by the merchants of Quebec to complete their fortifications—English unsuccessful—Outagamies suddenly make their appearance—In 1712, Outagamies and Mascoutins attack Detroit—Long siege—Garrison relieved by their allies—The enemy routed, and nearly all destroyed—Letter from Father Marest to the governor-general, giving an account of the attack—Urges the re-establishment of Michilimackinac—Memorial of M. Begon, opposing the immediate re-establishment of Michilimackinac.

The war between France and England, which continued until 1713, had a most disastrous effect upon the growth of their respective colonies in America. To keep the savages, especially the Iroquois, in a state of neutrality, seemed to be the greatest difficulty encountered by the English, while the French, more successful in making treaties, were no more fortunate in securing their observance.

Religious intolerance and jealousy kept the French outposts in a state of ferment, and prevented that decisive and united action which might have effectually controlled their savage allies, and repulsed their English enemies.

In the summer of 1710, the English resolved to end the war in America by the subjugation of New France. Extensive preparations were made for an expedition against Port Royal. About the middle of September the whole armament sailed from Boston. It consisted of thirty-six sail, having on board the land forces. The whole army numbered about three thousand four hundred. This force was under the command of General Nicholson and Adjutant-general Vetch.

On the 5th of October the fleet anchored before Port Royal. This fort, with a garrison of only two hundred men, was in no condition to withstand the great army brought against it. A show of resistance was made as the English advanced, and they were obliged to retire before the fire of the French artillery. For some time a cannonading was kept up on both sides, and an English fire-ship was blown up while entering the harbor. Aware that he could not long resist the invaders, M. Subercase, commandant of the fort, sent out a flag of truce, and a capitulation was agreed upon, by which the English became masters of Port Royal. In 1711, an unsuccessful expedition was made by the English against Quebec and Placentia; though Port Royal was still retained.

In 1712, the sum of fifty thousand crowns was raised by the merchants of Quebec, to complete the fortifications of that city.

The ill success of the English expeditions increased the attractions of the French in the eyes of the savages, and the Iroquois sent a deputation to Quebec to assure the governor-general of their sincere attachment. At first M. Vaudreuil gave them a cool reception, but finally dismissed them with numerous presents.

About this time the Outagamies, who for a number of years had scarcely been heard from, suddenly made their appearance. They formed an alliance with the Five Nations; and being won over to the English interests, engaged to surprise Detroit, and surrender it into their hands. Fort Pontchartrain was then commanded by M. du Buisson, who succeeded M. la Motte Cadillac .n the summer of 1711.

Early in May, 1712, a large body of the Outagamies and Mascoutins proceeded to Detroit, and threw up an intrenchment about fifty paces from Fort Pontchartrain. The French garrison consisted of only thirty men, and the Outawas and Hurons, their most reliable allies, had not returned from their winter hunt. Frequent sallies were made against the fort by the besiegers, keeping the besieged occupants in a state of constant anxiety and alarm. The church, storehouse, and some other buildings outside the fort, and so near as to endanger it if set on fire by the savages, were pulled down by order of the commandant.

When nearly worn out by unremitted watchings, the besieged garrison was relieved by the arrival of large numbers of their allies, who soon turned the tide of war. The Outagamies and Mascoutins were obliged to retreat to their own fortress, where they were in turn besieged. The siege lasted nineteen days, the firing being kept up day and night. Exhausted by hunger, thirst, and fatigue, they finally manifested a desire to capitulate. A great council was held, but no satisfactory arrangement could be made, and hostilities were resumed. At last the Outagamies took advantage of a dark rainy night, and escaped from their fort. They proceeded to Presque Isle, twelve miles above Detroit, where they again intrenched themselves. Thither they were pursued by the French allies, and, after a four days' siege, were obliged to surrender at discretion. No quarter was given; all the men were killed, and the women and children were made captives. The allies returned with their captives to Fort Pontchartrain, where they amused themselves with shooting four or five a day. Not one of those taken by the Hurons was spared.

As soon as the news reached Michilimackinac, Father Marest dispatched Koutaouiliboe to Quebec with letters to the governor-general. In these dispatches he makes use of the trouble at Detroit as an argument for the re-establishment of Michilimackinac.

Extract of a letter from Father Marest, missionary at Michilimackinac, to M. Vaudreuil, governor-general:

"June 21, 1712.

"No doubt you have already learned the news of the recent attack on Detroit, by the Sacs, Foxes, and Mascoutins, by a canoe sent from that place. The Rev. Father Recollet of Detroit informs me that about eight hundred men, women, and children of the Foxes and Mascoutins have been destroyed. Yet, in this large number, I presume he does not reckon forty warriors, sixty women, and more than a hundred children of the Mascoutins, who are reported to have been killed near the great river. I only give the report of others. Sakima is going to Montreal; he and Makisabe, a Pottawatomie, who is also going down from Detroit, were the chiefs principally concerned; they will give you their own account of affairs.

"Although the number of the dead is very great, the Fox nation is not destroyed. There still remain a great number of them near the Bay—some say there are two hundred warriors, besides those who have gone to the Iroquois. Their brothers, the Kickapoos, to whose villages ten families of the Mascoutins have retired, have more than a hundred good warriors; the Sacs, eighty men, boatmen; the Puans, sixty brave men, also boatmen. If these all unite, as is natural, they may yet excite terror, especially here. They would indeed be truly formidable, because so many of them are boatmen. Michilimackinac would no longer be a place of safety, as hitherto. It is not far from this post to the Bay, and the savages could come here both by land and water, and not only the savages, but the French, who were the first movers in this war, having joined with the Outawas to destroy the Foxes. We believe, however, that the Foxes at the Bay, having heard of the attack upon those at Detroit, will flee; and it is not difficult to believe that the Sacs and Puans will take the part of the Foxes against the French and Outawas; but these are only conjectures. It is certain that, in this region, there will always be cause to fear an attack, either from the savages at Detroit, at the Bay, or from the Illinois. The French, if they go, as is their custom—two men alone in a boat to make the tour of the lakes—will always be in danger, for the Foxes, Kickapoos, and Mascoutins are found everywhere, and they are a people without pity and without reason.

"If this country ever needs M. Louvigny, it is now; the savages say it is absolutely necessary that he should come for the safety of the country, to unite the tribes, and to defend those whom the war has already caused to return to Michilimackinac. The Indians of the great river, those of Saginaw and many from Detroit, have gone to Manitoulin with Le Pesant. But if M. Louvigny returns here, no doubt they will all quit Manitoulin, where they have planted but little, and return here.

"The savages told me that all the Outawas at Detroit would have come here, but for the recent arrival of fifty or sixty Frenchmen, who said they were soon to be followed by hundreds of others. This news, though probably not entirely true, has changed the purpose of many who wished to leave Detroit, and they have now invited the Outawas and Pottawatomies to come and establish themselves there. Sakima has had a quarrel with all the Outawas, both here and at the great river. I do not know what course the Pottawatomies will take; nor even what course those will pursue who are here, if M. Louvigny does not come, especially if the Foxes come to attack them or us.

"Sakima very much desired to come and present his respects to you; but the French have thought it best for him to remain for the safety of this village. In his absence, the enemy might attack us, while his presence would arrest all such designs, as he is greatly feared. They have believed it quite sufficient for Koutaouiliboe to go down and inform you of all that has passed: not deeming it expedient for both to leave Michilimackinac at such a time as this."

"July 2, 1712..

"This morning Koutaouiliboe came to see me, determined to prosecute a German quarrel. 'What does our father Onontio mean?' he demanded. 'It is already five years since he promised us M. Louvigny; still, he wishes to deceive us this year, as he has done in all the others. He tells us that the great Onontio, the king, especially loves his children of Michilimackinac, yet it seems that he abandons them entirely. Formerly, before the establishment of Detroit, we were a powerful nation. All the other nations were obliged to come here to obtain necessaries, and there was no trouble, as there is now. But the most savage and unreasonable of the nations, such as the Foxes, Kickapoos, Mascoutins, Miamis, and others, who do not use the canoe, have the power of going on foot to Detroit, in as great numbers as they wish, to buy their powder and trouble their allies. Yet the French desire more than ever to establish Detroit.

"'A canoe, which arrived yesterday from Detroit, brought the news that M. de la Forest had already arrived with fifty men. He has not come to remain, but only came beforehand to hold a council with the savages. Some time hence there is to come another French chief, a young man, who has bought all the movables of M. la Motte, his plate, his cattle, and other property; he has also bought all the land of Detroit. This chief is to come with four hundred French to build a city, in which, after four years, they are to sell goods at the same price as at Montreal. Only two canoes are ordered to come to Michilimackinac. It is also said that a few persons will steal away, and come here to settle. This, then, is the preference which the French give to Michilimackinac. It is because Detroit has always been a theater of war, and because it always will be so, that they think only of its establishment. Does our father wish that we should leave a place of security like this, and go to Detroit to be killed, ourselves and our children?

"'If our father loves us, why does he not establish us here, and give us him whom he has so long promised us, to give spirit to those who have it not, and to strengthen us against our enemies? Does not our father know that all the Outawas of the great river have returned here, almost all those of Saginaw, and many of those from Detroit, all except Jean le Blanc, whose wife is already here? Does he not know that all the Outawas of Detroit had already pitched their canoes, in order to come here, with half of the Hurons, while the other half of the tribe were to go to the Iroquois, not considering themselves safe at Detroit any more than the Sauteurs and the Mississaques, who all left that place after the attack made by the Foxes? But when they received the news of the coming of the French, they resolved to remain.' I could only tell him that you would know how to reply to him when he should come into your presence. He said that the only satisfactory reply which his father could make, was to grant him the commandant who had been promised long since, and whom he was now going to seek.

"Koutaouiliboe has also told me another fine piece of news; that there was peace in all Europe, and that 'the great Onontio of the French had given one-half of his children to the English, but that he had requested the English not to give them bad medicine.' He said he was indifferent whether he went to Boston or Montreal, as there was nothing but powder at Montreal, and that the French themselves went to purchase goods at the stores of the English. Already at Detroit, he said, they gave two hands of tobacco for a beaver, and a scarlet blanket for five or six beavers, and so with other goods.

"There is one thing, however, which makes all this news suspicious; those who told it brought no letters, and that makes many believe that it is news made expressly for the occasion, either by the French inhabitants of Detroit, or by the savages who remain there in such small numbers that they wish to cause others to return there for their safety. He also told me that M. la Motte had gone to Quebec, and that he told the people at Detroit, at parting, that he was not leaving them forever, but, at the expiration of four years, they would see him again. See how the savages make news according to their interests or inclinations!

"The Folle-Avoines have made an attack upon Chagouamigon and his wife, the adopted brother and sister of Durangé; they have killed the one, and carried off the other. Durangé is coming here to recover the prisoner. It is said that the people of Detroit are coming to make war against the Kickapoos, and that they have invited the Sauteurs to join them.

"Pardon me, sir, if I bring you only savage news; Koutaouiliboe will be able to tell you some other. He will be sure to make you remember that he is the only one who has observed your words; and that he had reason to tell you last year, that all your children would forget them as soon as they should be beyond the region of Montreal, and would not fail to kill each other. I am, with profound respect, sir,

"Your very humble, and
"Very obedient servant,
"JOSEPH T. MAREST,
"Of the Society of Jesus."

The request of Father Marest for the re-establishment of Michilimackinac seems to have excited but little attention until the following year, when the governor-

20

general began to feel the necessity of strengthening the northwestern frontier against the encroachments of the English. M. Begon, the intendant, to whom belonged the duty of deciding this question, then drew up the following memorial, fully discussing the subject:

"It appears from the letter of Father Marest, missionary of the Society of Jesus, dated July 19th, 1712, that the post at Michilimackinac had been abandoned since the establishment of Detroit, but its re-establishment would be useful to the colony; and that M. Louvigny is expected there to gather the savages together, which will be easily accomplished, as they have great confidence in him. M. Lignery, in his letter of the 20th of July last, also states that it is necessary that Michilimackinac should be reinforced with a garrison of trained soldiers, without which no commandant could succeed. There are at present at that post about forty deserters, who, in all their conduct, only consult their own interest. He expresses great impatience for the arrival of M. Louvigny, feeling assured that he will not come without a garrison. M. Lignery says the allied nations have gone to war with the Foxes, and he will give the result of the expedition when they return.

"It does not appear that the war among the nations requires much attention at present, as no action can be taken in the matter till the final result is known. Let us now examine the advantages which, there is reason to hope, will be derived from the re-establishment of Michilimackinac, and whether it is best to send M. Louvigny there with troops, or without. It is certain that troops cannot be sent there at present, because their expenses for clothing and other necessaries would be very great, and there is no order from the king for such an outlay. Nor does it seem best to send M. Louvigny without troops, as, by the letter of M. Lignery, it appears that the principal object of the journey of M. Louvigny would be to bring a garrison with him, that he might be able to overcome the forty *coureurs des bois*, who will remain masters there as long as there are no troops.

"Under existing circumstances it seems far better that the journey of M. Louvigny should be deferred until spring. If he should attempt the journey this fall, he must leave between this and the 15th of next month—and should he be two months in ascending the river, as the canoes were last year, he would not reach Michilimackinac before the 15th of November. The savages would then be hunting, and would not return till May, when they come to plant their corn; and not till then could M. Louvigny hold a council with them concerning the affairs of the colony.

"M. Louvigny could not undertake the journey at his

own expense. Provisions and clothing for himself and the troops, and presents for the savages, would require a considerable sum, and there are at present no funds, the storehouses are empty, and all kinds of merchandise are very dear. By waiting until spring, he would be able to supply himself from the stores which His Majesty will send this autumn. Besides, the principal object of the journey of M. Louvigny being the re-establishment of Michilimackinac—which has been delayed until the peace, because it was not considered expedient to weaken the colony during the war—it seems necessary, before proceeding further, to know the intentions of His Majesty. There must necessarily be great expense incurred for the officers, for the garrison, and in presents to the savages, and if the project meet His Majesty's approbation, he will appropriate funds for that purpose.

"Michilimackinac might be re-established without expense to His Majesty, either by surrendering the trade of the post to such individuals as will obligate themselves to pay all the expenses of twenty-two soldiers and two officers, to furnish munitions of war for the defense of the fort, and to make presents to the savages. Or, the expenses of that post might be paid by the sale of permits, if the king should not think proper to grant an exclusive commerce. It is absolutely necessary to know the wishes of the king concerning these two propositions;

and as M. Lignery is at Michilimackinac, it will not be any greater injury to the colony to defer the re-establishment of this post, than it has been for eight or ten years past.

"The conduct of the *coureurs des bois* is an evil which has lasted a long time, and we must learn whether the king will grant them a general amnesty, or punish them according to the rigor of the ordinance, which is corporal punishment, and the confiscation of their goods. Until this decision is made, their trading at Michilimackinac will not injure the colony any more than if they pursued the same course elsewhere. It seems necessary, in order to prevent the savages from going to trade with the English, where goods are cheaper than they are at Montreal, that our goods should be carried to them. Therefore, though the *coureurs des bois* deserve punishment for disobeying the orders of the king, no doubt the trade which they carry on with the nations is advantageous to the colony. This trade, during the war, has brought beaver and other furs to Montreal that would otherwise have gone to the English, had there been no French in the upper country. Besides, the principal object being to prevent any intelligence passing between the Outawas and Iroquois, the French should carry all that the savages might need, lest they be attracted to the English, first by necessity, and afterward by the cheapness of their goods; and it being impossible to prevent their going, the fur-trade in Canada, which is our principal dependence, would be ruined. The savages would also array themselves against us in the first war, as they always take the part of those with whom they trade.

"Written at Quebec, Sept. 20th, 1713.

(Signed) "BEGON."

There seemed good reasons for adopting M. Begon's suggestion, to defer sending men to Michilimackinac until another season; but early in 1714, M. Vaudreuil dispatched the long-wished-for garrison and commandant. New life was thus given to the settlement, yet the French could not regain their influence over the savages. English goods were cheaper and more abundant, and the low state of financial affairs in France was alleged as the reason that the merchants of Quebec and Montreal did not receive a supply of goods equal to the demand. Hence, the largest portion of the northwestern fur-trade passed to the English.

# CHAPTER XVII.

France cedes to England large portions of territory in New France—English attempt to conciliate the savages—Fail, through the influence of Father Rafle, a French Jesuit—English set a price on the head of the priest—Savages exasperated—Make incursions upon the English—Destroy their crops, but spare life—Outagamies trouble the French—In 1716, M. Louvigny proceeds to their country and obliges them to capitulate—Hostages die of small-pox at Quebec—M. Louvigny again visits the country of the Outagamies—Official report of M. Tonti's return from Quebec to Detroit.

By the treaty of Utrecht, ratified April 11, 1713, France ceded to England a large extent of territory, comprising Nova Scotia or Acadia, and Port Royal, with all the adjacent country included in the ancient boundaries.

Bancroft says: "On the surrender of Acadia to England, the lakes, the rivulets, the granite ledges of Cape Breton—of which an irregular outline is guarded by reefs of rocks, notched and almost rent asunder by the constant action of the sea—were immediately occupied as a province of France, and in 1714, fugitives from Newfoundland and Acadia built their huts along its coasts, wherever safe inlets invited the fishermen to spread their flakes, and the soil to plant fields and gardens. . . . . .

"From Cape Breton, the dominion of Louis XIV. extended up the St. Lawrence to Lake Superior, and from that lake, through the whole course of the Mississippi, to the Gulf of Mexico and the Bay of Mobile."

While the hardy Canadians were forming new settlements in the inclement North, the attention of the Court of France was more particularly directed to the settlement of Louisiana. Treasures were lavishly expended in fitting out expeditions to that El Dorado, while the already established posts of the whole northwest were left to struggle on, almost unaided.

After the treaty of Utrecht, no efforts were spared, on the part of the English, to conciliate the savages. The Abnaquais, who remained true to the French, continued to ravage New England. The English continued to use every means to win their favor, and among other projects, they established a free-school at the mouth of the Kennebec, where the young Abnaquais could be boarded and educated without expense. But all in vain. Father Rafle, an active, zealous Jesuit, had long dwelt among them as missionary, and so strongly were they attached to him, that they followed his dictates in every respect. Enthusiastically attached to his country, as well as to his religion, he used every means to excite in the minds of the savages a continued hostility to the English.

All remonstrances were unavailing. At last the English attempted to gain possession of his person, and, failing in that, they set a price upon his head. The savages were highly exasperated at this attack upon their favorite priest, and immediately sent out messengers to all their allies to meet them at Narrantsouak. From thence they made incursions upon the English settlements along the rivers, demolishing the houses and destroying the crops, but sparing the lives of the inhabitants. They took four or five prisoners, and held them as hostages to secure the lives of some of their messengers, who had been captured and retained prisoners at Boston.

Less forbearing than their savage enemy, the English broke down the fortifications about Narransouak, shot the offending missionary, burned the wigwams, and plundered the church. The destruction of this settlement, for a time, restored tranquillity to New England, but made the Abnaquais deadly foes to the British government.

The severe chastisement which the Outagamies received from the French in 1712, instead of subduing, only exasperated them. Their scouting-parties infested every line of communication between the distant posts, robbing and murdering the traders. So well did they succeed in their outrages, that the Sioux were induced to form an open alliance with them, and many of the Iroquois secretly favored them. Indeed, there seemed to be great danger of a general conspiracy among all the savage nations against the French. As the only means of safety, M. Vaudreuil resolved upon the utter extermination of the Outagamies. Accordingly, in the spring of 1716, an expedition was fitted out, consisting of an army of eight hundred men, under the command of M. Louvigny, lieutenant of Quebec. Proceeding to the country of the Outagamies, they found that nation intrenched within a fort of palisades, evidently aware of the enemy's approach, and expecting no mercy. There were about five hundred warriors, and nearly three thousand women and children.

M. Louvigny, having brought with him two or three small pieces of ordnance, commenced a formal siege. In spite of the governor-general's avowed determination to exterminate the Outagamies, he had given secret instructions to M. Louvigny, not to prosecute the war any farther than was necessary to obtain advantageous terms of peace. After a few days' siege, the Outagamies desired to capitulate. Their terms were rejected, and the siege was continued until, at last, the savages were compelled to accept peace upon the terms proposed by the French. By one of these stipulations, six sons of six of the principal chiefs were delivered to M. Louvigny, as hostages, to secure their sending deputies to Montreal the ensuing year, to ratify the peace. A written treaty was made, containing the cession to the French of all the country of the Outagamies. It is probable the savages were entirely ignorant of this clause in the treaty.

The following winter, the small-pox raged in Quebec and Montreal. Among the victims were the famous Outagamie chief, Pemoussa, and three of the hostages. Fearing the consequences of this mortality, M. Vaudreuil went on the ice from Quebec to Montreal, to give orders to M. Louvigny to set out for Michilimackinac at the earliest moment practicable.

M. Louvigny found it impossible to commence his journey till late in May, 1717. He took with him one of the surviving hostages, who had lost an eye by the small-pox, that he might convince his nation that his comrades had not died for want of care. Immediately after their arrival at Michilimackinac, the hostage and two French interpreters, well supplied with presents "to cover the dead hostages," were dispatched to the country of the Outagamies. The deputation was very cordially received, and the Outagamies expressed their gratitude to Onontio for his forbearance toward their nation, and gave repeated assurances of a lasting peace with the French. They said that for certain reasons they could not wait on Onontio till the next year, but they would never forget their obligations to him.

The hostage set out with the interpreters on their return to Michilimackinac, but, after traveling a few leagues, he left them, saying he must return home to make his countrymen keep their promise. No more was heard of him, nor did the deputies make their appearance at Montreal. The reason afterward given by the Outagamies for this breach of faith was, that "an enemy, provoked beyond a certain degree, could never become a reconciled friend."

About the time that M. Louvigny started on his journey to Michilimackinac, M. Tonti, commandant at Detroit, set out on his return to that post. An official report of his voyage was sent to M. Vaudreuil, bearing date October 12th, 1717. This report was submitted to the Council of Marine, and, as was customary, a summary was made by the secretary, and approved by the council. The following copy throws a ray of light upon the state of affairs at Detroit at that time:

"October 12th, 1717.

"At the same time that M. Louvigny left Montreal to go to Michilimackinac, M. Tonti also started for Detroit, the commerce of that post having been granted to him only on condition that he should not extend his trade beyond his own jurisdiction, nor employ others to carry goods to sell to more distant tribes.

"In conformity to the orders of the council, M. Tonti

took the route of the lakes, and met, on Lake Ontario, three canoes from Michilimackinac, three from Detroit, and three from Saginaw, which were going to Orange. He succeeded, by fair words and presents, in persuading them to follow him to Detroit. Two days later, when he was six miles from Niagara, he met seventeen canoes of savages bound for Detroit, but who were first going to Orange. He induced them also to abandon their design, by the promise that the price of merchandise at Detroit should be diminished, and he would also give them some brandy. Ten canoes followed him to Detroit, and seven took the route to Montreal. L'Oranger, the interpreter, was dispatched to accompany these last, and prevent their going to the English. He was only able to conduct six of them to Montreal; the seventh escaped and went to Orange.

"According to his promise, M. Tonti made satisfactory arrangements with the merchants. He also permitted the savages to buy two or three quarts of brandy each, to take to their villages. But they first agreed that it should be carefully distributed by a trusty person. He hoped the council would not disapprove of what he had done, nor of the continuance of the same course, as he had no other intention than merely to hinder the savages from going to the English.

"M. Tonti arrived at Detroit, July 3d, and immediately held a council with the nations which are established there, in order to engage the chiefs to come to Montreal, to testify concerning what had passed in the war with the Foxes; but they were unable to come, on account of an affair which occurred a short time before, which obliged them to remain in their own village. They have promised to come next year, without fail. They complained that the French had sold their goods too high, but they hoped the change of commandant would reduce the prices; if not, they should go to the English. M. Tonti then called a meeting of the merchants, and they all agreed upon a price for certain kinds of merchandise, with which the savages appeared satisfied.

"The difficulty which hindered the principal chiefs from going from Detroit to Montreal, was caused by an Outawa of this post and four other savages. All five of them pretended to start on a war excursion against the Flat Heads; but, while they were in the river of the Miamis, they killed an Iroquois and his wife, who was a Miami, and two children. This bloody deed would certainly have caused a war, for the Iroquois and Miamis took the part of their murdered people against the Outawas and other nations at Detroit. M. Tonti persuaded the nations at Detroit to join him and go to Saginaw for the murderers, and deliver them up to the Miamis. For this purpose the Outawas and Pottawatomies each sent a canoe, to which M. Tonti added one of the French, and placed the whole under the command of Lieut. Bragelonne. The three murderers were arrested and brought to Detroit, where M. Tonti kept them in custody till he obtained news from the Miamis, to whom he immediately made known the satisfaction the Outawas were ready to offer them. By this means, and by the presents which the nations of Detroit and even the French will make to the Miamis, M. Tonti hopes that nation will be conciliated, and the war prevented.

"Approved by the Council of Marine, January 18, 1718.

"L. A. DE BOURBON."

# CHAPTER XVIII.

Chiefs of the three villages at Detroit assembled in council—Orders of M. Vaudreuil—Speech of Sastarexy, the Huron orator—Unusual state of tranquillity in all New France—Increased number of settlers at Detroit—Enlargement of the stockade—Barracks erected—Canada in 1725—Commencement of "the old French war"—Extensive warlike preparations made in the colonies—Arrival of French and English fleets off the coast of Newfoundland—Quebec taken by the English—Montreal and all the French possessions in the northwest ceded to England—Major Rogers takes possession of Detroit—Lieut. Leslie takes possession of Michilimackinac—Description of Michilimackinac by Henry—Conspiracy of Pontiac—Massacre at Michilimackinac—Its reoccupancy—Removal of the fort to the island.

From 1717 to the close of 1724, there was a constant succession of difficulties between the French and the different tribes of Indians. As soon as one "bad affair" was adjusted, some other real or supposed injury would call forth savage indignation and revenge. The forts at Detroit and Michilimackinac, though still maintained, were in a very low state, and, to the savages, were objects of contempt rather than of terror. It is impossible to trace a connected chain of events at these posts, and only now and then can we find an isolated fact concerning them.

On the 7th of June, 1721, M. Tonti, who still commanded at Fort Pontchartrain, assembled the chiefs of the three villages in the immediate vicinity of Detroit—Hurons, Ottawas, and Pottawatomies—and communicated to them the orders of M. Vaudreuil, which he had just received. An important item in the business under debate, was a request from the governor-general to the three villages, to give their consent that no more brandy should be sold to them, as it had been expressly prohibited by the Council of Marine. It was also proposed that all the nations should unite with the French in a war against the Outagamies, who were again committing depredations upon the more remote posts. This warlike tribe had also driven the Illinois from their hunting-grounds on the Mississippi, and made dangerous the whole passage to Louisiana.

According to custom, the chiefs required two days "to consider the words of Onontio," when they reassembled in vast numbers at the council-house, and Sastarexy, the great Huron orator, replied to Onontio in an eloquent speech. He remarked that the French had a perfect right to do as they might think proper about selling brandy to the savages; acknowledged that it would have been far better for them if the French had never taught them to use it; and portrayed, in a vivid manner, the many evils it had brought upon all the nations; but they had now become so much accustomed to its use that they could not do without it. Hence, it was easy to infer that, if the French would not sell them their favorite beverage, they would obtain it of the English.

In regard to the war with the Outagamies, he said nothing could be determined, except in a general council of all the nations which acknowledge the authority of Onontio. Perhaps all would be agreed in thinking a war necessary, but they would have great difficulty in again placing confidence in the French. All would remember that, having once united the nations to assist in exterminating this enemy, the French had granted them peace without even consulting the allies, and without sufficient reason for such a proceeding.

Soon after this council at Detroit, the difficulties with the Outagamies were adjusted. The Mississippi scheme lost much of the enthusiastic interest it had awakened in France, and, with the exception of occasional outbreaks among the Indians, which were soon quelled, for many years New France remained in a state of unwonted tranquillity.

From this period until 1760, when the whole of the great northwest passed into the hands of the British, no very serious calamity of any kind befell the establishment at Detroit. As the number of settlers increased, the stockade that inclosed the town and constituted the fort, was enlarged and strengthened, until it inclosed eighty or one hundred small houses, closely crowded together and thatched with straw. The new palisades were twenty-five feet high, having a wooden bastion at each corner. Over each of the two gateways a block-house was erected. Barracks for the soldiers were also built on the spot where the first rude fort was constructed in 1701. Near these barracks was the council-house. The only other public building was St. Anne's Church, a small rude structure. The streets were very narrow, except a wide carriage-road called the *chemin du ronde*, which encircled the town just within the palisades.

In 1725, while all Canada was rejoicing in the rapid increase of its population and wealth, the loss of the French ship-of-war Camel, which was wrecked near Louisburg, produced the utmost grief and consternation. Besides the destruction of the rich cargo, the whole colony mourned the greater loss of many valuable lives. M. Louvigny, for many years lieutenant of Quebec, and afterward intendant of Canada, who had recently been appointed governor at Three Rivers, a son of the late governor of Montreal, a large number of colonial officers, and many ecclesiastics of all denominations, perished in the wreck.

In the autumn of the same year, an additional calamity befell the colony, in the death of M. Vaudreuil, the governor-general. This sad event took place October 10, 1725. M. Vaudreuil had governed Canada for twenty-one years, to the general acceptance of the people, who deeply mourned his loss. He was succeeded in the government by M. Beauharnais. The almost unbroken quiet of more than twenty years, though greatly enhancing the prosperity of the country, became at length very irksome to the restless spirit of the French. They had long been jealous of the rapidly increasing settlements of their English neighbors, and had often manifested their dislike by petty annoyances; but, in 1746, they made such encroachments upon the undoubted property of the English, that the British government was aroused.

By order of His Majesty James I., the Secretary of State required all the governors of the English colonies in America, to raise a large number of independent companies of soldiers. The troops of New York, New Jersey, Pennsylvania, Maryland, and Virginia, were to be formed into one corps, under the command of the Lieutenant-governor of Virginia, Brigadier-general Gooch. The colonies were to furnish levy money and provisions, and His Majesty was to bear the expense of arming, paying, and clothing the troops. The army was to be aided by a suitable armament sent from Europe, and the whole to be under the command of General Sinclair. The object was nothing less than the entire subjugation of Canada.

On their part, the French made equally extensive

preparations—collecting troops, erecting new fortifications, even within the British territory, and doing every thing in their power to harass the English. In the mean time, the French and English commissaries were at Paris disputing about the claims of their respective nations, but bringing about no adjustment. At length the English government received intelligence that a French fleet was about to sail from Brest, bound to America. Accordingly, Admiral Boscawen was ordered to set sail with twelve ships-of-war, and watch their movements. This armament was soon after reinforced by six ships-of-the-line and a frigate, under the command of Admiral Holbourne. The French king had instructed his ambassador that, should the British show signs of acting on the offensive, intimation was to be immediately given that the firing of the first British gun would be considered by the French as a declaration of war.

In due time, Admiral Boscawen arrived at Newfoundland, and took his station off Cape Race. Soon afterward M. Bois de la Motte arrived with the French squadron. On account of a dense fog, the English did not see the French fleet; but two French vessels, named the Alcide and the Lys, being separated from the rest, were captured. About 8,000 francs were found on board. Thus commenced the war known as the old French War, during whose sanguinary continuance the name of Washington was first recorded in the book of fame. For ten long years the war continued. With the exception of that rashness which resulted in Braddock's defeat, the war was conducted with marked success to the English. Yet Canada could never be conquered while Quebec and Montreal, the strongholds of the French, still remained in their possession, and thither the English force was gathered—the lion in search of his prey.

Every scene of the battle on the plains of Abraham, where fell the brave Wolfe, and his great adversary, the young and chivalrous Montcalm, is familiar as household words. On the 18th of September, 1759, Quebec, "the rock-built citadel of Canada," passed forever from the hands of the French.

Quebec, Niagara, Frontenac, and Crown Point, were now in the possession of the English; but Montreal and the adjacent country still held out, and early in the year 1760, three divisions of the British army entered Canada at three different points, and, conquering as they went, converged toward Montreal. By a singular coincidence, all three reached the neighborhood of that city on the same day. The enfeebled and disheartened garrison could offer no resistance, and on the 8th of September, 1760, Montreal and all its dependencies were surrendered to the British crown. This capitulation included not only the surrender of Montreal and its immediate vicinity, but of Detroit, Michilimackinac, and all other portions of Canada still in the possession of the French.

On the 12th of September, 1760, Major Robert Rogers received orders from General Amherst to advance, with a sufficient force, and take possession of Detroit, Michilimackinac, and indeed all the northwest, and administer the oath of allegiance to the inhabitants. During the war, the distant tribes of the northwest had continued allies of the French, and, as a consequence, Detroit and the other outposts in that region had remained unmolested. So entirely unacquainted with the progress of events were the soldiers, and even the officers, that Captain Bellestre, commandant at Detroit, was at first quite inclined to dispute the authority by which Major Rogers demanded the surrender of Fort Pontchartrain. Indeed, so sure was the French officer that the demand was informal, that he not only placed himself in a hostile attitude, but attempted to rouse the fury of the Indians, by erecting on a pole an effigy of a crow pecking a man's head, representing the manner in which the French would treat the English if they continued to advance.

At last, becoming satisfied by letters furnished by Major Rogers from the governor-general of Canada, that the fort must indeed be surrendered, Captain Bellestre, with ill-disguised chagrin, declared his garrison at the disposal of the English commander. The French garrison defiled upon the plain, and laid down their arms. The Canadian militia were called together, disarmed, and the oath of allegiance administered. The *fleur-de lis*, which had for sixty years waved over this little fortress, beneath whose folds had been acted many a stirring scene in life's drama, was lowered from the flag-staff, and the red cross of St. George became the symbol of the ruling power.

With that facile transfer of favor which is everywhere paid to power, seven hundred Indians, but a few days since the fast allies of the French, now sent up a shout of exultation, and tauntingly signified that the Englishman was the crow, and the French captain the victim. The French troops were sent as prisoners of war to Philadelphia, and the Canadian inhabitants were permitted to retain their houses and farms, on condition of taking the oath of allegiance. Major Rogers, with a small detachment of troops, attempted to prosecute his journey to Michilimackinac, but the advanced season rendered this impossible. Leaving Captain Campbell in command at Detroit, he set out on his return to Pittsburg, on the 23d of December, 1760.

In the spring of 1761, the British troops, under the command of Lieutenant Leslie, took possession of Michilimackinac, Green Bay, and the Saut Ste. Marie, and the whole northwest passed forever from under the dominion of France. The French troops gave place to the English, and, as at Detroit, the cross of St. George floated where the *fleur-de-lis* had so long held sway. The jealousy of the Indians was excited by this change of rulers; but the Canadian inhabitants, who had gathered within and around the fort at Michilimackinac, preserved their tranquillity, while the *coureurs des bois* were quite willing to enjoy the favors of their new allies. A fresh impetus was given to the fur-trade, by the reduced prices of English goods, and the whole trade at Michilimackinac was monopolized by four English traders. One of these traders, Alexander Henry, who arrived there just before the troops, and who was one of the few that escaped the massacre in 1763, thus describes the fort and its surroundings:

"Fort Michilimackinac was built by order of the governor-general of Canada, and garrisoned with a small number of militia, who, having families, soon became less soldiers than settlers. Most of thöse whom I found in the fort, had originally served in the French army. The fort stands on the south side of the strait which is between Lake Huron and Lake Michigan. It has an area of two acres, and is inclosed with pickets of cedar-wood; and it is so near the water's edge that, when the wind is in the west, the waves break against the stockade.

"On the bastions are two small pieces of brass cannon, taken some years since by a party of Canadians who went on a plundering expedition against the posts of Hudson's Bay, which they reached by the route of the River Churchill. Within the stockade are thirty houses, neat in their appearance and tolerably commodious, and a church, in which mass is celebrated by a Jesuit missionary. The number of families may be nearly equal to that of the houses, and their subsistence is derived from the Indian traders, who assemble here in their voyages to and from Montreal. Michilimackinac is the place of deposit, and point of departure, between the upper and lower countries. Here the outfits are prepared for the countries of Lake Michigan and the Mississippi, Lake Superior and the northwest; and here the returns, in furs, are collected and embarked for Montreal. . . . .

"At the entrance of Lake Michigan, and at about twenty miles to the west of Fort Michilimackinac, is the village of L'Arbre Croche, inhabited by a band of Ottawas, boasting about two hundred and fifty fighting men. L'Arbre Croche is the seat of the Jesuit mission of St. Ignace de Michilimackinac, and the people are partly baptized and partly not. The missionary resides on a farm attached to the mission, and situated between the village and the fort, both of which are under his care. The Ottawas of L'Arbre Croche, who, when compared with the Chippewas, appear to be much advanced in civilization, grow maize for the market of Michilimackinac, where this commodity is depended upon for provisioning the canoes."

Henry says Fort Michilimackinac and the Mission of St. Ignace were on the south side of the straits, which is corroborated by the ruins still visible, while Father Marest, M. Cadillac, and others, distinctly state that these places were on the *north* side. The exact period at which the change was effected, cannot be determined; probably it took place at the time of the re-establishment of Michilimackinac by the French in 1714. The spirit of disaffection with which the Indian tribes at first received their new rulers, was continually increased by the haughty and often unjust treatment of the English. Settlers took possession of the choicest hunting-grounds, without even a semblance of treaty or purchase. The Delawares and Senecas were most exasperated by these acts of aggression, and every means was used by the French to add fuel to the flame. A prophet arose among the Delawares. By his visions and interpretations he aroused the savage hordes, who had been brooding over their wrongs, but feared to avenge themselves.

In 1761, an abortive attempt was made to destroy the posts along the frontier. During the year 1762 many outbreaks occurred, but no decisive blow was struck. It was then that Pontiac, a celebrated chief of the Ottawas, conceived a plot for the extirpation of the English aggressors. Comprehensive in design, and minute in detail, the scheme of Pontiac would have reflected honor on any civilized mind. He possessed courage, resolution, a certain kind of wisdom, a quick perception and ready adaptation, and the gift of convincing eloquence. His plans once perfected in his own mind, he perseveringly addressed himself to their accomplishment. Revenge and ambition urged him on. With the close of the year 1762, Pontiac's arrangements were complete. Far and near he dispatched his swift messengers with gifts of tobacco and belts of wampum, to call the tribes to a great council on the banks of the River Ecorces, a short distance from Detroit. The villages of Pontiac's tribe, the Ottawas, and the wigwams of the Hurons and Pottawatomies, his more immediate allies, were near the place of meeting. Hither came deputations from the Iroquois, Delawares, and Senecas of the east, and from the Illinois, and all the other numerous tribes of the northwest. The council fire was lighted, and the pipe of peace was passed around the dusky circle. Then Pontiac, the tall and stately chieftain, arose and addressed the assemblage in strains of impassioned eloquence. He spoke of their former happiness under the mild sway of the French, and detailed the wrongs inflicted on them by the English. He repeated the fabrication of the traders, that Onontio, their great French father, was hastening on his soldiers to help them subdue the English. He described the numbers and prowess of the tribes represented in council, and spoke of the ease with which their united efforts could crush the English, and restore to the Indian tribes the undisputed possession of the hunting-grounds of their fathers. Then unfolding his plan, he assigned to the representatives of each tribe their part in the great tragedy. The destruction of Michilimackinac was allotted to the Ojibwas and Sacs, Fort St. Joseph to the Illinois, the forts east and south of Lake Erie to different tribes of the Six Nations, while Detroit, the most important of them all, was reserved by Pontiac for himself and his allied tribes.

The assembled chiefs expressed their approbation, other preliminaries were settled, and with war-dance and carousal the vast assemblage dispersed.

The destructive blow was to be everywhere simultaneously struck, each chief devising his own plan for the execution of his part of the scheme. Minavavana, chief of the Ojibwas, to whom was assigned the destruction of Michilimackinac, adopted a very simple expedient, which proved but too successful. On the morning of the 4th of June, the birthday of King George, a large number of Ojibwa chiefs came to the fort, and invited the officers and soldiers to be present at a great game of ball which was to be played between their nation and the Sacs. It being a holiday, the discipline of the garrison was relaxed, and the fort was soon half deserted. The gates were wide open, and the soldiers stood in groups near the palisades, watching the progress of the game, many of them unarmed. A large number of the Canadians were also present, and a multitude of squaws, wrapped in blankets, wandered about among the crowd. Captain Etherington and Lieutenant Leslie stood in the gateway, the former betting on the success of the players. The game progressed to its finale. Parkman thus graphically describes the scene:

"The plain in front was covered by the ball-players. The game in which they were engaged, called *baggattaway* by the Ojibwas, is still, as it always has been, a favorite with many Indian tribes. At either extremity of the ground a tall post was planted, marking the stations of the rival parties. The object of each was to defend its own post, and drive the ball to that of its adversary. Hundreds of lithe and agile figures were leaping and bounding upon the plain. Each was nearly naked, his loose black hair flying in the wind, and each bore in his hand a bat of a form peculiar to this game. At one moment the whole were crowded together, a dense throng of combatants, all struggling for the ball; at the next, they were scattered again, and running over the grounds like hounds in full cry. Each, in his excitement, yelled and shouted at the height of his voice. Rushing and striking, tripping their adversaries, or hurling them to the ground, they pursued the animating contest amid the laughter and applause of the spectators. Suddenly, from the midst of the multitude, the ball soared into the air, and, descending in a wide curve, fell near the pickets of the fort. This was no chance stroke. It was part of a preconcerted stratagem to insure the surprise and destruction of the garrison. As if in pursuit of the ball, the players turned and came rushing, a maddened and tumultuous throng, toward the gate. In a moment they had reached it. The amazed English had no time to think or act. The shrill cries of the ball-players were changed to the ferocious war-whoop. The warriors snatched from the squaws the hatchets which the latter, with this design, had concealed beneath their blankets. Some of the Indians assailed the spectators without, while others rushed into the fort, and all was carnage and confusion. At the outset, several strong hands had fastened their gripe upon Etherington and Leslie, and led them away from the scene of massacre toward the woods. Within the area of the fort the men were slaughtered without mercy."

A mere handful of men escaped from this dreadful

carnage. For a short time they were held prisoners by the Indians, but were finally set at liberty, or ransomed through the friendliness of the Ottawas of L'Arbre Croche. Captain Etherington, the unfortunate commander of Michilimackinac, was permitted to send a letter to Lieutenant Gorell, commander at Green Bay, acquainting him with the disastrous condition of affairs.

On the reception of these tidings, Lieutenant Gorell immediately resolved to evacuate his post, and return to Montreal. Accordingly, on the 21st of June, he embarked, with his troops, in batteaux, accompanied by about ninety Indians in canoes. They crossed Lake Michigan in safety, and arrived on the 30th at L'Arbre Croche. Here they found Captain Etherington, Lieutenant Leslie, and eleven men, detained as prisoners by the Ottawas, yet treated with great kindness. By dint of persuasion on the part of Lieutenant Gorell, the prisoners were set at liberty, and on the 18th of July, 1763, about six weeks after the massacre, the English left L'Arbre Croche, escorted by a fleet of Indian canoes. They reached the portage of the Ottawa river in safety, and arrived at Montreal on the 13th of August.

Saut Ste. Marie had been partially destroyed by fire the previous winter, and was at this time unoccupied by the English. The post at Detroit now contained the only British soldiers to be found in all the region of the lakes.

For a little more than a year, the forts at Michilimackinac, Green Bay, and Saut Ste. Marie, were only occupied by the *coureurs des bois*, and those Indian bands which chose to make them a temporary residence.

After the treaty of peace with the hostile Indians at Detroit, made by General Bradstreet in 1764, Captain Howard was dispatched with a sufficiently large detachment of troops, to take possession of these deserted posts; and once more the cross of St. George was the rallying point, and the protection of the adventurous traders.

In 1779, a party of British officers passed over from the point of the peninsula to the island of Michilimackinac, to reconnoiter, with the intention of removing the fort thither. After selecting a location, they asked permission of the Indians to occupy it. Some time elapsed before their consent could be obtained; consequently, the removal was not effected until the ensuing summer. A government house, and a few other buildings, were erected on the site of the present village, and the troops took possession on the 15th of July, 1780.

The removal of the inhabitants from the main land to the island was gradual, and the fort, which was built on the site of the present one, was not completed until

1783. This fortification, standing on a high cliff which overlooked the village, occupied a controlling and protecting position in regard to the assaults of the Indians; but, during the war of 1812, another fortification was erected on a still more elevated point, the apex of the heights, and named Fort George—subsequently called by the Americans, Fort Holmes, in honor of a gallant officer, a Kentuckian, who fell in the unsuccessful attempt of Colonel Croghan to retake the island in 1814.

Like Detroit, Michilimackinac has been the theater of many a bloody tragedy. Its possession has been disputed by powerful nations, and its internal peace has continually been made the sport of Indian treachery, and of the white man's duplicity. To-day, chanting *Te Deums* beneath the ample folds of the *fleur-de-lis*, to-morrow yielding to the power of the British lion, and, a few years later, listening to the exultant screams of the American eagle, as the stars and stripes float over the battlements on the "isle of the dancing spirits." As a military post in time of war, the possession of Michilimackinac is invaluable; but as a commercial mart, now that the aboriginal tribes have passed away, the location is one of little consequence.

In these later days, to the invalid and the pleasure-seeker, the salubrity of the pure atmosphere, the beauty of the scenery, the historical reminiscences which render it classic ground, and the many wild traditions, peopling each rock and glen with spectral habitants, combine to throw around Michilimackinac an interest and attractiveness unequalled by any other spot on the Western Continent.

# CHAPTER XIX.

Detroit in 1763—Description by Bancroft—Number of French inhabitants—Enumeration in 1764—French farms—English fort—Gladwyn commander—Pontiac's plan for its destruction—His attempt and defeat—Major Campbell's captivity and death—Continuation of the siege—Battle of Bloody Bridge—Indians obliged to disperse in search of food—Gladwyn provisions the garrison—Comparatively quiet winter—Fort le Noult built in 1778—Detroit in 1793—Description by Spencer—Americans take possession of Detroit in 1796.

Bancroft gives the following beautiful description of Detroit and its surroundings, in 1763, just before the consummation of the conspiracy of Pontiac :

" Of all the inland settlements, Detroit was the largest and most esteemed. The deep majestic river, more than half a mile broad, carrying its vast flood calmly and noiselessly between the strait and well-defined banks of its channel, imparted a grandeur to a country whose rising grounds and meadows, plains festooned with prolific wild-vines, woodlands, brooks, and fountains, were so mingled together that nothing was left to desire. The climate was mild, and the air salubrious. Good land abounded, yielding maize, wheat, and every vegetable. The forests were natural parks stocked with buffaloes, deer, quails, partridges, and wild turkeys. Water-fowl of delicious flavor hovered along its streams, which yielded to the angler an astonishing quantity of fish, especially the white fish, the richest and most luscious of them all. There every luxury of the table might be enjoyed by the sole expense of labor.

"This lovely and cheerful region attracted settlers, alike white men and savages; and the French had so occupied the two banks of the river, that their numbers were rated even so high as twenty-five hundred souls, of whom were five hundred men able to bear arms; three or four hundred French families. Yet an enumeration in 1764 proved them not so numerous, with only men enough to form three companies of militia; and in 1768, the official census reported but five hundred and seventy-two souls; an account which is in harmony with the best tradition. The French dwelt on farms which were about three or four acres wide on the river, and eighty acres deep; indolent in the midst of plenty, graziers as well as tillers of the soil, and enriched by Indian traffic.

"The English fort, of which Gladwyn was commander, was a large stockade, about twenty-five feet high, and twelve hundred yards in circumference, including perhaps eighty houses. It stood within the limits of the present city, on the river bank, commanding a wide prospect for nine miles above and below the city."

In maturing his plans for the destruction of the English posts, Pontiac had reserved Detroit for his own special field of action, partly because his village was on a little island just above "Ile au Cochon," or Belle Isle, as it is now called, but more especially because Detroit was the most important post, and would require the greatest degree of caution and skill to secure its capture. That he failed in this most important part of his vast project was not owing to any deficiency in his plan, nor lack of energy in its execution, but was entirely the result of circumstances beyond his control. The treacherous chief was himself betrayed. His well-arranged plot was divulged to the English. Catharine, a beautiful Ojibwa girl who dwelt in the village of the Pottawatomies, had become much attached to Major Gladwyn, and the day before the intended massacre she brought to the fort a pair of moccasins which she had wrought for him. Improving the opportunity thus afforded, she revealed to him the impending danger. The same afternoon William Tucker, a soldier at the fort, who had been captured in his boyhood, and adopted into the tribe of his captors, received from his Indian sister intimations of the designs of Pontiac, which he communicated to Gladwyn. Strict secrecy was enjoined on Tucker by the commander. The little time which remained was diligently employed in preparing for the assault. The guards were doubled, officers were on the alert, soldiers and inhabitants were ordered to be ready for immediate service, yet the nature and extent of the danger was unrevealed. The garrison consisted of only one hundred and twenty-two men, and eight officers. There were also about forty traders and *engagées* who resided in the fort. Two small vessels, the Beaver and the Gladwyn, lay anchored in the river, though it is not known that their commanders were apprised of Pontiac's design.

The day had been rainy, but toward evening the clouds were swept away, and the sun set gloriously. During the afternoon, the Pottawatomies, Hurons, and Ottawas had gradually withdrawn from their villages and congregated at the council-ground of their chief. Only a few squaws and little children remained. And now, when the light of day had departed, and the curtains of night, gemmed with stars, closed around the beautiful earth, fierce, discordant notes were borne on the breeze to the ears of the wakeful sentinels and anxious officers of that feeble fort in the wilderness. Not unfamiliar were the booming sounds of the Indian drum and the cadence of the war-song, now wailing out the dying agony of the victim, now shouting the fierce cry of triumph. Then, indeed, the garrison needed no explanation of the unwonted preparations; too well they understood the reason for the vigilance of their officers.

Aware of the vast superiority of the Indian force,

Gladwyn feared that, in the excitement of their fiendish orgies, they might break over the authority of their chief, and make an immediate attack on the fort. But the night of anxious suspense passed away, and the morning of May 6th, 1763, dawned upon a quiet landscape. The misty vail which hung over the river and obscured the southern shore was scarcely lifted, when a large flotilla of birch canoes was discovered crossing the river at some distance above the fort. Only two or three savages could be seen in each, yet the convoy moved slowly, as if deeply laden. Every canoe was indeed filled with warriors, lying flat on their faces, that their great numbers might not excite suspicion. Pontiac and his numerous chiefs landed just above Parent's Creek, out of sight of the fort, while the other canoes were drawn up along the shore nearer the town, and the occupants soon found their way to the common behind the fort. They were joined by the women and children from the villages, and while it was yet early, the extensive area presented an animated spectacle. The savage throng moved hither and thither as if preparing for a game of ball, a favorite pastime with the Indians. Yet there was an uneasy restlessness, then a suddenly assumed indifference manifested by the warriors, which was never apparent in peaceful times.

Meanwhile the brave Gladwyn was on the alert. No

one was permitted to leave the fort. The impending danger was fully known. Every soldier was under arms, and Sterling and the other fur-traders closed their storehouses, and armed themselves and those in their employ. Every thing was in the most complete readiness, and the little handful of brave-hearted men calmly awaited the result.

About ten o'clock, sixty chiefs, with Pontiac at their head, came marching down the river-road in Indian file. They moved slowly on, with solemn and stately tread, their faces begrimed with paint, and their heads fantastically adorned. All were wrapped to the throat in colored blankets, beneath which were concealed the rifles they had shortened for that purpose. Reaching the eastern gate of the fort, they demanded admittance. It was readily granted. As Pontiac entered the gate, and traversed the short distance which intervened between it and the council-house, he became half convinced that his plot was discovered. Around the gate, at the door of the council-house, and far down St. Anne-street, was an unwonted array of armed soldiers. The guns on the bastions were also manned, yet all was calm, sternly, fearfully calm.

When they arrived at the door of the council-house, the savages found Major Gladwyn and his officers waiting to receive them. "Why do I see so many of my father's young men standing in the streets with their guns?" demanded Pontiac. Gladwyn answered by M. la Butte, the interpreter, that it was customary to exercise the soldiers every day. After some hesitation, Pontiac and his chiefs seated themselves on the mats prepared for them, and the business of the council commenced.

The customary pause ensued, then Pontiac arose and began his harangue. He assured the English of his unchanging friendship, and, addressing the commandant, said he and his chiefs had come to smoke the pipe of peace and strengthen the cords of friendship.

At any other time, the great Ottawa might have commanded admiration. His tall, majestic form was drawn up to its full height as he spoke of the number and prowess of his braves, and the lightning flashed from his eye while he rehearsed their deeds of valor. When he spoke of the English, his reverence for their superior knowledge, and his desire to conciliate their favor, the subdued expression, bowed head, and half-supplicating gestures, were the very personification of graceful, appropriate eloquence. But life and death hung upon a single movement of the treacherous hand which held that sacred emblem of peace, a belt of wampum. With the keenest vigilance was every gesture watched by the officers as they listened to his hollow words. Once Pontiac raised the belt to give the preconcerted signal of attack, but the quick eye of Gladwyn caught the motion, and he passed his hand across his brow. A sudden clash of arms was heard without, the drum rolled the charge, and the rapid tramp of armed men resounded along the street. Pontiac stood in mute astonishment, while Gladwyn sat unmoved, with his calm eye fixed on the treacherous chief. A few more professions of friendship were stammered out, and the belt was presented in the usual manner.

After a pause, Gladwyn commenced a brief reply. He assured his savage auditors of the friendship and protection of the English so long as they continued to deserve it, but threatened the most fearful vengeance for any act of perfidy or aggression. The council broke up. The gates of the fort, which had been closed during the interview, were thrown open, and the baffled savages departed. No sooner were they beyond the precincts of the fort than their rage burst forth in most terrific yells. A small party rushed madly to a lone house on the common, where dwelt an Englishwoman and her two sons, whom they massacred. Others ran to the water's edge, sprang into their canoes, and proceeded to Ile au Cochon, and wreaked their vengeance on a discharged sergeant and his family, who resided there. Meanwhile, the main body of the Indians, consisting of about one thousand warriors, stationed themselves behind the picket fences, and the houses and barns on the common, and commenced firing upon the garrison.

It is said that Pontiac took no part in these demonstrations, but sullenly walked away alone, embarked in his canoe, and paddled to the Ottawa village on the southern shore. With every expression of demoniac rage, he ordered the immediate removal of the camp to the opposite shore. His commands were obeyed with the utmost alacrity, and before nightfall the wigwams of Pontiac's camp occupied the rising ground beyond Parent's Creek. No watery barrier now intervened between the blood-thirsty warrior and his beleaguered foe. Detroit was in a state of siege. Day and night an incessant firing was kept up by the Indians, and a simultaneous attack upon the fort was hourly expected.

When the council was held in the fort, Gladwyn was by no means aware of the extent of Pontiac's schemes, and considered the attack on Detroit merely as one of those impulsive outbreaks which frequently occurred; but he was soon undeceived by the commission of an act of treachery for which even the Canadians were unprepared.

Major Campbell, who had held the command since the country passed into the hands of the British, still remained at the fort. He was highly esteemed, both by the Canadians and Indians. Pontiac formed the design of getting this officer into his possession, and making his life an equivalent for the surrender of the fort.

The Canadians were the means of communication between the British and Indians. By them Pontiac sent a request that Major Campbell would visit him in his camp, that they might "settle all difficulties, and smoke the pipe of peace together." He gave the most positive assurances that Campbell should be permitted to go and return in perfect safety. Messrs. Godfroy and Chapoton were deputed to visit Pontiac, and assure themselves of his sincerity. Conversant as they were with the Indian character, they were deceived by his consummate duplicity, and advised Major Campbell to accept the invitation. Anxious to terminate this vexatious warfare, even at the hazard of his own life, Major Campbell, accompanied by Lieutenant McDougall, and a number of Canadians, repaired to Pontiac's camp.

At first they were well received, but soon became aware that they were in the power of a treacherous foe. The Canadians were sent back, with a message from Pontiac to Major Gladwyn, that Major Campbell and Lieutenant McDougall would be held as hostages for the surrender of the fort. The prisoners were detained at the house of M. Meloche, near the bridge which spanned Parent's Creek. They were permitted to walk out occasionally, and during one of these walks, Lieutenant

McDougall proposed making an attempt to escape. The Indians were so numerous that there was little prospect of success; and, fearing that his own defective vision might impede the progress of his friend, Major Campbell declined. They parted, and Lieutenant McDougall reached the fort in safety.

The weary days of Major Campbell's captivity passed on. All attempts at negotiation with Pontiac received but one reply: "Surrender the fort, and Major Campbell shall be set free." But those tedious hours were numbered—deliverance was near. One day, while taking his accustomed walk, he was met by an Ottawa, whose uncle, a celebrated chief, had been killed by the English at Michilimackinac. Fired with the spirit of revenge, the blood-thirsty savage rushed upon Major Campbell, and by one blow of the tomahawk put an end to his valuable life. Apprehending the vengeance of Pontiac, the murderer fled to Saginaw. In vain was every effort made by the indignant chief to apprehend the miscreant, whose own life would have paid the penalty of his temerity. The death of Major Campbell was a sad blow to the besieged and almost disheartened garrison.

On the 21st of May, the schooner Gladwyn was dispatched to Niagara, to hasten the arrival of the supplies which were daily expected. On the 30th, a convoy of boats was descried coming around the point, and the whole garrison joyfully flocked to the bastions. A salute was fired from the fort, but, instead of the answering guns, the Indian death-cry came wailing across the waters. The convoy, consisting of twenty-two batteaux laden with provisions and munitions of war, and manned by a re-enforcement of troops, was in the hands of the enemy. The prisoners were taken to Ile au Cochon, and put to death with all the horrors of Indian barbarity. This loss was a terrible calamity. Then came the news of the destruction of Michilimackinac and St. Joseph's at the north, and the capture of Forts Sandusky, Miami, and Presqu'ile at the south. West of Niagara and Fort Pitt, Detroit was the only remaining post.

About this time, a large body of the warlike Ojibwas joined themselves to the Pottawatomies, Hurons, and Ottawas, and Pontiac felt certain of success. Still the little fort held out. Every building outside the ramparts which could shelter the Indians, was burned with hot shot fired from the fort, or by sorties made for that purpose by the garrison. Every man was on duty. "For sixty days and nights," said William Tucker, one of the soldiers, "I was a sentinel on the ramparts, catching a few hours sleep, with my clothes on and a gun by my side."

The news of peace between France and England, and

the cession to the English of all the French possessions in Canada, reached Detroit on the 3d of June. It was immediately communicated to the French inhabitants, who found their relations essentially changed. From being prisoners by capitulation, they now had the power to continue their neutrality, or take part with the contending parties. They chose to remain neutral; nor could all the persuasions or threats of Pontiac induce them to join him.

On the 30th of June, the vessel which had been sent to Niagara for aid, after having been twice attacked by the Indians, succeeded in reaching Detroit in safety. She brought a re-enforcement of sixty troops, with provisions and ammunition.

Pontiac now saw the necessity of destroying the two vessels which again lay anchored before the fort. For that purpose, rafts were constructed of materials obtained by demolishing the barns of some of the inhabitants. Pitch and other combustibles were added. The rafts were towed to a proper position above the vessels, and set on fire, with the expectation that the current would bring them in contact, thus securing the destruction of these formidable foes. Twice was the attempt repeated, but by the precautions of the English, the rafts passed the vessels without inflicting the slightest injury.

On the 29th of July, another fleet of boats was seen

ascending the river. Former experience had moderated the hopes of the weary garrison, but had by no means diminished their anxiety. A gun was fired from the fort, and, to the great joy of the eager throng, an answering salute was returned by the boats, each of which carried four swivels and two mortars. On board was a detachment of three hundred regular troops, under the command of Captain Dalzell, an aid-de-camp of the British commander-in-chief, Sir Jeffrey Amherst.

On the very day of his arrival, Captain Dalzell sought an interview with Major Gladwyn, and asked permission to attack Pontiac in his camp. Fresh, vigorous, and enthusiastic, he endeavored to convince the more cautious Gladwyn that the time had come when one decisive blow would terminate this vexatious war. Gladwyn hesitated, explained the position of affairs, and the danger of such an attempt, but was, at last, persuaded to yield a reluctant consent.

By the carelessness of some of the officers, Dalzell's design became known to the Canadians, and Pontiac was soon apprised of it. He had recently removed his camp farther back from the river, beyond the *grand marais*, a locality subsequently well known to the citizens of Detroit. The camp was immediately broken up, and the Indians repaired to the vicinity of the creek, and stationed themselves along the route which their enemy would traverse. One party of warriors concealed themselves behind the outhouses and cord-wood on a farm just beyond the creek; another was stationed within the pickets that lined the road on the farm of M. Dequindre. Indeed, wherever there was a place of shelter, beyond the range of the cannon at the fort, there a band of Indians was concealed.

On the morning of the 31st of July, about two o'clock, the gates of the fort swung open, and three hundred soldiers marched silently forth. In double file and perfect order, they proceeded along the river road, while two large batteaux rowed up the river abreast of them. Each boat was full-manned, and bore a swivel in the bow. The advanced guard of twenty-five men was led by Lieutenant Brown; Captain Gray commanded the center, and Captain Grant's detachment brought up the rear. The night was dark, still, and sultry. On the right of the advancing troops lay the broad, placid river, and on their left the farm-houses and picketed fields of the Canadians appeared in dim outline.

Parent's creek entered Detroit river about a mile and a half from the fort. At that point its course lay through a deep ravine, and only a few rods from its mouth, where the road crossed, it was spanned by a narrow wooden bridge. For a little distance beyond the bridge, the ground was rugged and broken. Along the summit of the highest ridges were rude intrenchments, which had been thrown up by Pontiac to protect his former camp.

The troops pushed rapidly forward, unsuspicious of danger, till they neared the bridge. As they passed the farm-houses of the Canadians, the wolfish watch-dogs, roused from their slumbers, barked furiously, and sometimes a head would be seen cautiously protruded from a dormer window, but naught gave token of the presence of an invisible foe. The bridge was nearly gained. On the left stood the house of Meloche, where Major Campbell had been held prisoner; in front was the bridge, scarcely visible, and beyond rose the banks of the ravine, dark as a wall of night. Still onward—the advanced guard had reached the farther extremity of the bridge, and the main body was just entering upon it, when the fearful war-whoop burst forth, and Indian guns sent out a volley of leaden death. Half the advanced guard fell, and the survivors shrank back appalled. Captain Dalzell immediately advanced to the front, his clear voice rose above the din, and the troops rallied, and rushed madly across the bridge and up the ascent beyond. But their foes had fled. In vain they sought them in the gloom; yet their guns flashed almost incessantly, and the war-cry rang out with undiminished ferocity. The English were unacquainted with the locality, and were soon bewildered in the darkness. At every pause of the soldiery, the unseen enemy renewed their fire. Farther advance was useless, and the only alternative was to retire to the fort, and resume the attack by daylight.

Captain Grant withdrew his company across the bridge and stationed them in the road. A small detachment remained to keep the enemy in check while the dead and wounded were conveyed to the batteaux, which, during the action, had been rowed up to the bridge, and the remaining troops recrossed the bridge and joined Captain Grant. During these proceedings a sharp firing was kept up on both sides; and in attempting to dislodge the enemy from one of their positions, Captain Gray was killed. Suddenly, volley after volley was heard in Captain Grant's vicinity. A large body of Indians had taken shelter in the house of Meloche, and in the adjoining orchards. The brave Grant and his no less courageous troops advanced and dislodged the foe at the point of the bayonet. From two Canadians whom Captain Grant found in the house of Meloche, he learned that the Indians were resolved to effect the complete destruction of the English, and had gone in great numbers to occupy different points below. An immediate retreat was therefore necessary, and the men resumed their marching order. Captain Grant was now in advance, and Dalzell in the rear. About a mile from the fort, on the right as they descended, was a cluster of houses and barns intrenched within strong picket fences. The river ran close on the left, and there was no way of escape except along the narrow passage that lay between. To many of the retreating soldiers it was the way of death. Hundreds of Indians lay in ambuscade. The troops were suffered to advance unmolested till they were directly opposite, when, with terrific yells, the Indians poured volley after volley upon them. The troops broke their ranks, and but for the presence of Dalzell, himself twice wounded, they would have fled, and thus secured their complete destruction. Encouraged by the voice of their leader, the soldiers again rallied, and comparative order was restored. A little farther on, the brave Dalzell stepped aside from the ranks to aid a wounded soldier, and was shot dead by a ball from the enemy.

The Indians still pressed on in hot pursuit, and destruction seemed inevitable, when Major Rogers and his rangers succeeded in gaining possession of the house of M. Campau, which commanded the road and covered the retreat of the regulars.

Meantime Captain Grant had moved forward half a mile, and was able to maintain his position within the inclosure of an orchard until the arrival of the remaining troops. All the men he could spare were detached to different points below, and the constantly arriving troops enabled him to reinforce these posts till a line of communication was formed to the fort, effectually securing the retreat. But Major Rogers and his men found themselves besieged in the house of Campau by about two hundred Indians.

The two batteaux, which had brought the dead and wounded to the fort, now returned and opened a fire from their swivels, which dispersed the savages and covered the retreat of Rogers. At eight o'clock in the morning the survivors entered the fort, having lost seventy men killed and forty wounded.

Thus disastrously terminated the sanguinary battle of Bloody Bridge, the most terrible conflict on record in the annals of Detroit. Fearfully appropriate is the present name of that little stream. Though the bridge is gone, the way-marks are all there, and many an eastern traveler turns aside to call up reminiscences of the past on the very spot where trod the renowned Pontiac, and where the life-tide of many victims crimsoned the waters of Bloody Run.

No other battle was fought, but from early in May until the end of September, Detroit continued in a state of siege. Yet the garrison still held out. At last, when hope had almost expired, the advanced season obliged the Indians to seek in the chase that sustenance which they could no longer find in the vicinity of the fort. By great efforts the indefatigable Gladwyn obtained from the Canadians sufficient provisions for the town during the winter. This long, dreary, hopeless season was passed in comparative quietude.

With the opening of spring the Indian tribes again began to move toward Detroit, but the negotiations of Sir William Johnson, and the approach of General Bradstreet, a dreaded name among the Indians, induced them to relinquish their vengeful purpose. Treaties of peace were at length made, and Michilimackinac, Green Bay, and Saut Ste. Marie, were again garrisoned.

The war of the revolution had no other effect on Detroit and the more distant posts, than to subject them to greater annoyances from the Indian tribes, though the progress of the tide of war was watched with some degree of anxiety. The success of the American arms at Vincennes in 1778, and the prospect that the victorious troops would continue their course onward to Detroit, induced Major Le Noult, the commanding officer, to erect a fort on the rising ground, or "second terrace," outside of the palisades, and back of the city. This large and efficient fortification was called Fort le Noult until after the war of 1812, when it assumed the name of Fort Shelby.

By the treaty of peace made in 1783 between Great

Britain and the United States, it was claimed that Michigan was within American bounds; but minor questions sprang up between the two governments producing mutual dissatisfaction, and when President Washington sent Baron Steuben to Quebec to make arrangements for the transfer of the northwestern forts, he was informed by Sir Frederick Haldimand that the surrender of the forts could not take place at that time, and was refused passports to Niagara and Detroit.

The Indian tribes, greatly dissatisfied with the aggressions of the American settlers upon their lands, and probably instigated by the British, made frequent attacks upon the feeble settlements on the borders of Kentucky and Ohio. An Indian war was the result, and Harmar, St. Clair, and Wayne prosecuted their several campaigns before peace was established.

In 1787, the whole region claimed by the Americans lying northwest of the Ohio river, though still occupied by the British, was organized by Congress into a *Northwest Territory*, and Gen. Arthur St. Clair was appointed governor.

Under the British rule, there was a constant improvement in the appearance of Detroit, but more especially in the military appointments. New barracks for officers and soldiers were built, and a handsome esplanade, and two or three military gardens, were laid out between the fort and the town. The palisades which surrounded the town were extended so as to intersect the corners of the fort, and thus afforded additional protection to the inhabitants.

The following minute description of Detroit in 1793 is given by Rev. O. M. Spencer, who was then a lad twelve or thirteen years old. While at play with other boys near Cincinnati, Ohio, he was taken captive by a band of Miami Indians, and brought to their village, near the present site of Fort Wayne. By General Washington's request, General Simcoe, commander-in-chief of the British forces in the northwest, ordered Colonel England, who then commanded at Detroit, to ransom the lad. After a few months' sojourn with his kind British friends at Detroit, he was safely returned to his parents. Though a mere child, young Spencer kept a written journal during his captivity, which forms the basis of a narrative since published, and from which this remarkably correct extract is taken.

"Detroit," says Mr. Spencer, "was then a small town, containing only wooden buildings, but few of which were well finished, surrounded by high pickets, inclosing an area of probably half a mile square, about one-third of which, along the bank of the river, as the Strait was called, was covered with houses. There were, I think, four narrow streets running parallel with the river, and intersected by four or five more at right angles. At each end of the second street was an entrance into the city, secured by heavy wooden gates. North of this street, at the west end of the town, was a space about two hundred feet square, inclosed on a part of two sides with palisades, within which a row of handsome two-story barracks, for the accommodation of the officers, occupied the west side, and buildings of the same height for the soldiers' quarters, stood on the north and a part of the east side. The open space was occupied as a parade-ground, where the troops were every day exercised by the adjutant. In the northwest corner of the large area, inclosed with pickets, on ground slightly elevated, stood the fort, separated from the houses by an esplanade, and surrounded first by an abatis of tree-tops about four feet high, having the butts of the limbs sharpened and projecting outward; then by a deep ditch, in the center of which were high pickets; and then by a row of light palisades, seven or eight feet long, projecting horizontally from the glacis.

"The fort itself, covering not more than half an acre of ground, was square, having a bastion at each angle, with parapets and ramparts so high as to entirely shelter the quarters within, which were bomb-proof. Its entrance was on the south side, facing the river, over a drawbridge, and through a covered way, over which, on each side, were long iron cannon, carrying twenty-four pound shots, and which the officers called the 'British lions,' while on each of the other sides were planted two, and on each bastion four cannon of various caliber—six, nine, and twelve pounders. By the side of the gate, near the end of the officers' barracks, was a twenty-four pounder; and, for the protection of the south side of the town, there were two small batteries of cannon on the bank of the river.

"The fort was garrisoned by a company of artillery, under the command of Captain Spear, while two companies of infantry, and one of grenadiers of the twenty-fourth (Colonel England's regiment), were quartered in the barracks; the balance of the regiment was at Michilimackinac and other northern posts.

"In the spring of 1793, there were anchored in the river in front of the town, three brigs of about two hundred tuns each—the Chippewa and the Ottawa, new vessels, carrying eight guns each, the Dunmore, an old vessel of six guns, and a sloop, the Felicity, of about one hundred tuns, armed with only two swivels, all belonging to His Majesty George III., and commanded by Commodore Grant. There were, besides, several merchantmen, sloops, and schooners, the property of private individuals."

By the stipulations of the treaty of Greenville, made

by Gen. Wayne with the Indian tribes in August, 1795, Detroit and all the region of the northwest became the undisputed property of the United States.

Before evacuating the fort at Detroit, the British soldiery filled the wells with stones, broke the windows of the barracks, and locked the gates of the fort, committing the keys to the care of an old negro, in whose possession they were afterward found.

In 1796, Captain Porter, with a detachment of troops from General Wayne's army, took possession of Detroit, and flung out to the breeze the first American banner that ever floated over the soil of the Peninsular State.

HON. JAMES MAY.

First Chief Justice.

## CHAPTER XX.

Localities of Detroit—The city in 1701—In 1763 and 1796—River Savoyard—Settlements at Grosse Point, along the St. Clair river—French inhabitants—Domestic life—Increase of immigration—Settlements on the Detroit—Improved appearance of the country—Social life at Detroit—Business—French characteristics—Summer recreations—*Le grand marais*—Winter amusements—Easy life in the fort—Establishment of the civil government—Michigan territory organized—Detroit burned—Arrival of the government officers—Act of Congress for the relief of the sufferers by fire—Legislative board organized.

To enable the reader who is familiar with Detroit as it now exists, to trace the boundaries of the old town by the well-known localities of the new, we will describe as accurately as possible the site of Fort Pontchartrain in 1701; the boundaries of Detroit as it existed in 1763; and the localities indicated on the map of 1796.

Old Fort Pontchartrain, built by M. la Motte Cadillac in 1701, occupied the ground where now stand the "Cooper block," and the Farmers' and Mechanics' and Peninsular banks, and extended west a little below the "Michigan Exchange;" thence running south to Woodbridge-street, which was then the margin of the river, thence east and north to the place of beginning, including a space about equal to one square block of the present city.

At the time of Pontiac's conspiracy in 1763, the original fortifications had been greatly enlarged (the whole town was inclosed in palisades and was called the fort), and extended from the river bank, on Griswold-street, north to the alley between Jefferson Avenue and Larned-street, thence as far as the western boundary of the first fort, thence south and uniting with the old palisade, inclosing a space about twelve hundred yards in circumference. "Pontiac's Gate" was the eastern entrance to the town, and occupied the site of the United States Courthouse. This gate received its name from the fact that here the renowned chief entered when he came to hold a council with Major Gladwyn, and through it he retreated, crest-fallen, when he found that his perfidy was discovered. St. Anne's church, a rude chapel, stood on the north side of St. Anne-street, nearly in the middle of the present Jefferson Avenue, and in front of the "Conant block." Opposite the church, on the south side of St. Anne-street, was a large military garden, in which stood a blockhouse, where all the councils with the Indians were held. It was also the place of meeting for deliberative consultations among the officers of the garrison. These two were the only public buildings in the town.

In 1796, the eastern boundary of the town remained the same as far north as Congress-street, then taking an angular direction, intersected the southeastern angle of Fort le Noult or Shelby. The southern angle of the palisade, which marked the western boundary of the city, was at Cass-street. It extended from the river north, and intersected the western angle of the fort, giving the town a triangular form. The fort extended from Wayne-street to about half way between Shelby and Griswold streets, thence north to Lafayette-street. The south side fronted on Fort-street, the southeast angle extending across to about half way between Fort and Congress streets.

The River Savoyard ran between Congress and Larned streets, and emptied into the Detroit near "Kendrick's foundry." This stream was sufficiently large to float canoes, and parties of officers and their ladies often embarked from the beautiful esplanade, and passed down its rippling waters to the broad, placid Detroit. Hither and thither, ever within range of the protecting guns of the fort, danced the tiny barks with their light-hearted voyagers, and the wild song of the Canadian boatmen woke the slumbering echoes of the distant shore.

The large grants of land offered to actual settlers, with rations from the fort for a specified time after their arrival, had, during the British domination, induced a few Scotch and English families to immigrate, and settle along the banks of the Detroit and St. Clair rivers. The

French inhabitants, many of whom had intermarried with the Indians, had been permitted to retain and enjoy their farms above and below the city, and when the American eagle became the symbol of the ruling power, they were in a prosperous condition. They owned large herds of cattle and wild horses, and numerous flocks of sheep, and raised sufficient grain to supply their own necessities. Of the manufacture of wool they were entirely ignorant, using the fleeces to protect their cellar windows from the frost, and like strange appropriations of that valuable article. The women were indifferent housekeepers, sewing being their principal employment, many of them earning considerable sums by the manufacture of rude garments for the Indian traffic.

Soon after the stars and stripes began to wave above the fort, a number of emigrants from France, who had spent some years in the colonies, removed to Detroit, and about the same time a few Americans also ventured to find homes in this far-off wilderness. From 1796 to 1805 there was a constant, gradual accession to the number of inhabitants in the town and surrounding country. A small settlement had already been formed at Grosse Point, twelve miles above Detroit on Lake St. Clair, and a few adventurous farmers had even dared to find homes on the St. Clair river, in the vicinity of the present village of Newport.

Along the banks of the Detroit new farm-houses arose, and agriculture assumed a better character under a more enlightened cultivation; yet the progress toward independence was very much slower than in new settlements at the present day. The great number of Indians compelled the inhabitants to settle in close proximity along the rivers, and prevented them from selecting the richer lands of the interior. The lack of water-power also obliged them to depend solely upon the rudely constructed windmills of the French for the flouring of their grain; while their lumber was sawed by the slow and laborious method of whip-sawing. Six miles below the city, on the river Rouge, was a windmill known as "Baby's mill," afterward "Knoggs' mill," around which was gathered a considerable settlement. Another mill was built by a Mr. Peltier on the Savoyard, a little way from its entrance into the Detroit.

Within the town all was bustle and business; some of the French traders still remained, and they and the British merchants had full possession until 1799. Joseph Campau, Robert Gonier, George Moniot, Jean Baptiste le Duke, Gabriel Coté, Jacques Allaird, Conrad Ten Eyck, Hugh Martin, and Meldrum and Park, comprised the whole list, and they were very prosperous. All kinds of merchandise brought good prices and met with ready sales. Coffee sold for thirty-eight cents a pound, tea for two dollars; calico was seventy-five cents a yard, and all articles of wearing apparel were in like proportion.

Colonel Stephen Mack was the first American merchant in Detroit. He came in 1799, and with true Yankee independence erected a shanty in the very heart of the city, and spread out his goods to the admiring gaze of thronging customers. He had a large supply of that plaid cotton fabric called "apron check," for which he found ready sale at the moderate price of one dollar a yard. The narrow streets and alleys of the city were constantly thronged with savages hastening to the trading-houses to exchange their peltries for goods, or reeling about under the influence of the baneful "fire-water." At the wharves vessels were busy discharging their freights of merchandise, and receiving return-cargoes of furs from the well-filled storehouses. The prevailing style of the dwellings was one-story blockhouses with dormer windows, a few of which were covered with clapboards.

In social life, the French characteristics predominated. During the summer the days were devoted to business, and the evenings were spent by the older portion of the inhabitants in social visiting, and by the younger in dancing, promenading, and moonlight sailing on the beautiful Detroit. Barbecues were occasionally held in a grove near Baby's mill, almost the only daytime recreation during the business season.

In winter, when a vast sea of ice separated them from their eastern neighbors, and their Indian allies were far in the depths of the forest engaged in the chase, the denizens of the fort and of the crowded town gave themselves up to unrestrained pleasure-seeking. Three or four miles above the city was a large marsh, called by the French *Le Grand Marais.* It extended down to the river brink; and when the autumnal rains came the entire surface was submerged, and the wintry frosts soon converted it into a miniature sea of glass. In the absence of sufficient snow for sleighing, the *Grand Marais*, which could be readily gained from the icy margin of the river, was a favorite drive for the citizens; and late in autumn the young men of the town would erect on its border a long one-story building, with stone chimneys at each extremity, and furnished with rude tables and benches.

Every Saturday morning during the long, cold winter, carioles filled with gay young men and laughing girls might be seen gliding over the glassy surface of the ice-bound river, or, if there were snow, flying along the river road, where now extends the broad and beautiful Jefferson Avenue, each finally landing its freight of life and beauty at the *Hotel du Grand Marais.* The box-seats of the carioles were always well filled with mysterious baskets and packages, which were speedily transferred to the aforesaid long tables, and soon the rattling of the dinner-service was heard in the lulls of the gay chatter of the French girls; and the aroma of the fragrant Mocha escaped into the frosty air in delicate smoke-wreaths,—an incense of anticipation to the coming repast. As soon as the dinner was over, the tables and benches were removed, and dancing commenced, which continued until the booming of the evening gun at the fort warned the merry party that

> The evening shades might be but 'vantage ground
> For some fell foe.

The next day, Sunday, after morning mass, the gentlemen were accustomed to repair to the *Grand Marais* and spend the day in carousal, and feasting on the remains of yesterday's store. Sleigh-riding on the ice, and balls and parties in town, filled up the week's interim. The summer's earnings scarce sufficed for the winter's waste.

At the fort all went on prosperously: the troops had no other service than the usual military routine in time of peace, except, perhaps, the occasional punishment of some stray band of marauding savages. A gay, indolent life they were leading, very unlike that of their French predecessors a century before.

Meanwhile, the civil government was preparing to

supplant the martial law, by which Detroit from its first settlement had been principally controlled.

On the 11th of January, 1805, that part of the North-west territory lying between Lake Michigan on the west, and Lakes Huron, St. Clair, and Erie, and their connecting straits on the east, was organized into a separate territory by an act of Congress. William Hull was appointed governor, and Augustus B. Woodward, Frederick Bates, and John Griffin, judges. The winter passed, spring came and departed, and still the expected governor and his associates had not arrived.

On the 11th of June, 1805, just five months after Governor Hull's appointment, a fire broke out at mid-day in the midst of the crowded town of Detroit, and when darkness settled down upon the world, the whole town was one vast scene of smouldering ruins, and the entire population were homeless. Within the limits of the stockade, one small French-built dwelling-house, on St. Anne-street, and a large brick storehouse almost in range standing below, near the river, were all that remained of the city. During the conflagration, the utmost panic and confusion prevailed. The flames raged with such fury as to defy all control. There was no place of safety within the city. Furniture, once removed, was soon destroyed by the advancing fire, and, as a last resort, tables, chairs, bedsteads, and such other articles as would not be thus injured, were sunk in the river, as the only means of saving them from the flames. Every skiff and canoe was employed in conveying clothing and other easily removed valuables across the river. Two larger vessels were in port, but they were obliged to drop down the river for their own safety.

The day after the destruction of Detroit, the governor and other territorial officers arrived. A sad spectacle presented itself to the astonished gaze of these newly-appointed dignitaries. Instead of a flourishing town, growing rich by a lucrative traffic with the Indians, they found only a wide-spread waste of still smoking ruins. The inhabitants, suddenly impoverished and greatly disheartened, were gathered on the common within range of the guns of the fort, with no other abiding-place than cloth tents, or rude huts erected from such materials as they could obtain. The little children, and the sick and aged, had found refuge among the hospitable farmers on both sides of the river. The fort afforded an asylum for the governor and his suit.

On the second Tuesday of July, 1805, the oath of office was administered to the several territorial officers, and Michigan commenced its governmental existence. Again inspired with hope, the inhabitants of Detroit gathered together their remaining means, and began to build for themselves new homes. The first house in the new town was erected by Peter Audrain, secretary of the territory. Numerous other dwellings were soon built, and the town began to assume a less desolate appearance. Yet there was much suffering among those of the inhabitants whose whole available property had been destroyed.

On the 10th of October, 1805, an official statement of the destruction of the city, and the consequent deplorable condition of the inhabitants, was made to the Secretary of State, by Governor Hull and his associates. At the next session of Congress, the following act was passed for the relief of the sufferers, and to encourage an increased immigration:

"Be it enacted, by the Senate and House of Representatives of the United States of America, in Congress assembled: That the governor and judges of the territory of Michigan shall be, and they are hereby authorized to lay out a town, including the whole of the old town of Detroit and ten thousand acres adjacent, excepting such parts as the President of the United States shall direct to be reserved for the use of the military department, and shall hear, examine, and finally adjust all claims to lots therein, and give deeds for the same. And to every person, or the legal representative of every person, who, not owing or professing allegiance to any foreign power, and being above the age of seventeen years, did, on the eleventh day of June, one thousand eight hundred and five, when the old town of Detroit was burnt, own or inhabit a house in the same, there shall be granted by the governor and the judges aforesaid, or any three of them, and where they shall judge most proper, a lot not exceeding the quantity of five thousand square feet.

"§ 2. And be it further enacted, that the land remaining of the said ten thousand acres, after satisfying claims provided for by the preceding section, shall be disposed of by the governor and judges aforesaid, at their discretion, to the best advantage, who are hereby authorized to make deeds to purchasers thereof, and the proceeds of the lands so disposed of, shall be applied, by the governor and judges aforesaid, toward building a courthouse and jail in the town of Detroit; and the said governor and judges are required to make report to Congress, in writing, of their proceedings under this act."

The "Journal of the Proceedings of the Board of Governor and Judges of the Territory of Michigan," contains the following record:

"Pursuant to the above act of Congress, the governor and judges of the territory of Michigan convened at the house of Governor Hull, on Saturday, September sixth, one thousand eight hundred and six. Present, William Hull, Governor; Augustus B. Woodward, Chief Judge, and Frederick Bates, Senior Associate Judge. Peter Audrain was continued legislative secretary, and Asa Jones was appointed sergeant-at-arms, with a compensation of twenty-five dollars a month. After the business of organizing had been dispatched, the act of Congress was read, and referred to Judge Woodward as committee, with instructions to report from time to time, by bill or otherwise."

# CHAPTER XXI.

Judge Woodward's plan for the new city of Detroit—Survey of the city—Apportionment of lots—Incorporation of the Bank of Detroit—First code of laws published called the "Woodward Code"—Bank charter revoked in 1809—Land granted for St. Anne's church, Roman Catholic—Building lots granted for boys' and girls' schools—Resolution to grant building lots to foreigners—Peter Desnoyers—Building lot granted for a Protestant church—Tecumseh plans the destruction of Detroit—Disaffection of the Shawanese and Wyandots induces the inhabitants to build a stockade around the new city—Governor Hull effects a treaty with the Indian tribes in 1807—Facetious resolution of Judge Woodward—Resolution concerning American manufactures—Answer to an official communication from Governor De Witt Clinton, and others, of the State of New York.

The following is a copy of a bill presented by Judge Woodward, at the very next session of the Board, held September 8th, 1806:

"*Resolved*, That it is expedient immediately to lay out and survey a town under the said act of Congress, and to adjust the titles and claims to lands and lots therein.

"*Resolved*, That the basis of the said town be an equilateral triangle, having each side of the length of four thousand feet, and having every angle bisected by a perpendicular line upon the opposite side, such parts being excepted as, from the approximation of the river or other unavoidable circumstances, may require partial deviations.

"*Resolved*, That it will be expedient to allow and convey to individuals having legal claims, the lots within their respective limits, reserving so much as may be necessary for public squares or spaces, avenues, streets, and lanes, the increased value of the property as lots being considered as more than an equivalent for the same, excepting in some particular cases, where the proprietor, having but a small quantity, the whole or the greater part may be taken up, in which case special indemnification will be necessary; and reserving also to those having legal rights, and who may not think the benefit greater than the damage, the right of having their damage ascertained according to law.

"*Resolved*, That it will be expedient, in adjusting the titles and claims, to allow to every person the quantity to which he may have a good title; and when a person has been in possession of a farm without a good title, to allow him the quantity he was in possession of in front, by nine thousand feet in rear, provided that encroachment on public land, unusual and unjustifiable under the circumstances of the country, be not comprehended therein.

"*Resolved*, That it will be expedient to make deeds immediately to proprietors and purchasers, securing all sums due to the public by mortgages and bonds.

"*Resolved*, That it be requested of Mr. Joseph Watson to prepare the deeds, mortgages, and bonds which may be necessary, at the following charges, to be paid by the party receiving the title: that is to say, for a deed, one dollar; for a mortgage, one dollar; for a bond or other writing, twenty-five cents.

"*Resolved*, That the committee on this subject be instructed to report a bill or bills to carry into execution the preceding resolutions, and that the committee be farther instructed to collect a list of all claims, and from time to time report an opinion on the respective claims.

"*Resolved*, That it will be expedient immediately to incorporate the said town of Detroit into a city, and to provide by law for the government of the same."

On the 13th of September, 1806, we find the following record: "The engrossed bill relative to the city of Detroit was read a third time, and thereupon

"*Resolved*, unanimously, that the said bill do pass to be a law, and that the title of the said law be, 'An Act concerning the City of Detroit.'"

The plan of the new town of Detroit, said to be similar to that of Byzantium, was on a magnificent scale, and, if fully carried out, would have far surpassed the present city. Jefferson and Woodward Avenues, and some of the streets near the river, were immediately surveyed, and the adjudication of claims went on as rapidly as possible. Early in 1807 the whole survey was completed. The triangle around the fort was the military reservation, and was not divided into lots until about 1826.

The great scarcity of money in the territory, and the difficulties arising from using only specie as the commercial medium, had long been felt by the merchants, and on the very day of the organization of the "Board of Governor and Judges," a petition was presented by Russel Sturges, Henry Bass, Jr., Benjamin Wheeler, Samuel Coverly, Nathaniel Parker, and Bazillary Homes, and their associates, stating that they were merchants on the Atlantic coast, and interested in the peltry trade in Michigan, and that they had experienced great hazards and inconveniences in the transmission of specie to so great a distance, and praying, for that and other reasons, for the passage of an "act of incorporation for a bank at Detroit." The subject was referred to Governor Hull, as committee. On Monday, September 15th, 1806, a bill was passed incorporating the first "Bank of Detroit."

During the winter of 1805–6, the Legislative Board had been busy in establishing a more efficient judiciary system; and in May, 1806, the first code of laws for the territory of Michigan was adopted and published. They were drafted by Judge Woodward, and were called the "Woodward Code." These laws, with the Act of incorporation and plan of the city of Detroit, and the "Act incorporating the Bank of Detroit," were approved by

Congress at its next session, early in 1807. The existence of the Bank of Detroit was very brief; its bills were in circulation until 1809, when the charter was revoked by Congress. The bank was built on the northwest corner of Jefferson Avenue and Randolph-street, and two lots were sold to the directors for three hundred and ninety-five dollars and seventy-five cents.

The Franciscans had sustained a mission at Detroit from the period of its settlement in 1701, and at the time of the fire in 1805, St. Anne's church was the only house of worship in the town. In consequence of the widening of the street, in the new plan of the city, the old church site was found to be nearly in the center of Jefferson Avenue. It therefore became necessary to obtain a new location. Accordingly, on the 4th day of October, 1806, the governor and judges granted a petition to that effect, made by Rev. Gabriel Richard, Vicar-general of the order of Sulpitians, by the following enactment:

"*Resolved*, That the Roman Catholic church be built in the center of the little military square, on section No. 1, on the ground adjacent to the burying-ground; the said lot fronting on East and West Avenue,* two hundred feet wide, and running back two hundred feet deep, and bounded on the three sides by three other streets."

* Michigan Avenue.

The previous day a petition from Angelique Campeau and Elizabeth Williams (nuns), asking for the donation of a lot on which to erect an academy for young ladies, was received, and referred to the standing committee. A petition was also presented by Rev. Gabriel Richard, asking for a lot for an academy for boys. Subsequently, a lot was donated for the nuns' school, on what is now the corner of Randolph and Congress streets, and one for the boys' academy on Bates-street, opposite the site for St. Anne's cathedral.

The "governor and judges" found great difficulty in adjusting the claims of the inhabitants of the old town of Detroit, to the satisfaction of all parties; and, finally, a meeting of the citizens was called on the 14th of October, 1806, to devise some means by which this object could be accomplished. The following plan for adjusting the donation claims of the inhabitants of the old town of Detroit was finally agreed upon, and a committee appointed to present it to the Board, by whom it was adopted:

"The committee chosen by the inhabitants of the late town of Detroit, on Saturday, the 11th inst., recommend to the honorable Legislative Board the following plan for adjusting their donation claims in the first class:

"All those belonging to the first class who have improved the lots now in their possession, we conceive ought to retain them for their donation, or in exchange for an equal quantity of ground in the old town, paying for the surplus feet, agreeable to the conditions of sale: to wit, two cents for each square foot. All lots that the Legislative Board have disposed of since the Act of Congress, or that remain unsold, together with those that are improved, ought to be numbered and balloted for by the claimants of the first class who are not satisfied. All those persons who have built dwelling-houses on lots considered to be in the first class, and who are claimants in the second class, shall retain said lots by paying to the person in the first class who draws the lot, two cents for each square foot, in the course of twelve months. Those who are not claimants, having built a dwelling-house on a lot in the first class, ought to pay to the person drawing said lot, the same price that the Legislative Board were to receive. It is understood by the committee, that the lots for the first class should be those fronting on the Courthouse Avenue from the river, to the corner lots on the north side of Main-street, inclusive, and those on the street commonly called Main-street.

"The claimants in the second class ought to have the next choice of the best lots remaining after the first class is satisfied, and to have their claims adjusted on the same system with the first class.

"The claimants in the third class should have the next choice of the best lots remaining after the second class are satisfied, and the system taken to adjust their claims to be the same as recommended for the first class."

Then came petitions for "donation lots," from married women, minors, and persons residing outside of the palisades at the time of the fire, but now, by the new city survey, brought within the corporation, the result of which was the passage of the following resolution by the "Board:"

"*Tuesday, November* 11*th*, 1806.—On motion of Judge Woodward: *Resolved*, That the governor and judges will so construe the Act of Congress, that wives, and those who resided out of the old town, but within the corporation, shall be considered donees, and that the donations of married women, and persons residing out of the town, but within the corporation, shall, in all cases, be to the northward and westward of the Catholic Church Square, and not on the Avenue leading from the Catholic Church Square to the Statehouse Circus."

Notwithstanding this liberality, there still remained one class of sufferers unprovided for—the foreign residents, principally French, who had not sworn allegiance to the United States. In many instances they were among the most prominent citizens, and strong adherents to the American interests. To meet their necessities, we find the following record on the journal of the governor and judges:

"*Thursday*, *January* 22*d*, 1807.—On motion of the governor: *Resolved*, That any person or persons born in a foreign country, but having resided in this country since the independence of the United States, over the age of seventeen years, and having owned or inhabited houses at the time of the conflagration of the town of Detroit, and who produce no other evidence of their not owing or professing allegiance to any foreign power than their residence here, and their being subjected to the laws of the country, may, if they think proper, be heard before the Board on the question of their right to a donation lot under the Act of Congress."

In compliance with the above resolution, Peter Desnoyers appeared before the Board, and made the following statement:

"Peter Desnoyers, a native of France, of the age of thirty-four years, arrived at Detroit on the seventeenth day of August, 1796, in the quality of armorer, in the service of the public. He came from Paris to America in the year 1790, lived at Gallipolis several years, and afterward at Pittsburg, from which place he came to Detroit, where he has resided ever since. He has never professed allegiance to the government of France, or to any other foreign government, since his landing in the United States."

Henry Berthlet, John Gentle, George Smart, William McDowell Scott, and others, also obtained a hearing before the Board, and, after due consideration, donation lots were granted to the several applicants.

On Monday, April 27th, 1807, "a petition for a lot on which to build a Protestant church," was presented to the Board, and a lot on the corner of Larned-street and Woodward Avenue was granted, and a house of worship erected, known as the First Presbyterian church. Rev. John Monteith was the first Protestant clergyman employed by the citizens of Detroit, and through his instrumentality a Protestant church was organized, embracing all the different denominations then represented in the city. No distinctive creed was adopted, but the form of organization was Presbyterian.

In 1806, the celebrated chief Tecumseh, and his brother Ellshwatawa, or the prophet, belonging to the Shawanese tribe, devised a plan, quite similar to the famous project of Pontiac, to effect the destruction of Detroit and the other American settlements in the territory. They were probably encouraged in this by the British, whose allies they were. The disaffection soon manifested by the Wyandots and other Indians in the vicinity of Detroit, caused the governor, early in 1807, to order the inclosure of the inhabited part of the new town in a strong stockade. The eastern boundary of this stockade was along the eastern line of the "Brush farm," about where Brush-street now runs. There was a gate on Atwater-street, near the present Pontiac depot, and a blockhouse on Jefferson Avenue, a few rods east of the present site of the Biddle House. The western line of the stockade ran along the eastern line of the Cass farm, then known as the Macomb farm, and the western gate was on Jefferson Avenue, about one hundred feet below Cass-street. The northern line ran about in range with the fort. During the year 1807, General Hull effected a treaty with the Ottawa, Chippewa, Pottawatomie, and Wyandot tribes, yet the threatening movements of the Shawanese, and the little reliance that could be placed on Indian fidelity, had its influence in retarding the very rapid growth of Detroit. Still there was a constant progress. Many of those who have since given character and influence to this chief city of a prosperous State, were young, enterprising immigrants to Detroit, between 1807 and 1812.

"The Board of Governor and Judges" were busy adjusting land claims, and devising and perfecting such plans for the future prosperity of the city as came within their province. Their "Journal" contains no record of particular interest to the general reader, except the following extracts. On Friday, Oct. 14th, 1810, the facetious Judge Woodward offered the following resolution:

"*Resolved*, That the president of the governor and judges, sitting under the 'Act of Congress concerning the town of Detroit,' and under the ordinance, be respectfully requested to accommodate the said governor and judges with fire during their sitting; the expense accruing thereby to be defrayed, one moiety from the territorial funds, and the other in the same manner as other expenses attending the execution of the said 'Act of Congress,' or in such other equitable proportion as the said president, from his knowledge of the arithmetical rules of proportion, vulgar and decimal fractions, and the algebraic rules of equation, shall ascertain to be reasonable and conscientious."

The resolution did not pass, but we presume a fire was speedily provided.

The growing disaffection between the United States and Great Britain, its evident effect upon the Indians, and the probable result, were subjects of much interest to Detroit. Fully sympathizing with the general government, and imbued with the American spirit of resistance and independence, on Saturday, January 19th, 1811, Judge Woodward, clothed completely in American manufactures, moved the following resolution:

"Whereas, the encouragement of American manufactures is a duty imposed on all good citizens of the United States, by the dictates of benevolence as well as by the injunctions of patriotism; and whereas the consumption of domestic manufactures is, at the same time, the most simple and the most efficacious encouragement of them; and whereas it is at all times becoming that those who receive both honors and emoluments from the execution of public trusts should exhibit themselves the foremost in examples of utility; therefore,

"*Resolved*, That it be respectfully and earnestly recommended by the legislative authority of the territory of Michigan, to all the officers of this government, to appear clothed in articles the manufacture of the continent of North America, at all times, when engaged in the execution of any public duty, power, or trust, from and after the fourth day of July, 1813."

This resolution "was passed unanimously, and a copy thereof was signed by the members and attested by the secretary, in order to be deposited in the office of the secretary of the territory; and the secretary was ordered to take such measures for the further publication and communication of the same, as he might judge expedient." In accordance with the above direction, James Watson, Secretary of the Board, wrote the following letter to an editor in Pittsburg, Penn.:

"DETROIT, MICH., January 29th, 1811.

"E. PENTLANE, Esq.,

"Editor of the Commonwealth:

"SIR—In obedience to directions received from the legislative authority of the territory of Michigan, I hereby take the liberty of requesting that you will insert the annexed resolution, at an early period, in your paper; and have the honor to be

"Your fellow-citizen, and

"V. O. H. S.,

"JAMES WATSON."

"*Thursday*, *January 9th*, 1812.—The committee, to whom was referred the communication from the commissioners of internal navigation in the State of New York, made the following report, which was unanimously adopted:

"Whereas, the commissioners of internal navigation in the State of New York have addressed to the governor and judges of the territory of Michigan certain communications relating to a canal in the State of New York, which have been duly considered; therefore,

"*Resolved*, That in the opinion of the undersigned, the canal contemplated by the commissioners, from Black Rock to Rome, would not be so desirable as a canal around the cataract of Niagara, and another by the Falls of Oswego."

On Tuesday, January 14th, 1812, a letter inclosing the above resolution, was signed by the governor and judges of Michigan, addressed to Governeur Morris, De Witt Clinton, Simeon Dewitt, William North, Thomas Eddy, Robert R. Livingston, and Robert Fulton, Esqrs., commissioners of internal improvement in the State of New York.

HON. JAMES WITHERELL.

One of the first Judges.

# CHAPTER XXII.

Renewed disaffection of the Indians—Resolution to increase the military force—William Hull appointed commander-in-chief of the military force of the northwest—Army of twelve hundred raised in Ohio—Gen. Hull proceeds to Detroit—Vessels containing valuables captured by the British—Orders from the Secretary of War—Army cross the river to Sandwich—Col. Cass takes Canard Bridge—Gen. Hull returns to Detroit without attacking Malden—Surrenders Detroit to the British —Facts concerning the surrender obtained from an eye-witness—Col. Lewis Cass appointed governor.

During the year 1811, the Indians, probably instigated by the British, had occasioned some trouble to the inhabitants of Michigan, and no sooner had winter set in, separating this thinly-populated region from eastern aid, than their savage neighbors showed symptoms of increasing disaffection. This state of affairs caused the Legislative Board to pass the following resolution, which was subsequently carried into effect:

"Whereas, the turbulent disposition manifested by the savage tribes in the vicinity of this territory, menaces it with danger:

"*Resolved*, That if, in the opinion of the governor of this territory for the time being, it shall be deemed necessary to call any part of the militia of this territory into actual service, should not the general government provide for their pay and subsistence, this government will do it, provided that, previous to incurring such expense, an estimate thereof, and the number proposed to be called into service, be laid before the governor and judges of the Territory of Michigan, acting in their legislative department."

War was declared by Congress against Great Britain on the 18th of June, 1812, but by a most culpable neglect on the part of the War Department, the northwestern frontier was not apprised of it until the enemy was upon them. Indeed, the first intimation of the declaration of war, received by Lieut. Hancks, commandant at Michilimackinac, was a demand from the enemy to surrender the fort, which occurred on the 17th of July.

Previous to the declaration of war, and in anticipation of such an event, General William Hull, governor of Michigan, was appointed commander-in-chief of all the forces of the northwest. An army of twelve hundred men, drafted from Ohio by the President, and considerably augmented by volunteers, was collected at Dayton, Ohio. This force was divided into three regiments, which were placed under the command of Colonels McArthur, Cass, and Finelly. A fourth regiment of infantry, numbering about three hundred men, under Colonel Miller, completed the Ohio army. General Hull was commanded to proceed to Detroit, and there await farther orders. The army left Dayton about the middle of June. They were obliged to cut their way through a trackless forest, and, after enduring many hardships, arrived at Detroit on the 5th of July.

A vessel which had been hired to convey to Detroit a few sick soldiers, hospital stores, General Hull's baggage, and many valuable documents, took the usual course up the river, by the Malden channel. On arriving opposite Malden, the vessel was captured by the British, the astonished crew being informed by the boarding officer that war was actually declared.

On the 9th of July, General Hull received the following orders from Mr. Eustice, Secretary of War: "Should the force under your command be equal to the enterprise, and should it be consistent with the safety of your own posts, you will take possession of Malden, and extend your conquests as circumstances will allow." The army, whose numbers were increased by the Michigan militia, manifested great anxiety to engage in this undertaking, and urged upon their commander its immediate prosecution. Malden was the key to that portion of the British provinces, and its possession was of great importance to the Americans. The garrison was weak, and seemed an easy conquest.

Having made arrangements for the expedition, General Hull crossed the Detroit river on the 12th day of July, and encamped at Sandwich. Here he issued a proclamation to the inhabitants, urging them to enroll themselves under the American banner. "Had I any doubt of ultimate success," says this proclamation, "I should ask your assistance; but I come prepared for every emergency. I have a force which will break down all opposition, and that force is but the vanguard of a much greater."

Day after day passed, and the army still remained encamped at Sandwich. Weary of the monotony of the camp, Colonel Cass, with a detachment of about two hundred and eighty men, left the camp to reconnoiter the ground toward Malden. He found a picket of the British army stationed at Canard Bridge. A skirmish ensued; the enemy were routed, with the loss of ten men, and the Americans took possession of the bridge. It was only four miles from Malden, and Colonel Cass, deeming it an important post, urged General Hull to retain it as a good position for a future attack. His suggestion was disregarded. After remaining nearly a month at Sandwich in a state of inactivity, with a brave, vigorous army chafing under the restraint, General Hull was so much intimidated by the hostile manifestations of the Indians, and the report that a large British force would soon arrive at Malden, that he recrossed the river to Detroit, on the 9th of August, without having made a single attack upon Malden. Here he remained until the 15th, the day of his inglorious surrender. Every circumstance connected with this most unaccountable and disgraceful affair is too well known to need repetition. The course pursued by General Hull seems more strange, from the fact that, in the army of Washington, he had distinguished himself by his bravery.

The facts contained in the following account of the surrender, were given me by Mrs. M. McCarty, one of the daughters of Peter Audrain, first secretary of the territory, who then resided at Detroit. It presents a social and domestic picture of that eventful time. I have preserved the narrative form, but am unable to give the language of the narrator.

"Detroit, in 1812, scarcely deserved the name of town, for it was, in reality, but a small village. The old town had been burned to the ground, and the inhabitants were obliged to build such houses as their means would allow, and but few of these were either elegant or convenient. Atwater was then the principal street, and the dwellings there were quite compact. A few houses were scattered here and there on the other streets; and around the whole town—small, compared with its present dimensions—was a stockade of tall pickets, as a protection from the Indians. Between the town and the fort there was no stockade, but the space was laid out in a beautiful esplanade, where the troops were drilled and exercised. Then came the fort, with its grass-covered sides, surrounded by a deep moat. All around the top of the fort, on the inside, were placed the cannon, alike for destruction and defense. On the west side of the fort was the cantonment, built around a neat court, with gravel walks and shade-trees. Two sides of the cantonment were dwellings of the officers' and soldiers' families, and the other two sides were barracks. At the west end of the town, near the gate of the stockade, stood the citadel, a strong blockhouse, used also for a guard-house. Along the river, above and below the city, were the farms of the inhabitants, mostly French, some of whom were devoted to the British, and some to the American interests.

"The morning before the surrender was sultry in the extreme. The sky was overspread with a thick haze, not a breath of wind lifted the drooping foliage, and the straggling rays of sunlight which now and then pierced through the gloom, were pale and sickly. Humanity seemed, for once, in unison with nature—listless and unhappy. Men gathered in groups about the market-place, and talked gloomily of the war, and their own future prospects; old women rocked to and fro, recalled their superstitions, and prophesied evil at hand; children were uncommonly peevish; and the usually bustling housewife, languid and depressed, shrank from the burden of her daily duties.

"We had scarcely breakfasted, when the clatter of a horse's hoofs was heard along the streets, and the stentorian voice of an officer warned the inhabitants to seek a place of safety, as the batteries recently thrown up at Sandwich would probably soon open their fire upon the town. Immediately all was panic and confusion; women bustling about, packing their valuables for removal; men running to and fro, seeking a retreat for those dearer to them than life; crying infants clinging to their half-distracted mothers, and older children everywhere but where they should be, made the town a second Babel. About noon the inhabitants began to leave the town; but, alas! where is safety in the midst of the stirring scenes of war? Our enemies were near us with their missiles of destruction; the forest swarmed with Indians, professing friendliness—yet who would vouch for savage integrity, should the enemy gain the ascendency? A deep ravine on the 'Cass farm,' a short distance below the city, then owned by General McDonald, seemed to offer the best security, and there the women and children were assembled, with a few of the sterner sex for protectors.

"The cannonading commenced at four o'clock in the afternoon, and continued at intervals during the night, keeping us in constant alarm, but doing little injury on either side. Often, while we sat huddled together in the ravine, did the ill-directed balls from the enemy's cannon plow through the orchard, tearing up the ground, but, fortunately, doing no other damage. A few shells also burst near us, harmlessly. Near midnight, those remaining in the ravine were persuaded to remove to a large stone root-house in the orchard, that we might be protected from the chilly dews of the night.

"My health had been failing for some time previous, and the fright, fatigue, and bad air of the crowded root-house, brought on an illness so violent that my friends were obliged to convey me to the dwelling-house, the basement of which we found already crowded. I was placed in an upper room, a most dangerous position, as, it being nearly daybreak, the firing was more frequent. Alarmed for the safety of my two children, who with my mother had accompanied me, I prevailed on my mother to leave me alone, and seek a more secure place for herself and my little ones. My father and husband were at the fort, and, though my wants were all supplied, none else were willing to peril their own lives by remaining with me, as their presence would be no safeguard to my life. Hour after hour I passed thus alone, listening to the booming cannon, and now and then starting and shrieking as a ball whizzed by the house, sometimes feeling almost sure that it was a mark for the enemy, and thinking perhaps the next shot would terminate my existence.

"Day dawned at length, and the cannonading ceased. Presently my mother came to tell me that the 'red-coats' were crossing the river at Springwells. 'Now,' said she, 'we shall be between two fires, and where to go for safety I cannot tell.' Her voice trembled with emotion, but her tearless eye flashed forth the determination of a resolute heart. She seated herself by a window that looked out on the beautiful Detroit. Unlike yesterday, not a cloud appeared on all the face of heaven; the cool breeze came sweeping up from its lake-bathings, rippling the river, and refreshing poor humanity. The glad song of birds hailed the rising sun, and the green herbage and the bright-eyed flowers nodded assent to their hymn of praise. But the *reveille* at the fort broke harshly on the ear amid the peaceful beauty of nature. It proclaimed the fearful truth that, for glory or mammon, man will murder his fellow-man, desolate the homes of the happy, and even himself rush into the presence of his Judge. The river below us was thickly dotted with canoes and barges, filled with scarlet-clad soldiery, and the reflected sunbeams flashed from burnished implements of war. There was a bustle at the fort, but no forming of troops on the esplanade. At length a cannon was placed at the west gate, and small detachments of troops were stationed here and there, behind the strong picket-fences that lined the road-side from Springwells to Detroit. The British troops, having breakfasted only a mile below us, formed and commenced marching toward the town.

"'What ails our men!' exclaimed my mother, as the troops continued to advance; 'why don't they fire upon them?'

"'Perhaps they might kill us,' I suggested.

"'We might as well be killed,' she replied, 'as to fall into the power of the "red-coats" and Indians. But we must try to find a safer place than this, for if General Hull is not a coward, we shall have bloody work to-day.'

"Supported by my mother, I succeeded in reaching the foot of the stairs, where my father, who had obtained leave of absence from the fort for half an hour, met us, and, taking me in his arms, carried me to our old retreat in the ravine. After telling me that my husband was on duty at one of the outposts, he returned to the fort. Kind friends made me a bed on the cold damp earth, my children were brought to me, and, when all was done for my comfort that could be, my restless mother again sought the house, to watch the movements of the belligerents.

"A flag of truce was sent from the fort across the river, and presently one of General Brock's aids galloped by, toward the fort, also bearing the white flag. After a short absence he returned, and was sent a second time, when he was met outside of the gate by a deputation from the fort. Soon after, to our utter dismay, the American banner was hauled down, and a white flag, in token of surrender, run up in its place. In the mean time orders had been issued to recall the detachments, and Captain Snelling, who stood at the cannon by the gate, with a lighted match in his hand to fire the gun, the report of which had been agreed upon as a signal of attack by those in ambuscade, had the match struck from his hand by a superior officer, who, pointing to the flag of surrender, told him not to fire, at the peril of his life.

"Scarcely were the terms of capitulation signed, before the British took possession of the town and fort, and an officer rode through the lanes and orchards, assuring the trembling inhabitants of protection from the Indians, who were swarming in vast numbers in the rear of the British troops. There was one universal burst of indignation from officers, soldiers, and inhabitants, at this disgraceful surrender, this stain on our national honor. General Hull's son, more brave than his father, raved and swore most fearfully. My father saw many of the officers break their swords, and weep over their disgrace like little children.

"I wish you could have heard the opprobrious epithets that were heaped upon the head of General Hull by the indignant women. I really believe they then felt that they preferred victory, or even an honorable defeat, at the expense of life, to this ignoble surrender. Nor could they, even now, anticipate any safety for themselves and their families. They well knew that the Indian allies of the enemy, greater in number than the white force, could not be entirely controlled by the most strenuous efforts on the part of the commanding officers, and constant annoyance, pillage, and perhaps massacre, were seen in the murky vista of the future. Nor were they mistaken; the ensuing year was one of terror.

"It is true that the orders of General Brock were very strict; he did all he could to protect us, and probably prevented a general massacre of the Americans. Many supposed that he dared not provoke the hostility of the Indians, by punishing petty grievances; and whenever a murder was committed, the murderer was kept out of the way till the affair was forgotten. Human life in time of war is little valued, and it required but a few days for a single murder to be forgotten, except by the immediate friends of the deceased.

"When my father went to his house in town, the day

after the surrender, he found that it had been broken open, and plundered of every valuable article. Mr. McCarty owned one of those narrow farms, about a mile below the city, to which my father removed what little he had left, and my father's family and our own remained together till the close of the war. My husband and my father were prisoners of war, but were permitted to be at home most of the time on parole. Three several times during the year our house was plundered, and we fared quite as well as our neighbors.

"When winter came, the difficulty of obtaining fuel in the city induced many families to remove to their farms in the vicinity. Scarcely would they begin to feel secure in the enjoyment of their comforts, when, perhaps at midnight, a band of savages would enter the house, and carry off every thing that tempted their cupidity. Happy were the helpless families if they escaped with life, for the slightest offense was sure to be punished by tomahawking the offender.

"During the whole period that the British held possession of Detroit, while the Americans were suffering so much, the Canadian families in the vicinity were unmolested. A red mark on their sheep and cattle, and red doors to their dwellings, insured them the respect of their Indian allies. But the Americans would not adopt this expedient. Perhaps I can best give you an idea of the feeling upon this subject that prevailed among them, by telling you a little anecdote of Mr. McCarty. Some time in the month of October, a friendly Indian came to our house, and had a long talk with my husband. My sister and I saw him glance at us, then point to Mr. McCarty, and encircle his own crown, significant of scalping, but he spoke so low that we could not understand a word he said. When he was gone, we anxiously inquired what news the Indian brought.

"'Do not be alarmed,' said my husband; 'Ocomo has only been trying to convince me that, if I wish to escape the tomahawk, I must go to the fort. He says you women are safe, because you are French, and have black eyes and hair; but my blue eyes and light hair are against me.'

"'Why don't you paint your door red?' asked my sister.

"'No British red about me, if I die for it!' he indignantly exclaimed. This was the general feeling among the inhabitants.

"The British held possession of Detroit about a year. They did not seem to expect to retain it so long, for the very next day after the surrender, they commenced removing the military stores to Malden, and for a whole month the river was covered with small boats engaged in the transportation. After two or three months the

British troops were withdrawn, except a detachment at the fort, and quite too many of their Indian allies remained prowling about the country, like ravening wolves.

"It was a long, weary year to us poor inhabitants, and a joyful time when General Harrison came to the rescue. The news of his approach was first brought by an old citizen of Detroit, whom we had suspected of being a tory, because he was allowed greater privileges than others who had not taken up arms. This gentleman, who had been a few weeks at Malden, came riding by, early one morning, on his way home, when my mother called to him through the lattice, and inquired the news.

"'Good,' he replied, without looking toward the house. He passed on to his own residence, put his horse in the stable, and seated himself on the front piazza, without entering the house, lest he might possibly excite suspicions that would lead to a forcible communication to the British of General Harrison's movements. If our neighbor was indeed a tory, he seemed by his conduct to have become sick of British rule.

"About an hour afterward, my brother James sprang through the gate at the foot of our garden, which extended down the sloping bank to the river's brink, and ran with all speed into the house. My father immediately barricaded the door, and begged my daring brother not to go too near the window-blinds, lest he should be seen by the Indians. James was an officer in General Harrison's army, and so great was his anxiety to know the fate of his father's family, from whom he had long been separated, that he obtained permission to cross the river a little in advance of the army, and thus was the first of our deliverers who set foot on shore.

"General Harrison and his army soon arrived. The Kentucky soldiers, who formed a part of the force, were tall, robust men, clad in blue hunting-shirts, red belts, and blue trowsers fringed with red. This singular uniform gave them a demi-savage appearance. The fort was surrendered after a mere show of resistance; the American flag again floated in triumph over the spot where a year before it had been so shamefully dishonored, and our joy was now as enthusiastic as then our indignation was unbounded."

In October, 1813, Colonel Lewis Cass, who had rendered essential service to the territory, was appointed Governor of Michigan. The country was in a most deplorable condition. Devastated by war, overrun by tribes of hostile savages, and very thinly settled, it presented a most discouraging theater for the gratification of a youthful ambition.

Immediately after the ratification of peace with Great

Britain, in 1815, Governor Cass devoted his energies to the conciliation of the Indian tribes, and so successful was he in controlling these savage hordes, that the period of his accession to the government was the commencement of a new and prosperous era in the EARLY HISTORY OF MICHIGAN.

THE END.

www.ingramcontent.com/pod-product-compliance
Lightning Source LLC
LaVergne TN
LVHW020058110826
845151LV00001B/13

* 9 7 8 1 4 2 5 5 4 5 2 1 5 *